The Homosexual Tradition in American Poetry

The Homosexual Tradition in American Poetry

BY ROBERT K. MARTIN

University of Texas Press, Austin and London

Copyright © 1979 by the University of Texas Press
All rights reserved
Printed in the United States of America

Requests for permission to reproduce material from this
book should be sent to Permissions, University of Texas
Press, Box 7819, Austin, Texas 78712.

Library of Congress Cataloging in Publication Data
Martin, Robert K   1941–
    The homosexual tradition in American poetry.
    Bibliography: p.
    Includes index.
    1. American poetry—History and criticism. 2. Homosexuality
in literature. I. Title.
PS310.H66M3   811'.009'352   79-16769
ISBN 0-292-73009-8
ISBN 0-292-73011-X pbk.

Due to the lengthy copyright data, an extension of the
copyright page is given on page 259.

To the memory of my father, FRANK H. MARTIN, JR.
1907–1971

Cur dextrae jungere dextram
Non datur, ac veras audire et reddere voces?
—AENEID I. 412–413

. . . I confidently expect a time when there will be seen, running like a half-hid warp through all the myriad audible and visible worldly interests of America, threads of manly friendship, fond and loving, pure and sweet, strong and life-long, carried to degrees hitherto unknown . . .

—WALT WHITMAN

Contents

Acknowledgments

Some books are conceived without one's awareness. It is only now, looking back, that I can see where it all began—in a very bad seminar on Whitman in which I enrolled as a graduate student. I must, paradoxically, be grateful to its instructor, for, in his unwillingness to acknowledge Whitman's homosexuality or its part in the literary relationship between Whitman and Crane, he sowed despite himself the seed that grew into this book. Still, it might never have come to fruition without the continuing efforts of my students, who have repeatedly urged that I remain honest in my presentations, honest to myself and to Whitman. I am grateful to them for their vigilance.

My years as a graduate student were rendered bearable, even pleasant, by the presence of several fellow students with whom I shared a very large part of my life. Let me recall here, and acknowledge publicly, Clare Beghtol and Louise Habicht, faithful readers and good friends for many years. Another friend from graduate school is in large part responsible for the fact that this book is appearing in this form at this time. It has been many years since Iris Tillman Hill and I endured an American poetry course together, but the memory of that course, and its ensuing breakfasts, is still bright.

When I returned to Brown University in 1977 to undertake the research that led to this book, I found a university that had changed substantially. Fortunately, friends change less than institutions, and several old friends contributed greatly to my work and to the pleasures of a year in Providence. I want to thank especially Robert Dickenson, Henry Majewski, and Simone Blanchard for their generous hospitality and the warmth of the *accueil* that they reserved for me. I also want to thank David Hirsch and George Monteiro, both of whom encouraged me to undertake this project and helped to see it through. Despite the fact that I must often have been a disappointment to them in past years, they have continued to believe in me, and I hope that this time at least they have not been disappointed. I am grateful to them for their bibliographic help and their acute criticism. Research for this book was conducted largely at the Harris Collection and the John Hay Library, Brown University. I appreciate the help given by the staff there, as well as the hospitality offered by the Beinecke Rare Book and Manuscript Library, Yale University.

Several other friends have been kind enough to read parts of this manuscript and to offer comments on it. While they cannot be held responsible for its flaws, it is likely that they have contributed to its felicities, such as they may be. I am deeply grateful to J. D. McClatchy, Linda Rahm Hallett, and Francis Murphy for an attentive reading of the text and for numerous helpful suggestions. Other who read parts of the text, or at least put up with me while I discussed it at great length, include my friends Lillian Bulwa, Jerry Bernhard, and Jean-Claude Klein. All of them were kind enough to encourage me in this project, and I owe them thanks for having enabled me to continue.

I am grateful as well to several people who have shared their knowledge on this topic, or on related topics, with me. When one is writing in a field that has been relatively untouched by scholarship, one is glad of the opportunity to exchange ideas and to learn from others. While I cannot now name everyone whose ideas have contributed to this study, and while some are acknowledged in the notes, I should like to mention especially Joseph Cady, Michael Lynch, Will Aitken, and Jacob Stockinger.

The staff at the University of Texas Press has been exceptionally thorough and competent. I am fortunate to have worked with Christine Gever, who displayed unusual skill and a warm interest in my work.

My colleagues have also been helpful, and I acknowledge Concordia University's continued support and financial aid. No one, however, could wish for a better colleague than Judith Scherer Herz. Her mark is on all the writing I have done for the last ten years, and it is a mark of a discriminating critic and a dearly valued friend.

I believe that I have been helped over many years by good schools and fine teachers. I have been fortunate in my education and in the intellectual, critical, and humane spirit that it fostered. That I have had such an education is due to the interest and love of my parents. The part that my father played is indicated by the dedication of this book to him. I also want to express my thanks to my mother, whose understanding has made this a much easier book to write.

While he will probably not read it, this book is nonetheless offered in love to Pierre Ollier, without whose daily presence it could never have been written.

Introduction

LET ME BEGIN by saying what this study will *not* do. It is not a study of the poetry of any author who happens to be homosexual. Nor is it the study of homosexual incidents in American poetry, in the manner of Leslie Fiedler's *Love and Death in the American Novel*.[1] Instead it considers the extent to which an author's awareness of himself[2] as a homosexual has affected how and what he wrote. It is restricted to authors who, to some degree (and that degree is specified in the text), may be considered to have defined themselves as homosexuals and to have given expression to their sexuality in their work.

Specifically, I argue that essential texts of major authors such as Walt Whitman and Hart Crane have been misread because readers have not understood the ways in which the poets used their texts as ways of announcing and defining their homosexuality. I also argue that the sense of a shared sexuality has led many gay writers to develop a particular tradition, involving references to earlier gay writers. This tradition has been formed partly out of a need for communication (in which allusions can serve as code references) and partly out of a feeling of exclusion from the traditions of male heterosexual writing. The existence of a homosexual tradition in American poetry, even if it is not fully defined, indicates the ways in which gay writers of the last one hundred and twenty years have sought to explore the consequences of their homosexuality and to express them in their creative work. While it is not possible to identify the exact delineations of a gay poem, it is possible to suggest several ways in which the author's homosexuality becomes a part of the text. If there is no single gay poem (any more than there is a single "straight" poem), there are specific ways in which a poem may reflect the homosexuality of its author.

Most writing has traditionally been heterosexual, not by declaration but by implication. Men and women are assumed to be heterosexual until proved otherwise. And heterosexual assumptions are presumed to be universal. For a heterosexual man, then, the adoption of a social definition of sexuality is likely to be unconscious. But for the homosexual man, who must repeatedly observe the differences between his own sexuality and the prevailing assumptions about "everyman," sexual definition is a matter of individual struggle and personal decision. Not all homosexuals are so introspective, of course; but the homosexual is confronted with the obligation to consider the implications of his sexual nature. It is not surprising, then, that gay poets have often used their poetry as, among other things, a forum for the exploration of sexuality and a way of speaking to the past and future, creating viable bonds of love linking themselves to the poets who have gone before.

It is not easy to define a homosexual poem. At the simplest level, it is what most anthologies of gay poetry proclaim it to be: a celebration of a sexual act with another man. And yet it must be obvious that very little of what we think of as great heterosexual poetry is concerned simply with heterosexual activity *per se*. Rather, it uses heterosexuality as a means toward larger concerns, whatever they may be. It has been, and continues to be, necessary to insist upon the homosexuality of a homosexual poem because it has so often been ignored or invalidated. It is essential, then, for a better (more accurate) reading of the poem, not because it makes the poem better. A homosexual poem is neither better nor worse than a heterosexual poem (although it is, arguably, different); a dishonest poem is, however, almost certain to be inferior to an honest one. During the last one hundred years homosexuals have gained more and more courage to be honest about their lives and this change is reflected in their art.

The study of homosexuality in American poetry begins with Walt Whitman. No other poet, until the present time, has so clearly defined himself in terms of his sexuality and so clearly defined his poetic mission as a consequence of his homosexuality. This remains true despite the attempts Whitman made, late in his own lifetime, to conceal his homosexuality from outsiders. It may be, of course, that in part he was telling the truth: that he never gave physical expression to his love for men. The textual evidence makes that seem unlikely, however; Whitman was fully aware of the possibilities of sexual expression between men, and he celebrated them not only as an end in themselves but also as a means to a mystic penetration of the universe and a more democratic vision of the American future.

It is also Whitman who provided the epigraph for this study: "I confidently expect a time when there will be seen, running like a half-hid warp through all the myriad audible and visible worldly interests of America, threads of manly friendship, fond and loving, pure and sweet, strong and life-long, carried to degrees hitherto unknown . . ."[3] Whitman's metaphor is important in that it suggests the coexistence of homosexuality with heterosexuality to an extent undreamed of by the ordinary observer. Whitman never suggests that homosexuality (which he terms "manly friendship" or "adhesiveness") has anything of illness or imperfection about it. On the contrary, in the same passage he speaks of the opportunity which the development of friendship between men provides for the realization of the democratic potential of America.

But if such ideas have run like a thread through the woof of (heterosexual) American literature, they have been at least "half-hid." The need for the present study has arisen from the critical refusal to consider homosexuality as a factor (in any but the most clinical way) in the makeup of the literary self. In the case of Whitman, there has been a deliberate and sustained effort to falsify the evidence and to present Whitman as a heterosexual. Even those few critics who have recognized his homosexuality have usually done so by adopting the medical model, according to which homosexuality represents an illness or a maladjustment.

In the case of Hart Crane, total neglect would almost seem preferable to the distortions which have prevailed. Since the study of Crane has almost always taken a biographical turn, the poet's homosexuality has been discussed repeatedly. But the discussion has almost always assumed that there is something wrong about homosexuality and traced Crane's "failure" to his "neurosis." One myth about Crane is particularly persistent: that he was "saved" from homosexuality in Mexico by Peggy Baird Cowley. Crane's unpublished letters do not seem to support this statement; he wrote in February 1932, "The old beauty still claims me, however, and my eyes roam as much as ever. I doubt if I'll ever change very fundamentally."[4] But this letter is not included in the published *Letters* and so has not influenced critical judgments. One question remains unanswered: if Crane was saved by his affair with Peggy Cowley and was on his way back to marry her, why did he jump overboard? The complete story of Crane's life has not been told; the evidence would suggest that he was hounded by his friends into a desperate acceptance of a heterosexuality that went against his nature.

In Crane we are confronted with the "reluctant" homosexual, in the view of his friend Allen Tate (although this is not quite the image that emerges from his letters, even those published). Crane lived daily with the societal oppression of homosexuality, and his poetry reflects the ways in which he internalized that oppression. For him the recognition of his homosexuality meant a recognition of himself as an outsider, what he repeatedly portrayed as a tragic clown of love. What would homosexual poetry be like without oppression? It is impossible to answer that question, since there has not been a society which did not suppress homosexuality since classical Greece. It seems likely, however, that a society without oppression would allow for the development of a frankly erotic poetry of male love; beyond that, it would probably be difficult to tell a homosexual poem from a heterosexual one. We are in any case far from the day when we shall know the answer to that question.

One possible answer comes from Whitman, for whom homosexuality meant a heightened political awareness, a sensitivity to the situation of women in a patriarchal society, and a belief that a homosexual society, freed from the impulse to power, might devote itself to pleasure. This aspect of Whitman's work has become important in the last twenty years, as pressures increasingly have been brought to bear upon the power structure headed by heterosexual men. We can now see how Whitman (and Melville) questioned some of the most fundamental assumptions of their times, in ways that we have only recently come to understand.

Among modern poets the possibilities are more varied. One can find homosexual poets writing in every mode from the most conservative, academic verse to the most experimental. Certainly the growth of "confessional" poetry has made it easier for the homosexual poet to talk of his sexuality, but few of the poets considered in this study may be said to be influenced directly by the confessional poets. There have been certain non-American influences, notably the work of Cavafy, the modern gay poet whose work has had the most impact on a large number of readers. But whatever forms the poets have adopted, they have almost all been aware of their place in a particular tradition. An awareness of the homosexual tradition has been a way for the homosexual artist to survive in a heterosexual world. Since the homosexual must feel himself at best indirectly connected to the "great tradition" of heterosexual literature, it has been especially important for him to establish his lineage, to validate himself by appeal to the past. All art builds upon previous art, of course—or tears it down; but homosexual art has constructed its tradition with particular care. It is for this reason that such poets as Whitman and Crane recur so often as informing spirits in the poems of their successors. These more recent poems are works which acknowledge those that went before and made them possible.

This study makes no attempt to be inclusive, particularly among contemporary poets where there are so many examples from which to choose. Two omissions should perhaps be noted. The first is Auden (if he may be considered at least partly American). I have not included him since he insisted so often that his poems must not be seen as homosexual, that they were universal. Although he wrote explicitly sexual poems, he concealed them, and when he spoke of love in his published poems it was always with a deliberate vagueness. Insofar as Auden used his public career as a way of defining his own sexuality, it was through his criticism, not his poetry, although the later poems do celebrate the domesticity he had come to cherish with Chester Kallman. The second is Frank O'Hara. He is not included, not because he attempted to conceal his homosexuality (it was a frequent subject of his poetic conversation) but because he does not seem to me to use his homosexuality as an element of self-definition in the way, say, that Whitman or Crane does.[5]

Obviously, many other poets could have been included. My criteria have been personal preference, inherent interest, and intertextuality (the ways in which texts build upon other texts). I have deliberately chosen not to consider works which are representative or which would distract attention from my principal line of development. Thus, for instance, one could not discuss Thoreau's poem "Sympathy" without considering the extent to which his journals and even *Walden* are informed by a repressed homosexuality—obviously far too ambitious a project for this context. Likewise, Melville's "After the Pleasure Party," which reflects bisexuality at least, cannot be considered without attention to *Typee*, *Moby-Dick*, and *Billy Budd*. In any case, omission of these two poems is justified by the fact that neither of them may be said to have entered the history of American poetry in the sense that the poems of Whitman or Crane did. They remain instead footnotes to other careers.

One final absence. I considered including T. S. Eliot, with a discussion of such early poems as "The Death of St. Narcissus," and of *The Waste Land* as an elegy for Jean Verdenal. Some of this material has already been covered in a recent book,[6] which emphasizes the way Eliot used Whitman in the construction of *The Waste Land*. That Eliot was building on a homosexual tradition, however, remains for the moment an assertion that cannot fully be substantiated. For this reason it seemed wiser to restrict my study to writers about whose sexuality there could be little question. Those who follow my argument will observe that Eliot fits in between Santayana and Crane, structurally similar to Crane but with emotional affinities to his fellow Harvard student and expatriate.

The Homosexual Tradition in American Poetry

1. Walt Whitman

Whitman, the Critics, and Homosexuality

Although Whitman intended his work to communicate his homosexuality to his readers, and although homosexual readers have from the very beginning understood his homosexual meanings, most critics have not been willing to take Whitman at his word. A charitable interpretation of this failure might suggest that these readers were simply unable to perceive the homosexual meanings, which were so divorced from their own experiences. But such charity is not justified. The record of lies, half truths, and distortions is so shameful as to amount to a deliberate attempt to alter reality to suit a particular view of normality. If Whitman is to be a great poet, he must be straight. If the poetry shows something else, Whitman must be made to alter his own poetry, censor himself. The considerable concessions made by Whitman during the course of his career, and the removal of a number of passages, have not satisfied such critics: Whitman's life must be betrayed, rewritten, and his poems reread in a "safe" manner. Whitman must be saved from himself.

The first phase of the creation of a new, false Whitman was directed toward biography, toward proving that Whitman was actively heterosexual in his personal life. In part this was provoked by Symonds' famous letter to Whitman and Whitman's famous (and comic) reply, in which he boasted of having fathered six illegitimate children. Whitman had played the role of good citizen, especially in his old age, despite his barely concealed friendships with younger men, and his older friends continued the fiction of his life. But the first critics were not content with an absence of open homosexuality; they needed proof of heterosexuality. So the New Orleans story (that Whitman had a mulatto or common-law wife in New Orleans) was invented, out of nothing but a desire to prove that Whitman was normal. In some versions, Whitman's "wife"·was even given a name, Fernande Desmoulins.[1] Even otherwise sensitive readers of Whitman, such as Emory Holloway, William Carlos Williams, and Babette Deutsch, continued to believe in the story long after its total fictitiousness had been demonstrated. Doubtless many still do.

The case of Holloway was particularly disappointing, since it was he who was responsible, in 1920, for revealing[2] that the poem which seemed to give rise to the New Orleans story, "Once I Pass'd Through a Populous City," had been changed prior to publication by Whitman to alter "I remember only the man who wandered with me there for love of me" to "I remember only a woman I casually met there who detain'd me for love of me." One would think that such evidence would have been conclusive. But by 1926 Holloway was citing the revised version to prove Whitman's heterosexuality.[3] The New Orleans story blooms again whenever someone refuses to believe that Whitman loved other men. Even those critics who must admit the textual evidence refuse to accord any significance to it: James E. Miller, Jr., in his important book on *Leaves of Grass* published in 1957, commented, "Although Holloway's discovery may be biographically revealing, the poem has the 'meaning,' surely, of its final version."[4] How convenient when a new-critical principle can be used to buttress what is essentially nothing more than a refusal to admit an unpleasant truth! One wonders what argument would have been used if the homosexual meaning were in fact the published version—as is the case with large numbers of poems scattered throughout *Leaves of Grass*.

In one sense, of course, Miller is right. What matters for a literary critic is ultimately the text and not the life. But when two texts exist (or a manuscript and a printed text), it is certainly valid to ask why the change was made and if the change can be traced to aesthetic considerations. In the case of the changed pronoun of the poem in question, the poet has simply protected himself by concealing the biographical source of the poem. In such a case, the change in text must be ascribed to social pressure and not to aesthetics, and the manuscript text must inform any reading of the printed text. But the real issue is not, of course, whether or not Whitman had sexual relations with a woman in New Orleans or anywhere else. The question, which has not been asked, is: Does the text of *Leaves of Grass* reflect the poet's awareness of himself as a homosexual? If the answer is yes, it makes no difference

what Whitman did in New Orleans, or what he told John Addington Symonds. The text does, as we shall see, reveal Whitman's
homosexual consciousness—his sense of himself as marginal, his
search for a form for the expression of love between men, his joy
at sexual experiences with other men, and his exploration of the
social and political consequences of his homosexuality. To adopt
Jacob Stockinger's witty and useful term, *Leaves of Grass* is ho-
motextual.[5]

Many critics have at least been honest about their prejudice.
Whitman criticism is full of the vocabulary of social opprobrium
and the clichés of undigested psychoanalysis. Even homosexuals
themselves have used such words—Newton Arvin spoke of a "core
of abnormality."[6] Others have been even harsher. Mark Van Doren
in 1942 was able to write, "Manly love is neither more nor less
than an abnormal and deficient love."[7]

Since that time the heterosexual attacks on Whitman have
become more subtle and perhaps ultimately more damaging. Critics have used sophisticated techniques of literary analysis to demonstrate that sexuality is not an important aspect of Whitman's
poetry. The most insistent of these arguments has been advanced
by James Miller, who reads "Song of Myself," for instance, as an
"inverted mystical experience"[8] (the pun is unintentional). By
seeing patterns of mystic symbolism at crucial points in the poem,
Miller diverts the reader's attention from the poetry's frankly and
directly sexual nature. Miller's argument, however, at least has
the virtue of making us look again at the mystical Whitman and
thus return to the visionary poet. In the hands of his less talented
followers, the arguments seem evasive and euphemistic, as in this
recent example from Thomas E. Crawley's *The Structure of Leaves
of Grass* (1970):[9] "To associate ["These I Singing in Spring"] with
any crude, sensuous interpretation of the calamus-symbol is to
miss the mystical beauty"; or, again, he denounces "the gross interpretation . . . that the root is a symbol of the male sexual
organ."

A recent version of Whitman's poetry illustrates the failure
of the "liberal" reading. Walter Lowenfels' edition of *The Tenderest
Lover: The Erotic Poetry of Walt Whitman* purports to be honest.
Lowenfels maintains with pride, "Our text . . . is unexpurgated;
erotic lines and passages that Whitman changed or deleted have
been restored." But although the text is restored, the editor feels
obliged to insist on the interchangeability of the sexes. He writes
of the famous "Once I Pass'd Through a Populous City" text,

"What is intrinsic to the poem is not the sex of the loved one but the love itself."[10]

Lowenfels strives to universalize Whitman by eliminating the specifics of his vision and to romanticize, i.e., render abstract, a sexuality which he finds distasteful. He writes, "Whitman was a prophet of today's sexual revolution. . . . In his love poems, youth speaks to youth of all ages, across all centuries and languages." But he goes on to ignore crucial and obvious evidence and refers to "the unnamed him or her whom Whitman identified only by the number '16' or '164.'" The rankest amateur in cryptography knows that Whitman meant P or PD, Peter Doyle.[11]

The history of Whitman criticism in this connection is shameful. I know of no parallel example of the willful distortion of meaning and the willful misreading of a poet in order to suit critics' own social or moral prejudices. It should be added that the very few critics who spoke against this tradition of distortion were generally Europeans, who perhaps did not share American society's total and relentless hostility to the homosexual.

One recent study has made an attempt to come to terms with Whitman's homosexuality—Edwin Miller's *Walt Whitman's Poetry: A Psychological Journey*.[12] But Miller's Freudianism leads him to place far too much emphasis on the life and too little on the text. Too often the text becomes a mere illustration of what has already been "observed" in the life. Furthermore, the psychoanalytical bias of the study prevents Miller from looking at homosexuality in a neutral way. He sees homosexuality as an illness, an arrestment of normal development, never as an option. Consequently he follows the medical model and condemns Whitman repeatedly for evasions or childishness. When Whitman speaks of manly love as fulfilling man's highest aspirations, Miller comments on this "dubious reasoning, welling out of an absence of experience and personal frustration,"[13] without presenting any evidence to support his assertion of Whitman's frustration and lack of experience. Miller's prejudiced study barely conceals his dislike for what he terms Whitman's "deviancy." Apparently one can now recognize that Whitman was homosexual; but one still cannot say that his homosexuality contributed to his art except to flaw it.

The debate in America over Whitman's sexuality has never been as fierce or as open as in Germany. It was in Germany that the first elements of a homosexual liberation movement developed, through the efforts of Magnus Hirschfeld and his attempts to establish the scientific study of sex. One of the earliest champions of Whitman in Germany was Eduard Bertz, who sent a copy of his article on Whitman to the poet in 1889.[14] Bertz had already used citations from Whitman in his novel *The French Prisoners*, and his friend George Gissing had captured Bertz's admiration for Whitman in *Thyrza*. Bertz published a monograph on Whitman in 1905 in Hirschfeld's *Jahrbuch*,[15] in which he asserted Whitman's homosexuality and explained his reluctance to speak of this matter during the poet's lifetime. He stated that Whitman's positions as expressed in his poetry would be sufficient to prove his homosexuality even if one knew nothing of his life,[16] but he nonetheless proceeded to follow the method adopted by Hirschfeld and his followers of looking for outward physical signs of homosexuality. (Such reformers were anxious to demonstrate that homosexuality was innate, not acquired, and therefore worthy of legal and social toleration.) The following year Bertz was attacked by Johannes Schlaf, in his book *Walt Whitman homosexueller?*[17] Bertz responded with two further studies of Whitman's homosexuality[18] in which he continued to maintain that Whitman was homosexual but also now condemned Whitman for his homosexuality, calling him a "false prophet"[19] who had denied the noble Uranian love for a more physical love of the lower classes. All these works convey Bertz's own inner confusions—it appears likely that he approved a "spiritual" but not a physical homosexuality—but they also illustrate the far greater openness of intellectual debate that prevailed in Germany in the early part of this century, as compared to the almost total silence in American criticism. (When Bertz's monograph was reported in *Current Literature*, the author praised Schlaf as a "healthful protest against the morbid tendency of the modern German mind" who "refuses to see the abnormal in Whitman, not only denying his asserted femininity, but proclaiming him the arch-type of strong virile manhood.")[20]

Whitman's own life was marked by the same pressures toward sexual conformity that now lead to critical distortions. He seems to have felt the need to act out a role, to hide behind the mask of the "tough." And he had to learn the strategies of concealment, which, at least until recently, all of us had to learn as homosexuals in a heterosexual world. The changing of texts, the excision of passages, are but the most obvious of what must have been an enormously painful series of acts performed almost daily to conform to someone else's version of normality. And how painful they must have been to the man who was able to give another man a wedding band, who from his youth on wrote with passion only of friendship between men, who cried out in suffering "O unspeakable passionate love" ("Song of Myself," sec. 21), for the love, "the secret of my nights and days," which lay hidden "in paths untrodden."

One important consequence of his homosexuality is that Whitman, unlike so many male poets, does not regard women as sexual objects even in his ostensibly heterosexual poems. The homosexual, whose sexuality is directed toward other men, is free to see women as human beings, and thus we find in Whitman a strong sense of compassion for figures of suffering women— the mother, the prostitute, the spinster. Further, not only does he not see women as sex objects, but he thus can celebrate his own sexuality. Whitman's poetry is frequently autoerotic in the sense that he takes his own body as a source of sexual pleasure much as Freud's polymorphously perverse child does, and derives pleasure from his own orgasm rather than from any sense of aggression or conquest.

Whitman makes no distinction between subject and object (a distinction necessary for women to be taken as "other" and as property). All experience becomes a part of himself—"Absorbing all to myself and for this song" (sec. 13)—as total egotism of the child is restored. The "Song of Myself" is the song of the world, as seer and seen, male and female, become one. If Whitman's vision is regressive, it looks back to an earlier ideal of play. We need to see the sensitivity, the finesse of Whitman, which has too long been obscured by the image of him as

> Walt Whitman, A Kosmos, of Manhattan the son,
> Turbulent, fleshy, sensual, eating, drinking, and breeding
> ("Song of Myself," sec. 24)

This was what Whitman wanted to seem to be; but the poetry reveals the happy truth that he was indeed a much deeper, more sensitive person than he dared admit.

The Dream-Vision Poems

The great debate over homosexuality in Whitman's poetry has generally centered on the poems in the "Calamus" section or those poems which, although not actually placed in that section, seem to belong there by similarity of theme or imagery. But this emphasis is somewhat unfortunate. First, it tends to isolate the "homosexual" poems of Whitman in one neat category which can be labeled and then safely be put away and forgotten. Second, it tends to assume that Whitman's sexuality is only relevant to his most explicit and frequently didactic poems. While not ignoring the "Calamus" poems, it is important to begin by discussing another mode of Whitman's poetry which is slightly more elusive, yet essential to an understanding of the whole body of his work. That mode may be termed the dream-vision poems, those poems written in a state of mind somewhere beneath full consciousness, which invoke the experience of the mind in that state.

"The Sleepers" has received a fair amount of attention in recent years, probably as a result of the general interest in stream-of-consciousness techniques as well as a new willingness to look more carefully at explicit sexual imagery. There are helpful comments in the readings of Leslie Fiedler, Edwin Haviland Miller, and James E. Miller.[21] What I wish to stress at this point is that "The Sleepers" is similar to "Song of Myself" in its sense of wavering consciousness, its use of cosmic observation, its shifts through time and space, and its sexual imagery. Both poems contain the seeds of what would develop in the poems of 1856 and 1860 into the full expression of homosexual love.

"The Sleepers" is explicitly about a vision, as the first line informs us, and its action is the movement of the poet within his vision:

> I wander all night in my vision,
> Stepping with light feet . . . swiftly and noiselessly step-
>   ping and stopping
> Bending with open eyes over the shut eyes of sleepers;
> Wandering and confused . . . lost to myself . . . ill-assort-
>   ed . . . contradictory,
> Pausing and gazing and bending and stopping.[22]

The light and rapid movements of the poet deftly suggested by the assonances ("stepping and stopping"), Whitman's introduction evokes his role as gatherer of experience, through whose dream-mind (or unconscious) the apparent contradictions of the world are resolved.

The first section of the poem is agitated, marked by continual movement. The poet uses the game metaphor to evoke the atmosphere of levity which prevails as the covers are lifted and the genitals are revealed:

> Well do they do their jobs, those journeymen divine,
> Only from me can they hide nothing and would not if they
>   could;
> I reckon I am their boss, and they make me a pet besides,
> And surround me, and lead me and run ahead when I walk,
> And lift their cunning covers and signify me with stretched
>   arms, and resume the way;
> Onward we move, a gay gang of blackguards with mirth-
>   shouting music and wildflapping pennants of joy.

The mood of sexual (phallic) arousal is suggested through the use of metaphors, the "cunning covers" and "wildflapping pennants," which continue this section's concern with the motifs of concealment and revelation. The "cache" of line 35 is both the action of hiding and the hiding-place; what is hidden is ultimately sexuality. In the world of night and the dream, the covers are lifted, and the triumphant power of joy which Whitman situated in the phallus is freed. The "gay gang of blackguards" does not evoke, of course, the modern meaning of "gay," but it might as well: what is evoked is the pleasure of men together, a triumphant repossession of childlike joys, with Whitman as Pan in the procession back to a natural world of innocence.

The last third of the first section is devoted to a presentation from the point of view of a woman—a strategy echoed in the famous section 11 of "Song of Myself." This permits Whitman to give expression to deep sexual desires and passions, in an all-consuming love for the world. The "I" of these lines is both active and passive: "I roll myself upon you as upon a bed. . . . I resign myself to the dusk." The pretense that a woman is speaking is quickly abandoned, as the section concludes with a remarkable depiction of orgasm in which it becomes clear that the naked speaker, who has been exposed, is using his body as a metaphor for his penis, and that the entire exposure motif of the poem operates on these two levels: the exposure of the poet for what he is—the fear of being revealed as a homosexual—and the exposure of the penis, which may provoke castration anxiety in a hostile world.

In later editions Whitman ended this section with "I fade

away," but in the 1855 edition sexual fear and sexual pleasure are made explicit:

> O hotcheeked and blushing! O foolish hectic!
> O for pity's sake, no one must see me now! . . . my clothes
>   were stolen while I was abed,
> Now I am thrust forth, where shall I run?
>
> Pier that I saw dimly last night when I looked from the
>   windows,
> Pier out from the main, let me catch myself with you and
>   stay . . . I will not chafe you;
> I feel ashamed to go naked about the world,
> And am curious to know where my feet stand . . . and what
>   is this flooding me, childhood or manhood . . . and the
>   hunger that crosses the bridge between.
>
> The cloth laps a first sweet eating and drinking,
> Laps life-swelling yolks . . . laps ear of rose-corn, milky and
>   just ripened;
> The white teeth stay, and the boss-tooth advances in dark-
>   ness,
> And liquor is spilled on lips and bosoms by touching glasses,
>   and the best liquor afterward.

The progression is clear: shame gives way to curiosity, then hunger, and finally satisfaction. Whitman's lines recapitulate a sexual coming of age. The "bridge between" childhood and manhood is, as in classic psychoanalytic theory, the penis itself. Frightened of sexual exposure, the poet nonetheless realizes himself, driven by his sexual hunger.

The final stanza quoted here depicts the sexual experience which accomplishes the poet's "manhood." James Miller[23] manages to see vaginal imagery here, but I am not convinced. It seems clear that what is being depicted is the act known politely as fellatio—the penis protrudes from the foreskin, the balls are sucked, the penis is sucked, and finally there is ejaculation in the mouth. It is, of course, possible that the scene described is an act of fellatio performed on a man by a woman, but this seems extremely unlikely in view of nineteenth-century attitudes. It is more likely that Whitman chose to give his sexual explicitness a degree of acceptability by making the speaker apparently a woman (without, however, any personality or identity) but then remained sufficiently embarrassed by these lines to remove them from later editions.

In such a situation one can see clearly the difference between the Whitman of the 1855 edition and the Whitman of the 1860 edition: while the earlier Whitman presents scenes that are probably homosexual in origin, they are never defined as homosexual. What mattered to Whitman at this time was the role of sexuality in the establishment of a mystic sense of unity; the kind of sexuality involved was relatively unimportant. Whether this was due to a deliberate act of evasion, or to a relatively underdeveloped homosexual consciousness, it seems impossible to know at this time. It is likely that Whitman felt it dangerous to reveal himself, in a poem devoted to the portrayal of universal union, as an outsider. In any case, what is important here is to recognize that the starting place for the poem is the sexual experience. The poet's vision begins in the second section, after orgasm, when "my sinews are flaccid / Perfume and youth course through me, and I am their wake." The physical experience leads to the spiritual, the dream, which is also in its turn physical and sensual.

The third section brings a fantasy of the destruction of the "beautiful gigantic swimmer," a warning in dream terms of the dangers in the unconscious world of the sea with its "swift-running eddies." The swimmer seems to be a sexual object but is also an ideal presentation of the self. The dream of the third section is a dream of the destruction of the self—the clue lies in Whitman's surprising line, "Will you kill him in the prime of his middle age?" (Whitman was thirty-five at the time). The relatively open presentation of sexuality which gives rise to the dream state brings with it its own anxieties. The dream is of castration fears, brought on by indulgence in forbidden sex and exposure of self, hence the swimmer is "naked." At the same time the dream is erotic, implying sadistic or masochistic fantasies in which the beauty of the swimmer's body seems actually to increase as he is buffeted by the "ruffianly" waves. The "brave corpse" becomes an icon of male love, smashed on the rocks, its early death testifying to its poignant intensity.

"I turn but do not extricate myself." The poet-dreamer turns in his sleep, seeking to escape from his dream, but the nightmare is not yet over. (It should be mentioned that "extricate" refers primarily to the dream but also, perhaps, to the body of a beloved.) Death and disaster are multiplied, but there is also a suggestion of victory, as in the farewell of Washington to his troops, with his embraces and kisses that seem to continue the theme of male love and the possibility of a successful "revolution."

The sixth section links the theme of slavery to sexuality, as the poet moves from the mother's vision of the "red squaw":

> My mother looked in delight and amazement at the stranger,
> She looked at the beauty of her tallborne face and full and
>   pliant limbs,
> The more she looked upon her she loved her

to his own identification with the black slave. Both evoke guilt because of the (implicit) double violation of taboo: homosexuality and miscegenation are crimes deeply feared in American life. (We recall that Whitman's famous letter to Symonds implied that he had committed the lesser of the two, lest he be found guilty of the greater!) Whitman's deep sense of caring for those he felt to be victims (here the red woman and the black man) was undoubtedly genuine and can be seen throughout his life, from his love for his retarded brother through his Freesoil politics to his work as a nurse during the war. But it also seems likely that his self-image as healer had an erotic basis. Whitman's love was redemptive and restorative; such a love is difficult to reconcile with a relationship between equal partners.

Starting with section 7 there is a drastic change brought about by the poet's acceptance of the world, an acceptance made possible by his perception of unity in time and space. The agitation of sexuality, the sensation of guilt immediately following it, and the fantasy of death and loss accompanying its completion give way to a sense of sexual calm and peace. The poet learns to accept the daytime world of disunity ("the rich running day") as part of the cycle which always leads back to the night and love and the Great Mother. His love of experience and diversity leads him not to forget the world of unity and calm but, rather, to accept both:

> I love the rich running day, but I do not desert her in whom
>   I lay so long:
> .   .   .   .
> I will stop only a time with the night . . . and rise betimes.
>
> I will duly pass the day O my mother and duly return to you

Edwin Haviland Miller emphasizes such passages as evidence of Whitman's regressive patterns and what he implies to be an unresolved oedipal conflict.[24] But there are no *personal* maternal qualities in this poem. The mother addressed here is a universal mother, goddess of the night, the dream, the vision, of all that is excluded from the daylight world of jobs, reason, and father. Reading the poem in terms of personal psychology misses the essential significance of Whitman's vision, which returns to a state of primal consciousness that is prepatriarchal, cyclical rather than linear. His essentially matriarchal vision leads the poet back to the Night-Mother (forces of darkness, mystery, and the unknown) to be reborn from her. The Mother is the death-sleep which follows upon the male striving of sexuality but, also, the repose which heals and out of which the fallen penis may rise again:

> Not you will yield forth the dawn again more surely than
> you will yield forth me again,
> Not the womb yields the babe in its time more surely than
> I shall be yielded from you in my time.

The vision of the eighth section is deliberately eschatological and has something in common with the "Peaceable Kingdom" paintings by the Quaker artist Edward Hicks.[25] It represents the transformed world, a world redeemed by the Spirit and ruled by love. For Whitman this world could be attained here and now through an exploration of the possibilities of love. Like the Quakers, Whitman believed human regeneration and reconciliation to be possible in this world, and like them he had a radical vision of love as the way to that regeneration—although few Quakers would have thought of love in the explicitly sexual terms adopted by Whitman. The repeated phrase "hand in hand" almost certainly derives from the ceremony which closes the Quaker meeting for worship and which symbolizes brotherly love. Whitman provides a catalog, a series of examples of such love (as Hicks does in his paintings); and it is worth noting that Whitman includes in his universal vision the love of men: "friend is imarmed by friend, / the scholar kisses the teacher and the teacher kisses the scholar." (The last phrases recall Whitman's fictional treatment, in "The Half-Breed," of his teaching days, in Master Caleb and his pupil Quincy Thomas, "the one whom he loved.")[26] The power of love begins with the personal but extends to the social as well and is ultimately political, since it affirms a deep-rooted democracy and brotherhood across racial and national lines.

The sexual experience is revealed by "The Sleepers" to be the gateway to the visionary experience—literally because ejaculation leads to sleep and thus to dream and metaphorically because it is the realization of the possibility of transcending the self through sexual ecstasy which leads to an acceptance of the world. As we fall off to sleep following orgasm, we see a kind of inner sense in the world—a world, freed from the pressures of the day, in which we have regained the kind of repose that Freud thought found its only model in intrauterine existence. Through this vision Whitman would come to his understanding of the world and greet all women and men as sleepers, each dreaming their own dream, yet each dream like the others.

Whitman's most important poem by virtue of its length and the themes broached there, is clearly his "Song of Myself." Critics have attempted to find an adequate way of understanding the poem's strength and sense of inner unity despite an appearance of disorder, but no one has fully explained the poem's patterns by looking at it, in the light of "The Sleepers," as a dream-vision based on sexual experience. I propose such a reading now, with the understanding that I am not denying any epic, mystic, or democratic elements. Clearly they are all there; but they do not explain how the poem works, nor do they account for any of the sexual structure.

The poem appears, at first glance, to be very unlike "The Sleepers" in that it seems to be the product of a wholly conscious mind engaged in a number of identifiable traditional poetic functions—e.g., singing, as an epic poet, and debating, as a metaphysical poet. But a careful look at the poem reveals that it is a monologue posing as a dialogue, or perhaps a dialogue which turns out to be a monologue: a dialogue for one speaker, to put it nicely. The second role is clearly nonspeaking.

The mode of the poem seems to be a body/soul dialogue, such as those popular in the Renaissance. The poet repeatedly insists upon the equality of the body and the soul—"I am the poet of the body / And I am the poet of the soul." Nonetheless, the major thrust of the poem is toward a recognition of the claims of the body. If Whitman was to establish the equality of body and soul, it was necessary to insist upon the goodness of the body. There was a long tradition of art in America and Europe which spoke on behalf of the soul. But in the American 1850s there had been few poets who spoke for the body.

In most of the poem, it is the body which speaks: the soul does not seem to respond, and the readers are addressed so often and so insistently as "you" that they indeed become part of the poem. The poem is cast as a love poem; it involves a seduction, a growing desire which leads finally to fulfillment, and then to the vision which follows on sexual experience and which, as in "The Sleepers," permits the poet to perceive the unity of all things. The poem also ends with a sense of contentment brought on by acceptance, but not until the poet has marked the end of the night by bidding farewell to his lover.

The first section is a very brief introduction, particularly in the 1855 edition, where it consists of only five lines which provide a setting and the argument. (Section numbers were not used in 1855, of course; they are used here for convenience in locating passages. Citations are taken from the 1855 text.) In the second section, the process of natural intoxication has begun. The poet concludes this section by asking the reader to "stop this day and night with me." It is clear that, in fantasy at least, the request is granted, and the rest of the poem is an account of that day and night. At this very early stage in the poem it is clear that the poet has a sense of acceptance—"I am satisfied," he writes—and that his acceptance is based on the vision of God as the lover who sleeps with him by night, leaving him "baskets covered with white towels bulging the house with their plenty." The idea of God as the "loving bedfellow" is important throughout Whitman's work, from "the beautiful god, Jesus" of "Blood-Money" (1850) to the "Elder Brother" of "Passage to India" (1871), in whose arms "the Younger melts in fondness." In "Song of Myself" God is seen as the Spirit, breathing new life into the poet in a transferal of spiritual energy and, as Whitman's metaphor suggests, impregnating the poet with the word of God.

It is a mistake, however, to insist, as Edwin Miller does,[27] on the "bisexual" nature of the poet in this episode. Impregnation by the Spirit, after all, need not take place through the vagina; there may be penetration of the anus (as in the poems of Allen Ginsberg) or, as in the traditional iconography of the Annunciation, impregnation through the ear. The sexual metaphor of baskets "bulging" suggests a phallic plenty, rather than actual pregnancy; the genitals are hidden by white towels not unlike the "cunning covers" of "The Sleepers." It is also useful to recall that the Greek terms for the "active" and the "passive" male lover meant "breathing out" and "breathing in." The older lover quite literally inspired the younger.

The coming of God at night fills the poet with sexual energy, and enables him to accept the day in the knowledge of a forth-coming night and to ask whether in fact he should

> . . . postpone my acceptance and realization and scream at
>   my eyes
> That they turn from gazing after and down the road,
> And forthwith cipher and show me to a cent,
> Exactly the contents of one, and exactly the contents of two,
>   and which is ahead?

In the world of nighttime vision there is no counting, one and two are the same, real and imaginary lovers are equal.

The poet continues his address to "you," through the recol-lection of a previous sexual experience which is the source of his first knowledge of peace:

> I mind how we lay in June, such a transparent summer
>   morning;
> You settled your head athwart my hips and gently turned
>   over upon me,
> And parted the shirt from my bosom-bone, and plunged your
>   tongue to my barestript heart,
> And reached till you felt my beard, and reached till you held
>   my feet.

As in the sexual experience described in "The Sleepers," the gen-der of the poet's partner is unspecified, although it is apparently another man. It seems unlikely that a man would describe him-self in such a passive position, apparently a part of fellatio, with a woman. The absence of specification of gender may be itself a strong indicator. Whitman wrote a few lines earlier of "real or fancied indifference of some man or woman I love." The double reference is consistent with Whitman's desire to be universal, but it is, I submit, one that no nineteenth-century heterosexual male would make. The failure to indicate the gender of the beloved is a frequent and similar strategy, which allows concealment with-out outright duplicity and deception. It merely supposes that most people will misunderstand. From this sexual experience comes the first of the mystical states, moments of insight which have their source in heightened sensuality and release. The state is announced clearly and concisely—"Swiftly arose and spread around me the peace and joy and knowledge that pass all the art and argument of the earth"—and is followed by a catalog of the new knowledge of the unity and interrelatedness of all life. The source of such knowledge is the ability to love and be loved.

When, in line 137,[28] Whitman calls out "Undrape," he addresses not merely the "you" but also the hidden self embodied in the penis. Once undraped, the loved one is the subject of one of the most interesting passages of the poem, section 8, which depicts through a sexual metaphor the progress of life:

> The little one sleeps in its cradle,
> I lift the gauze and look a long time, and silently brush away
>   flies with my hand.

> The youngster and the redfaced girl turn aside up the bushy
>   hill,
> I peeringly view them from the top.

> The suicide sprawls on the bloody flow of the bedroom
> It is so . . . I witnessed the corpse . . . there the pistol had
>   fallen.

From childhood to adolescence to death, from birth to reproduction to death, from the "little one . . . in its cradle" to "the bushy hill" to "the bloody floor" with the pistol "fallen." The sight of nakedness leads in visual terms to a realization of death and suggests an ambivalent attitude toward the male genitals. But it is crucial to see that if one "cannot be shaken away," then one must accept all. One must accept the penis beneath the foreskin, the erect penis, and the penis after coitus. The acceptance of these three stages may lead to an acceptance of the same three stages of life and thereby to an acceptance of life itself in all its multiplicity. Whitman's catalog technique derives from the recognition of that multiplicity; for him the catalog expresses the ultimate unity of things seen not on their surface but *sub specie aeternitatis*, a point of view that for Whitman was most often arrived at through sexual experience.

The following sections of the poem go out, literally, into the world and lead, for instance, to the celebrated section 11, where the abstract vision of section 8 is transformed into a very specific vision of masturbation and fellatio:

> Twenty-eight young men bathe by the shore,
> Twenty-eight young men, and all so friendly,
> Twenty-eight years of womanly life, and all so lonesome.
>
> She owns the fine house by the rise of the bank,
> She hides handsome and richly drest aft the blinds of the window.
>
> Which of the young men does she like the best?
> Ah the homeliest of them is beautiful to her.
>
> Where are you off to, lady? for I see you,
> You splash in the water there, yet stay stock still in your room.
>
> Dancing and laughing along the beach came the twenty-ninth bather,
> The rest did not see her, but she saw them and loved them.
>
> The beards of the young men glistened with wet, it ran from their long hair,
> Little streams passed all over their bodies.
>
> An unseen hand also passed over their bodies,
> It descended tremblingly from their temples and ribs.
>
> The young men float on their backs, their white bellies swell to the sun . . . they do not ask who seizes fast to them,
> They do not know who puffs and declines with pendant and bending arch,
> They do not think whom they souse with spray.

This poem, or part of the poem, is exquisite in its evocation of the mood of sexual arousal. As many readers have pointed out, Whitman achieves the feat of being both subject and object, of being the female voyeur as well as the men who are masturbated. Not only is this one of the loveliest sexual poems I know, it is also a clear defense of the anonymity of sexual encounter. In the dream-vision of Whitman there are no persons but, rather, a general feeling of the delight of sexual experiences regardless of the partner. They are totally tactile, since they take place in the dream-world of closed eyes. Such experiences could well be repeated in almost any steam bath of a modern large city. But the important point is that not asking, not knowing, and not thinking are integral parts of Whitman's *democratic* vision, and anonymous sexuality is an important way-station on the path to the abolition of distinctions of age, class, beauty, and gender. Whitman loves all being and will love and be loved by all being. It is perhaps at this juncture that the implications of his perspective become most revolutionary.

It is a measure of the difference between the Whitman of the 1855 edition and the Whitman of the 1860 edition that in these lines Whitman relies upon the device of the female point of view in order to present an essentially homosexual vision. What is eroticized is the image of the men themselves, and the shift in point of view comes about when Whitman moves from describing the woman's feeling of sexual longing to describing the men's response. At this point the woman disappears completely from the poem, since she is not present in the men's consciousness (nor, one suspects, the poet's). That the woman is a device for the "safe" presentation of homosexual desire does not make her any less a representation of the repressed sexuality of Victorian women. Whitman seems to have sensed the relationship between the thwarted desires of women and those of homosexual men, for the homosexual in mid-nineteenth-century America was also obliged to look at life from "aft the blinds," secretly glimpsing the desired bodies of young men. Like so many Victorian women, the majority of nineteen-century homosexuals appear to have concealed their sexuality for the sake of respectability—a gentility which contrasts sharply with the exuberant playfulness of the young men bathing. It will be noted, of course, that the bathing scene became in the nineteenth century almost a cliché of homosexual literature and painting.[29] It offered an opportunity to display the male body naked and to display men together, even touching each other, at the same time remaining totally "innocent." The image became an icon because it combined the opposed elements of sexual attraction and moral purity. Whitman, however, who in some sense invented the image, worked against the idea of moral purity, as the last three lines of the cited passage make clear. Whitman's celebration of sexuality is not veiled but open, and the sexuality itself is not potential but realized.

The "white bellies" which "swell to the sun" have been read as an image of pregnancy.[30] It seems more likely, however, that they are a direct representation of the body's response during cer-

tain sexual activities. In general, throughout Whitman, readers
have been unwilling to look carefully at his sexual figures to see
if any real activity is taking place; instead, out of embarrassment
or ignorance, they have moved quickly to a symbolic interpretation. In this case, the bulge of the men's bellies comes from the
arching of their backs, which is the usual position for men who are
being fellated. The scene which Whitman depicts begins as a masturbatory fantasy, as the hand "descended tremblingly," but it
concludes with a fantasy of mass fellatio, as all twenty-eight men
apparently climax and shower the sky, and their sexual partners,
with sperm: "They do not think whom they souse with spray."
The exuberance of this final image comes partly from sexual desire but also from Whitman's buoyant belief in the possibility
of distributing sexual energy. The "spray," the life force of the
twenty-eight young men, is released into the world and becomes
a token of the value in multiplicity of the world. Against nineteenth-century medical theories of the conservation of energy
through the withholding of sperm, Whitman proposes a radical
redistribution of that energy through the release of sperm. To the
"capitalism" of heterosexual intercourse (with its implications of
male domination and ownership) Whitman opposes the "socialism" of nondirected sex.

In such sections of the poem Whitman displays the development of a political consciousness which bases its call for social
reorganization upon a major change in sexuality. Whitman, like
his contemporaries Engels and Lewis Morgan,[31] appears to have
seen a connection between the organization of society (concentration of capital and power) and the organization of sexuality (marriage and the subordination of women). Whitman's democratic
society, as outlined throughout his poetry and made more explicit
in *Democratic Vistas*, would require the suppression or elimination
of the aggressive forces which lead to capitalism, imperial power,
and the domination of women by men, and their replacement by
the loving forces which lead to an economic system of sharing,
a political system of universal participation, and a sexual system
that allows for the full expression of sexual energy in ways that
are neither aggressive nor directed toward use. In other words,
Whitman's ideal society requires socialism, democracy, and homosexuality. For the homosexual impulse, as Whitman depicts
it in his poetry and essays, is inherently nonaggressive, based on
sharing rather than the drive for power. It is not directed toward

the creation of a product (the child) which will continue to feed the economic system. For these reasons, although Whitman's images do not exclude the more traditional sexual acts, they give primary importance to the caress, symbol of a love which does not destroy but preserves the integrity of the individual selves.

Whitman's celebration of undirected sexual energy leads him, appropriately, to a very long catalog, a rejoicing in the things of the world. Prominent among the things celebrated is male beauty. Immediately following the moment of sexual release we see the "butcher-boy" and a few lines later "blacksmiths with grimed and hairy chests." These images demonstrate that Whitman did not confine himself to pastoral dreams, as many have charged. As we shall see, he made use of the pastoral tradition in "Calamus," but he was also an effective poet of urban life. The call to the country in Whitman is not an idyllic yearning for a return to the past but, rather, a call for escape from the oppressions of life in the city. Whitman's erotic figures are not Greek shepherd boys, nor are they traditional pederastic figures at all. They represent Whitman's ideal of energy and commitment; they are men at work, ordinary and democratic. They are to be the heroes of the new epic, the new lovers to replace Achilles and Patroclus. Whitman rejoices in the colorful mosaic of the city, with its rapidly changing scenes and its constant offering of young men, who will become the "lovers and comrades" of "Calamus." For the time being they are merely glimpsed while at work. In a memorable image— worthy of Hopkins, who learned a great deal from Whitman— Whitman calls attention to the blacksmiths and the "lithe sheer of their waists." Whitman's ability to combine two adjectives here so that each modifies the other and becomes in part a noun illustrates his verbal strength, strikingly combined with his awareness of male beauty. As is well known, Hopkins made use of the image of boys bathing in his "Epithalamion" (directly influenced by section 11 of "Song of Myself" in such lines as "By there comes a listless stranger; beckoned by the noise / He drops toward the river unseen / sees . . .") and borrowed something of Whitman's exuberance here for the young workingmen in such poems as "Harry Ploughman." The affinity between Whitman and Hopkins is due partly to a sense of shared sexuality and partly to a sense of poetic indebtedness: Whitman's lines often seem like primitive precursors of Hopkins' meters, and "lithe sheer" must strike us now as "sprung rhythm."

Throughout the catalog Whitman expresses his relationship to the world in terms of love; but it is a nonselective, divinely promiscuous love:

> Adorning myself to bestow myself on the first that will take
>   me,
> Not asking the sky to come down to my goodwill,
> Scattering it freely forever.

The final metaphor, suggesting as it does generation ("We plow the fields and scatter," in the words of the hymn for rogation), emphasizes Whitman's distributive sexuality and recalls the final words of the earlier passage ("souse with spray"). In both cases the poet emphasizes that the sense of pride and power must be eliminated from sexuality and that this is to be accomplished by a deliberate acceptance of the passive role, by allowing oneself to be made love to rather than seeking out someone to make love to (note "the first that will *take* me"—my emphasis).

In section 21, Whitman makes use of the body/soul contrast to express his desire to restore the bodily. He returns to the earth in its plenitude ("rich apple-blossomed earth!"), rendering back the love that the earth has given him. This love that he feels for the earth is evoked in his passionate cry "O unspeakable passionate love!" That this love is not unspeakable simply because it is too great to be spoken is made clear by the following lines:

> Thruster holding me tight and that I hold tight!
> We hurt each other as the bridegroom and the bride hurt
>   each other.

Here as so often in "Song of Myself" the content appears to be heterosexual, though only in symbolic terms (the earth is imagined as female), while the context, when closely analyzed, reveals itself to be homosexual. Just as in the first image of lovemaking in the poem, we can see that the scene is one of love between two men. The "thruster" is an unmistakable image of the male lover, and the simile of the second line indicates a deliberate comparison with heterosexual love. The poet makes love to the world, in the sense that he imposes upon the world his mark, his art, and also in the sense that the world makes its mark upon the poet. The poet, leaving himself open and receptive to the sensual experiences of the world, becomes the receptacle into which the world pours itself in order to find expression. Whitman makes use of the male marriage metaphor in order to suggest his closeness to experience and his role as a passive receiver of inspiration (he is, to be blunt, fucked by the earth, as a man may be fucked by his "thrusting" partner). At the same time, he is both giver and receiver ("we hurt each other"), as an artist imposing an order upon the experience that he receives.

As the poet imagines himself making love, his assertions become bolder. There is a clear transition from the passages of sexual awareness to those of political awareness. Recognizing his position as an outsider, as marginal or criminal, he asserts his rights and those of others who have been made victims of arbitrary ethical codes. Whitman rejects the whole notion of good and evil, returning to a (Quaker-based?) idea of the goodness of all being. "What blurt is it about virtue and vice?" he exclaims. Instead of such categories he proclaims a code of behavior based upon inner standards, a profound antinomianism which asserts the rights of the individual: "What we do is right and what we affirm is right." His language is fully engaged, a call for the realization of the full potential of self, through metaphors of revolution and escape from slavery: "Beat the gong of revolt, and stop with fugitives and them that plot and conspire." While the revolution of which Whitman speaks is not specifically identified with homosexuality, it is linked to a recognition of full sexual identity: "[I] make short account of neuters and geldings, and favor men and women fully equipped." If one cannot identify Whitman's call with the call for homosexual liberation, one must admit that it seems at least to include it and that the language he chooses is strikingly similar to that used later by those speaking for homosexual liberation. Whitman gives voice to "many long dumb voices," "forbidden voices / Voices of sexes and lusts," and calls for a new openness and self-revelation:

Unscrew the locks from the doors!
Unscrew the doors themselves from their jambs!

One cannot help hearing the similarity of Whitman's metaphor for the exposure of the hidden, the ending of the secret life, to "Out of the closets into the streets!"—a more modern call for a turn from private sexuality to political action.

As his ire increases, the blood and sperm rise ("You my rich blood, your milky stream pale strippings of my life") and are asserted to be part of his sacred self. The calamus symbol ("Root

of washed sweet-flag, timorous pond-snipe, nest of guarded duplicate eggs") is introduced as a metaphor for his own genitals, and
he is able to sing all of the body, with penis and sperm. The use
of the calamus symbol here gives the lie to Whitman's later attempts to claim that his use of the plant was merely fortuitous.
This line, present in the first edition of "Song of Myself," is the
source of the central image of the "Calamus" section, written in
1859 or 1860. The symbol of male friendship, of adhesiveness,
is the male genitals: it is impossible to believe that Whitman,
at the time he conceived this as a major symbol for his poems,
wished to imply a love which was merely fraternal and not physical. The following lines continue the phallic associations, evoking another image important for Whitman:

> Winds whose soft-tickling genitals rub against me it shall
>   be you,
> Broad muscular fields, branches of liveoak, loving lounger
>   in my winding paths, it shall be you,
> Hands I have touched, face I have kissed, mortal I have ever
>   touched, it shall be you.

Edwin Miller, pursuing his oedipal reading of Whitman,
finds that the first of the lines cited "evokes the child-mother motif."[32] But surely he is insensitive to the text. Do mothers rub
their genitals against their children? The encounter is clearly with
another man (men's genitals rub and tickle each other's as women's
do not), and all the associations are of male love. The "broad muscular fields" are not merely those of the earth but those of a lover,
a lover who has become the entire universe, filling the poet ("loving lounger in my winding paths") and transcending a personal
role to become all lovers ("mortal I have ever touched"). The use of
the "branches of liveoak" is particularly interesting, since, as Fredson Bowers had demonstrated, it was the live oak which was originally planned as the central symbol of what became the "Calamus"
poems. Here the live oak and the calamus are used in closely related passages, which recount the poet's coming to sexual awareness and culminate in a sexual climax: "Seas of bright juice suf-
fuse heaven."

And yet, suddenly the passage comes to an end with the apparent arrival of dawn, which would destroy the night. The reference is at the same time ambiguous, since the physical dawn
would end the nighttime vision, but the daybreak of sexual ecstasy

would show the poet the possibility of ultimate victory over the day through his sexual powers:

> Dazzling and tremendous how quick the sunrise would kill
>   me,
> If I could not now and always send sunrise out of me.
>
> We also ascend dazzling and tremendous as the sun,
> We found our own my soul in the calm and cool of the
>   daybreak.

Man can make his own sunrise and, thereby, master the natural world and escape the necessity of the cyclical pattern; recall the first sexual experience, section 5, which also took place in the morning. Making love in the morning seems to break the tyranny of the day. It asserts the power of the inner light to triumph over the outer, the triumph of the "ascension" of the human.

The next few sections record the poet's playful reluctance to give in, to let himself be brought to orgasm, a coyness which is ended by the rebirth of section 28:

> Is this then a touch? . . . quivering me to a new identity,
> Flames and ether making a rush for my veins,
> Treacherous tip of me reaching and crowding to help them,
> My flesh and blood playing out lightning, to strike what
>   is hardly different from myself,
> On all sides prurient provokers stiffening my limbs,
> Straining the udder of my heart for its withheld drip,
> Behaving licentious toward me, taking no denial,
> Depriving me of the best as for a purpose,
> Unbuttoning my clothes and holding me by the bare waist,
> Deluding my confusion with the calm of the sunlight and
>   pasture fields,
> Immodestly sliding the fellow-senses away,
> They bribed to swap off with touch, and go and graze at
>   the edges of me,
> No consideration, no regard for my draining strength or my
>   anger,
> Fetching the rest of the herd around to enjoy them awhile,
> Then all uniting to stand on a headland and worry me.
>
> The sentries desert every other part of me,
> They have left me helpless to a red marauder,

> They have come to the headland to witness and assist against
>   me.
>
> I am given up by traitors;
> I talk wildly . . . I have lost my wits . . . I and nobody else
>   am the greatest traitor,
> I went myself first to the headland . . . my own hands car-
>   ried me there.
>
> You villain touch! what are you doing? . . . my breath is
>   tight in its throat;
> Unclench your floodgates! you are too much for me.

The "new identity" is specifically based on sexual awareness. The "provokers," ironically viewed as a raiding party, only complete an action begun by the poet himself, with his "own hands." Whitman's view is comic, as it rests upon an exaggeration of the provocation and plays upon the contrast between the apparent loss of "my wits" and the simultaneous acquisition of a "new identity." The passage records the transition from a sudden recognition of the "rush" caused by "a touch" to the playful "confusion" and "anger" and finally to the almost unbearable desire for sexual release.

Two lines follow this passage in the printed version of 1855:

> Blind loving wrestling touch! Sheathed hooded sharptoothed
>   touch!
> Did it make you ache so leaving me?

The pain at the moment of sexual withdrawal—a pain both spiritual and physical—is assuaged by the realization of the spiritual growth that has come with lovemaking. Hating to quit the individual lover, one recognizes nonetheless that one can now turn to the entire world with love. These lines appear to refer specifically to anal intercourse; Whitman is reborn as he takes into himself the seed of the unnamed lover. The references to "sheathed" and "hooded" seem almost certainly to refer to the uncircumcised penis. The "floodgates" must be "unclenched" in line 640, orgasm apparently occurs between lines 640 and 641, and lines 641–642 look back upon the pain of withdrawal, which is particularly sharp in anal intercourse.

If one returns to the manuscript from which this passage apparently derived, a different sexual act seems to be described. The manuscript describes the act of fellatio, thus making sense of the word "sharptoothed" retained in the printed version:

> Grip'd Wrestler! do you keep your heaviest grip for the last?
> Must you bite with your teeth with the worst spasms at part-
>   ing?
> Will you struggle worst when I plunge you from the thresh-
>   old?
> Does it make you ache so to leave me?
> Take what you like, I can resist you no longer,
> I think I shall sink.
> Take drops of my life, if that is what you are after.
> Only pass to someone else, for I will contain you no longer.
> Pass to someone else; leap to the nearest landing.
> Little as your mouth is, it has drained me dry of my strength.
> I am faintish.[33]

As in the published version, it is the experience of orgasm, the fainting away of sexual satisfaction, which gives rise to Whitman's "cosmic consciousness." But in this version the act described is far more explicit than in the published version. Nonetheless, despite the fact that this text was first published in 1942, it seems to have had almost no impact on the critics' reading of Whitman. "Song of Myself" is still read as if it were a poem without "real" sexual content, and Whitman's homosexuality continues to be considered "spiritual" only. A close examination of such passages reveals that Whitman was depicting specific sexual activities, that an act of fellatio is the prelude to and precondition of the floating state which Whitman enters and which provides his sense of universal unity.

It is not, of course, of great importance to determine whether Whitman is describing fellatio or anal intercourse or is joining the two in a single fused image. It is necessary to insist upon the question here in order to show the sexual basis of Whitman's spiritual vision. Sexuality, in Whitman, is not a metaphor but an act; its value comes both from its inherent pleasure and from the spiritual growth it can bring. Whitman's manuscripts include both the passage cited above and another related passage, which seems to depict anal intercourse:

> Fierce Wrestler! do you keep your heaviest grip for the last?
> Will you sting me most even at parting?

> Will you struggle even at the threshold with spasms even
>   more delicious than all before?
> Does it make you ache so to leave me?[34]

In all cases the sexual analogy is used to make a philosophical or political point. Just as in lovemaking the lovers strive to prolong their orgasm and preserve their brief moment of union, only to learn that release brings with it its own pleasures of reflection and calm, so the drive of one individual toward another is the first step toward a perception, in visionary terms, of one's union with the world. The move is always from the particular to the general, from love of one person to love of all. Learning to separate is difficult, for it brings pain, the pain of sexual withdrawal; but for Whitman it remained one of the principal lessons of "Song of Myself," since it was essential to self-realization.

Whitman's insistence upon the intensity of the physical encounter, as well as its brevity, is made clear in section 32, where he turns to the stallion, symbol of the male lover. Here the poet, who has often been the so-called passive partner in sexual intercourse, becomes the active partner, as Whitman makes vivid the banal sexual metaphor of "riding" someone:

> Picking out here one that shall be my amie,[35]
> Choosing to go with him on brotherly terms,
>
> A gigantic beauty of a stallion, fresh and responsive to my
>   caresses,
> Head high in the forehead and wide between the ears,
> Limbs glossy and supple, tail dusting the ground,
> Eyes well apart and full of sparkling wickedness . . . ears
>   finely cut and flexibly moving.
>
> His nostrils dilate . . . my heels embrace him . . . his well
>   built limbs tremble with pleasure . . . we speed around
>   and return.
>
> I but use you a moment and then I resign you stallion. . . .

Whitman's "brotherly" love is explicitly sexual and explicitly momentary. The moment is brief but fulfilling; it leads not to possession but to the vision, in this case to the famous section 33, where the poet is "afoot with my vision," recalling the first lines of "The Sleepers."

In this vision, as in those of "The Sleepers," the poet is not able to separate sexuality from guilt. Death images are pervasive and culminate, in section 38, in his vision of himself as crucified. His racial memory includes all experience and all suffering. He becomes a sacrificial victim, taking upon himself the sins of the world and thereby assuring the safety and sleep of his beloved. Reborn like the resurrected Christ, he can begin his journey across the continent—"Ohio and Massachusetts and Virginia and Wisconsin and New York and New Orleans and Texas and Montreal and San Francisco and Charleston and Savannah and Mexico"— and beyond. His poetic mission will be carried on by his "élèves," the poet's disciples, who can learn the meaning of the words only if they have followed out the sexual patterns of the poem and have in fact become the poet's lovers. Whitman acknowledges his inability to be totally honest, the necessity he has felt to be somewhat circumspect about his own sexual nature:

Man or woman! I might tell how I like you, but cannot,
And might tell what it is in me and what it is in you, but cannot,
And might tell the pinings I have . . . the pulse of my nights and days.

The passage is itself less than totally frank, with its initial "man or woman," although it seems clear that "or woman" is added as a fairly transparent dodge; there is no reason why the poet could not tell of his love for a woman or, at least, identify her as a woman. As so often, Whitman's universal references serve at least in part to conceal the specifically homosexual sources of his poetry. He "cannot" tell what he feels because of the social pressure that weighs upon the homosexual. He can hint, he can indicate, but he must always withhold confirmation of his sexual nature.

That what cannot be told directly is Whitman's homosexuality is substantiated by his appropriation of these lines for "Not Heaving from my Ribb'd Breast Only," included as "Calamus" 6, in 1860. There Whitman acknowledges that adhesiveness is integral to his poetry as to his life, exclaiming "O adhesiveness! O pulse of my life!" In 1855 "the pulse of my nights and days" could not be spoken, partly because of social pressure and partly because of the absence of a vocabulary. As we shall see, Whitman only began using the term "adhesiveness" in 1856, out of his need

for a word to express the love of men for each other. But before
that time, as Whitman put it at the end of "Song of Myself,"
"There is that in me . . . I do not know what it is . . . but I
know it is in me / . . . it is without name . . . it is a word unsaid / it is not in any dictionary . . ."

It is unfair, nonetheless, to consider "Song of Myself" duplicitous or dishonest to any significant degree. Whitman was clearly
seeking to give the fullest possible expression to the sexual origins
of both his mystic vision and his belief in a new democratic society.
He constantly sought honesty. But it was difficult to achieve when
the honest word, had it existed, would have been misunderstood
as a sexual perversion and sin. Even now many critics defend Whitman against the charge of homosexuality by claiming that he was
not "unwholesome," implying that homosexuality is unwholesome. Whitman concluded that his message could only be delivered to his "élèves"—his lovers and readers—for only they would
understand.

The last sections of the poem portray the poet assuring his
sleeping lover of love and protection:

> Sleep! I and they keep guard all night,
> Not doubt, not decease shall dare to lay finger upon you

He brings his message of salvation, his Christ-like role, to the
world, and feels certain of the correctness of his mission. Thus
assured, he awakens the lover in section 44: "It is time to explain
myself—Let us stand up." He realizes that he has escaped the trap
of reality through his acceptances, including Death, hardest of all
to accept. But once he has accepted it (and acceptance was already
implied in section 8), he is already "out of time and out of space"
(to quote Poe, who sometimes seems surprisingly like Whitman).

Having achieved that state of ascension, he can now say goodbye to the lover, recognizing his transitoriness. The acceptance of
death means that no earthly love is final, that all lovers will part;
and so he parts from his lover, prepared to give himself to the
world rather than to any one individual. He cannot take the lover
with him but must ask him to make his own journey:

> Not I, not any one else can travel that road for you,
> You must travel it for yourself.
> .   .   .   .
> Here are biscuits to eat and here is milk to drink,

But as soon as you sleep and renew yourself in sweet clothes
   I will certainly kiss you with my goodbye kiss and open
   the gate for your egress hence.
.   .   .   .
Long have you timidly waded, holding a plank by the shore,
Now I will you to be a bold swimmer,
To jump off in the midst of the sea, and rise again and nod
   to me and shout, and laughingly dash with your hair.

Whitman's homely communion of biscuits and milk is a priestly
offering of his own body and blood, the transfer of his own spiritual potential to the young lover. It is in the lover's achievement
of selfhood that the act of love finally will be complete: "The boy
I love, the same becomes a man not through derived power but
in his own right." Through his love Whitman gains the strength
to confront the nightmare image of "The Sleepers" and triumph
over it. The swimmer of "The Sleepers," although "courageous,"
is a "brave corpse." The swimmer of "Song of Myself" has every
hope of success; he fulfills Whitman's mission, ensuring its continued life and bearing the word into the future.

Having made love, learned about the world, and then bid
the world adieu, the poet is calm again. He has found happiness.
Characteristically Whitman's image is physical and sensual:

Wrenched and sweaty . . . calm and cool then my body becomes;
I sleep . . . I sleep long.

It is only after the experience of sexual gratification, achieved
through the dream, that the visionary experience becomes possible. It is the euphoria of the satisfied lover which gives rise to
the unity of Whitman's poetry of vision, the poems of realization
of unity. Its needs fulfilled, the body expands to encompass the
world. One can accept the death of the world only after transcending individual death, overcoming the fear of the "little death" in
the conviction that all death brings resurrection, that the penis
shall indeed rise again.

Whitman went on to express this central idea in "Calamus"
2, but it runs through his poetry from "Song of Myself" to "Out
of the Cradle":

Every year shall you bloom again, out from where you retired
   you shall emerge again;

O I do not know whether many passing by will discover you
    or inhale your faint odor, but I believe a few will;
.   .   .   .
Do not fold yourself so in your pink-tinged roots timid leaves!
Do not remain down there so ashamed, herbage of my breast!
Come I am determined to unbare this broad chest of mine,
    I have long enough stifled and choked;
Emblematic and capricious blades I leave you, now you serve
    me not,
I will say what I have to say by itself,
I will sound myself and comrades only, I will never again
    utter a call only their call

Out of the cycle of the penis is born the cycle of the soul; out
of his erections, ejaculations (the pun is crucial), and reerections
comes Whitman's faith in a cycle of the world which will comprehend and conquer death. The real sleep is the sleep of the contented
lover who will not die. Whitman's first poems were an important
announcement of his central theme, the relationship of the individual and personal experience of love to the perception of a universe of love.

"O a word to clear one's path": Adhesiveness

It is to the development, identification, and general prevalence of that fervid comradeship, (the adhesive love, at least
rivaling the amative love hitherto possessing imaginative
literature, if not going beyond it,) that I look for the counterbalance and offset of our materialistic and vulgar American
democracy, and for the spiritualization thereof. Many will
say it is a dream, and will not follow my inferences: but I
confidently expect a time when there will be seen, running
like a half-hid warp through all the myriad audible and
visible worldly interests of America, threads of manly friendship, fond and loving, pure and sweet, strong and life-long,
carried to degrees hitherto unknown—not only giving tone
to individual character, and making it unprecedently emotional, muscular, heroic, and refined, but having the deepest
relations to general politics. I say democracy infers such loving comradeship, as its most inevitable twin or counterpart,

without which it will be incomplete, in vain, and incapable of perpetuating itself.[36]

Despite Whitman's extraordinary statement of the significance of what he called "adhesive love" or "adhesiveness," this has remained one of the least understood aspects of his thought. Over forty-five years ago, a scholarly article[37] pointed out that the term "adhesive" came from the language of phrenology, the pseudoscience of reading the bumps of the head to determine character. Since that time most of Whitman's editors have felt that it was sufficient to refer to phrenology to explain Whitman's meaning. As a result, the concept has never been examined in the context of Whitman's own words.

In the passage from *Democratic Vistas* cited above, Whitman uses a series of synonyms which clarify the meaning of adhesive love: "fervid comradeship," "manly friendship," and "loving comradeship." In no case is "comradeship" itself an adequate substitute, unless modified by an adjective of strong affect, such as "fervid" or "loving." Nor apparently is "friendship" an adequate translation of adhesiveness; Whitman must specify "manly" friendship. Manly friendship is both friendship between two men and friendship which remains manly, that is to say, is not effeminate. It is significant that adhesive love does not include, then, the friendship of a man for a woman or of a woman for another woman.[38] Finally we must note Whitman's definition by antonym: adhesive love is not "amative" love. It is therefore clear that Whitman's term "adhesive," although it may derive from the terminology of phrenology, does not function in a phrenological context. It is its connotations, not its denotation, that Whitman calls upon.

Phrenology says nothing about adhesive or about amative love. Its categories include adhesiveness and amativeness, the propensity to friendship and the propensity to love. These are independent entities, not complementary halves of one whole, love. Nor does the development of one preclude the other; the two are simply unrelated and may coexist or not, depending on the bumps on an individual's head, or, as we would say now, his or her psychological makeup.

Whitman took his term "adhesive" from the language of phrenology but gave it an entirely new meaning by contrasting two kinds of love which he called adhesive and amative. These two loves had been recognized for thousands of years; they are implied in the language of the Bible: David loved Jonathan with "a love passing the love of women." [39] But there was no word for this love. For that reason, in fact, not so many years after Whitman wrote the lines cited at the beginning of this essay, Lord Alfred Douglas spoke of "the love that dare not speak its name." [40] Not even when his poem was used to help convict Oscar Wilde was its name spoken. By the refusal to "name," to create a word, language had been used to deny the existence of any other love. But Whitman was indeed Emerson's "poet as namer." He gave that love the first name it had of its own, albeit a poor and borrowed one.

Whitman himself was aware of the problem of namelessness, as he revealed in his notes on words and language, later gathered together as *An American Primer*. He was struck by the fact that although "passionate fondness" flourished among young men, particularly those of the "muscular classes," "they yet have remarkably few words or names for the friendly sentiments." Although such words apparently existed, "they are words which the muscular classes, the young men of these states, rarely use, and have an aversion for." [41] The words for the other love have almost always been scientific—"homosexuality"—or religious—"sodomy"; they have never been ordinary words that Whitman's muscular young men could use for themselves. They have not described a "friendly sentiment" but a forbidden sexual act. The words which have characterized that love have been part of the process of distancing and objectifying it. For this reason, in the twentieth century the term "gay" gained acceptance, first by gays themselves and then by a larger public. As blacks have preferred that term to "Negro," which they consider condescending, so gays have rejected the clinicism implied by "homosexuality," or "inversion," or any other term which they have not chosen themselves.

Whitman found in the vocabulary of phrenology a term which he could use and make his own. His appropriation of the word "adhesiveness" was an essential part of the process of validating love between men. As he used it, it lost its phrenological associations and took on new ones; it evoked the qualities Whitman admired—loyalty, fidelity, sharing, touching. It was to be the new word of a new religion. Whitman gave the word and made it flesh; it was for others to acknowledge it, to take it up, to make it a banner, a pennant, a sign of the new order and the new faith. Under its sign they would conquer.

It has frequently been suggested that Whitman's awareness of his adhesiveness dates from the "Calamus" sequence. This theory has the advantage of placing two of Whitman's major poems— "Song of Myself" and "The Sleepers"—before such an awareness developed, and the other major poems such as "Lilacs," "Out of the Cradle," and "Passage to India" long after his "adhesive" period. In other words, the theory has isolated the "Calamus" poems from the central body of Whitman's work. Very few contemporary critics are prepared to argue that there is no homosexuality[42] in the "Calamus" poems, as early critics did; they now take a more subtle line. The argument is that "Calamus" represents a transitory period, an interlude of homosexual awareness not to be found in the "major" poems. Textual study has shown that a central group of the "Calamus" poems was composed at a single period and designed as a group, with the central symbol of "live-oak with moss," and so it has been supposed that this cycle of poems arose from a "crisis."[43] (It should be noted that this view, although presented as the conclusion of literary and even textual study, corresponds nicely with the prevailing psychoanalytic theory of homosexuality as a "phase.")[44] In fact, however, Whitman's use of the term "adhesiveness" dates from at least three years before the so-called crisis of 1859, and his awareness of himself as adhesive, although without yet applying the word, dates as far back as his early fiction.

Whitman's first use of the term "adhesiveness" occurs in the "Song of the Open Road" (1856). In section 5 of that poem the poet declares himself free in a radical proclamation: "From this hour I ordain myself loos'd of limits and imaginary lines / Going where I list, my own master total and absolute." The "open road" is metaphor, not place; it stands for a way of life without restraints, without ends or predetermined goals, and without boundaries, as wide as one likes, as pointless as organic growth. The discovery of that road and the sensation of that freedom are necessary for the growth of the self. The poet, "divesting myself of the holds that would hold me" (cf. Stephen Dedalus' "I shall fly by those nets"), expands, "inhaling" space and realizing "I am larger, better than I thought." From that freedom and assertion of the inner man (what Friends call the "light within" or the "inner light"), the poet turns in section 6, to self-examination: "Here is realization, / Here is a man tallied—he realizes here what he has in him." This self-realization is also a process of liberation, a shedding of the social self and a stripping to the naked reality—in Whitman's metaphors, tearing "off the husks" and undoing "stratagems and envelopes." Now, after this preparation, this process of turning within, he can proclaim:

> Here is adhesiveness, it is not previously fashion'd, it is
>   apropos;
> Do you know what it is as you pass to be loved by strangers?
> Do you know the talk of those turning eye-balls?

Adhesiveness is the "kernel" of the poet's self, that which "nourishes" but which cannot be known until after a process of self-examination and self-definition. Then Whitman can announce it, offer it—"Here it is," he says, and proposes both the word and the life it signifies.

Whitman was fully aware that he was offering something new, something unknown and unnamed. Thus he writes, "It is not previously fashioned"; he is the maker, the creator or fashioner, of the new word. Lest there be any doubt of its meaning he gives two examples, both of which admit of no other meaning than an erotic and physical attraction between two men. Whitman explains that the adhesive is rescued from his isolation and confirmed in his existence by the love "of strangers," expressed by an admiring glance, "those turning eye-balls." Adhesiveness in these lines has nothing whatever to do with phrenology. Whitman's subject is not friendship, long-lasting affection between human beings; it is instantaneous sexual attraction between two strangers as they pass in the street. Of course this is not to say that such attraction may not flower into friendship. But it is essential to see that its foundation is sexual *and* democratic; it is not of the salon, nor is it a meeting of intellectual mates. It is random, physical, and joyful; and it yearns for physical expression: "the shuddering longing ache of contact."

The announcement in section 6 of adhesiveness is the dramatic center of the "Song of the Open Road." The following two sections elaborate on the physical nature of desire in terms specifically phallic: "Why when they leave me do my pennants of joy sink flat and lank?" But seeing desire as "the efflux of the soul" the poet must accept what will be seen by others as unduly gross and crude; he must accept physical desire as a part of universal spirit. There follow six sections each beginning with "Allons!" and one section beginning "Listen!" which acts as a warning to

would-be disciples. Each of the "Allons!" sections is a revolutionary call to arms echoing the "Marseillaise," a call to the freedom
of the soul. That call has a particular urgency for those who live
lives of shame and concealment. For the new gospel is to be one
of exposure, as exposure is necessary to self-realization: "Out of the
dark confinement! out from behind the screen!" The price of concealment is terrifying isolation, self-deception, and duplicity: "No
husband, no wife, no friend, trusted to hear the confession, / Another self, a duplicate of every one, skulking and hiding it goes."
As section 13 reveals, such men and women are everywhere: "in the
parlors, / In the cars of railroads, in steamboats, in the public
assembly." The mutual recognition of this community is essential,
for it brings a sense of solidarity and the possibility of release from
isolation. The word can finally be spoken; the truth can be told.

Whitman is not politically naive about the possibilities for
a change in the attitudes of homosexuals themselves and of others
toward homosexuals. He recognizes that the path will be "through
struggles and wars"; yet he retains his faith that adhesiveness can
be attained: "The goal that was named cannot be countermanded."
Each struggle will bring a new struggle, as each victory brings
renewed opposition. But the open road is not the safe path: it is
the way of "active rebellion." The form of that rebellion is largely
personal. Echoing Christ's call to his disciples, Whitman calls
upon his to abandon their lives and careers and to come with him.
The test of adhesive love is not in intellectual discourse, nor in
the sermons of churches, nor in the arguments of law courts; it
is in individual experiences of love. Thus the conclusion of the
poem is the joining of hands, a clasp of revolutionary solidarity
that is at the same time a touch of love. The poet addresses his
comrade: "Will you give me yourself? will you come travel with
me? / Shall we stick by each other as long as we live?" Whitman's
final line calls attention to the root meaning of "adhesiveness"
and thus shifts the reader's attention from the abstract concept
to the actual experience of love, as the two lovers "stick by each
other."

The 1860 edition uses "adhesive" or "adhesiveness" five ad-
ditional times. Three of those passages were retained in all suc-
ceeding editions, and only one of them occurs in "Calamus." Thus
it is clear that Whitman did not reject the idea or the word "adhesiveness" (although he never used it again in the composition
of a poem). Had he been seriously embarrassed by his earlier uses

of the concept, he surely would have eliminated every reference, including those in "Song of the Open Road" and not merely those in "Starting from Paumanok" (then called "Proto-Leaf"). It is also clear that adhesiveness is not a concept associated exclusively with "Calamus," as most critics suppose; it predates the "Calamus" sequence and, despite Whitman's frequent revisions, continues long after it.

Whitman's only use of "adhesiveness" in the "Calamus" poems occurs in the sixth (of the 1860 series), "Not Heaving from my Ribb'd Breast Only." The poem is structured rather like a catalog, with sixteen lines beginning "Not" or "Nor." Each of these lines mentions a sign of adhesiveness, all in terms of unfulfilled physical desire. The cumulative effect is highly negative, suggesting an impulse seeking expression but denied it by the conscious, moral self. But in the penultimate line there is a sudden shift and reversal: "Not in any or all of them O adhesiveness! O pulse of my life! / Need I that you exist and show yourself any more than in these songs." The contrast is between the involuntary expression of adhesiveness in sighs, pounding blood, panting, and other physical phenomena and the voluntary expression of adhesiveness in "these songs." Whitman draws together all the images of bodily energy in his phrase "pulse of my life!" to suggest not merely the presence of adhesiveness but its necessity. It is his very heart-flow; without it he would die. As he gives expression in his dreams to his adhesive desires, so too shall he give expression in his songs. The poem operates subtly to undercut an apparently negative catalog of physical symptoms, by suggesting that these are but signs of his "pulse," the flow of life within him. By so doing he elevates adhesiveness to the central fact of his being, a fact which for him must not only "exist" but also "show yourself." The expression of adhesive love in the poems of *Leaves of Grass* or of "Calamus" is essential to his survival. The point is important, for Whitman is suggesting that his adhesive nature is no mere incident in his life, no accidental and minor attribute, but the very source of his energy as a man and poet. He declares that he cannot be understood without his adhesiveness.

In the 1860 edition Whitman printed a number of "Thoughts." These are brief passages of reflection, based presumably on Pascal. They stand at the boundary between poetry and prose and offer a single insight. The full text of the seventh "Thought" is:

Of obedience, faith, adhesiveness:
As I stand aloof and look there is to me something profoundly affecting in large masses of men following the lead
of those who do not believe in men.

Whitman's thought is drawn, I suppose, from the military, but
it could as well have come from almost any group of men—in a
factory, sports, or politics. The point is, of course, that these men
commit themselves to the leadership of someone who is not adhesive, that is, who feels no affection or fondness for them. The
relationship therefore remains one of competition and power.
Whitman questions the effect of adhesiveness on situations in
which men are seen as part of a mass. He poses an ironic contrast
between obedience and adhesiveness, emphasizing the lack of love
in such situations. By implication one sees the transformation accomplished when the leaders of men "believe in men," when the
generals love the privates and the privates love the generals, as
in certain ancient armies. With adhesiveness obedience will be
based on love, not fear.

Whitman's final poem, "So Long!" is also a poem of adhesiveness. Here the statement is quite straightforward. Whitman concludes his work with an announcement of "what comes after me."
Like Christ taking leave of his disciples, Whitman foresees the fulfillment of his mission. Among those of his doctrines to be realized
is adhesiveness: "I announce adhesiveness, I say it shall be limitless, unloosen'd, / I say you shall yet find the friend you were
looking for." Whitman's placement of adhesiveness here among
his political and spiritual goals is significant. For he did not see
adhesiveness as a private matter, whose realization was merely a
matter of personal satisfaction. He recognized that the goals of
American democracy would always be unrealized as long as adhesiveness had no place and that full spiritual development could
not take place until women and men were free to develop their
potential for love of members of the same sex. To say this is not
to "sublimate," as some critics have thought, or to weaken his
statement. It is to enlarge it and insist upon its importance. The
reader who has already read the "Song of the Open Road," "Calamus," and the 1860 version of "Proto-Leaf" does not need to be
told of the personal significance of adhesive love. But he does perhaps need to be reminded that the expression of adhesiveness is
not merely the personal need of a few but a national priority.
While Whitman's vision would render justice to the adhesive,

it would also make adhesiveness "limitless," spreading it throughout the nation and thereby working toward greater democratization and spiritualization (as Whitman stated again in *Democratic Vistas*).

The 1860 edition of *Leaves of Grass* thus was framed by statements of adhesive love. The introductory poem in that edition, now known as "Starting from Paumanok," contained two references to adhesiveness, both of which were revised in preparing the 1867 edition.[45] It is important to look at these passages and their place in the poem as a whole if we want to know to what extent, if any, Whitman renounced his adhesive goals after 1860. (There is other evidence, of course, to suggest that he did not: the strongly adhesive nature of the *Drum-Taps* poems, the notebooks recording encounters with young men who spent the night, and the long friendship with Peter Doyle. We shall confine our discussion here, however, to Whitman's use of "adhesive" and "adhesiveness.")

In section 22 of "Proto-Leaf" (section numbers refer to the 1860 edition), Whitman establishes a relationship between the political theme of American unity and the sexual theme of "manly love," and considers the expression of his own desires as a way of signaling the new ideal to others. Out of this motivation comes his decision not to repress and conceal but to proclaim:

> I will therefore let flame from me the burning fires that were
>   threatening to consume me
> I will lift what has too long kept down those smouldering
>   fires,
> I will give them complete abandonment

Prior to these lines Whitman's manuscript included another line, "I believe the main purport of America is to found a new ideal of manly friendship, more ardent, more general." This line was eliminated in preparing the 1860 text and reappears in "Calamus" 35, composed later. Thus a clear link between "Proto-Leaf" and "Calamus" could be established by textual evidence, if the thematic relationship were not sufficiently clear. It is interesting to note that in section 22 Whitman suggests a positive effect of openness: the "smouldering fires" had threatened to consume him as long as they were suppressed; now that they are allowed to burn in "complete abandonment" he is no longer in danger. It is the repression of manly love which is destructive, not its expression.

The section continues, "I will write the evangel-poem of

comrades and of love." Since this statement is made in the "Proto-
Leaf" or Proem, it is clear that *Leaves of Grass* is meant and not
merely "Calamus." As I have suggested earlier, Whitman often
compared himself to Christ. (This comparison is felt by many to
be blasphemous and a sign of arrogance on the part of Whitman.
It must be remembered that Whitman was not a Christian and
that his reference therefore cannot be blasphemous. Whitman
compares himself not to a divinity but to a moral teacher.) He
meant his poem to fulfill the mission begun by Christ, the gospel
of love, which was uncompleted or misunderstood. (It is quite
possible, of course, that Whitman was aware of the theory that
Christianity had in fact begun as a homosexual cult, with the relationship between Jesus and St. John, the Beloved Disciple, as its
paradigm.) *Leaves of Grass* was to be the *new* New Testament, the
gospel of "comrades," revealed by Whitman just as Christ revealed
a new religion of love to replace the harsher Judaic code. The New
Jerusalem of brotherly love was to be located in America, founded,
likewise, by Whitman.

Whitman returns to this theme in section 33, "O I see the
following poems are indeed to drop in the earth the germs of a
greater Religion." Here all three elements come together: love,
democracy, and religion. Whitman is addressing his "comrade"
(in 1867 this was changed to "dear son" just as "dear son" replaces
"mon cher!" in section 31) and expressing his role as interpreter
of the divine: "I take to your reckless and composite chords—I
add to them, and cheerfully pass them forward." The source of
that divine energy is sexual, and like sexual energy it is transmitted without exercising a permanent hold. From the sense of the
physical ("contact daily and hourly") comes a receptiveness to experience and an awareness of the unity of the world, a unity equally
expressed by love, democracy, and religion. That unity takes prec-
edence over the particular moment of union, whether it be the
union of a man with his lover or of a man with his God:

> Not he, adhesive, kissing me so long with his daily kiss,
> Has winded and twisted around me that which holds me to
>   him,
> Any more than I am held to the heavens, to the spiritual
>   world,
> And to the identities of the Gods, my unknown lovers,
> After what they have done to me, suggesting such themes.
>   (1860 ed. sec. 36)

Finally man is responsible to his own life, not to any lover or any god, no matter how much they may have helped him find his way. The point of such love affairs is always, for Whitman, self-reliance.

In manuscript the first line quoted above read, "Not he whom I love, kissing me . . ." Whitman substituted "adhesive" for "whom I love," not, I think, to censor himself in any way but in order to make greater use of his new word. He clearly felt that "adhesive" would convey the love which had been explicit in the manuscript version. An intent to censor the passage seems unlikely since the other physical details ("winded and twisted around me") are left intact. Then when revising the printed text for reprinting, Whitman changed his text again: the first line became, after several attempts at wording, "Now he with a daily kiss onward from childhood kissing me." Whatever Whitman's motivation in making these changes, it is certain that they do not improve the line. The 1867 text is awkward and ponderous; either of the earlier versions is preferable. The modern reader might well prefer the first, as being the most direct; but this preference would not take into account Whitman's desire not merely to celebrate love between men but also to invent a word for it. Unfortunately the use of that word has resulted not, as Whitman hoped, in the proclamation of that love and the unification of men under its banner but in the suggestion of a secret code or esoteric reference— as if he had used a Masonic symbol. The deletion of "adhesive" may reflect some awareness of this problem on Whitman's part, although it does not explain why he left "adhesiveness" elsewhere in the poem. The effect of its removal is not, in any case, a significant diminution of the sexuality of this section. A more serious deletion, in fact, is that of the fourth line quoted above, probably out of fear of blasphemy. Whitman had already lost his position in the Department of the Interior, and it is far more likely that government censors would look for heresy or blasphemy than signs of "adhesiveness." A similar deletion of a related passage occurred in "Song of Myself," where God is "a loving bedfellow" in 1855; when the passage was revised the bedfellow is still loving, but he is no longer identified as God.

The last two sections of "Proto-Leaf" were also heavily revised and eventually made into a single stanza. In both the manuscript and the 1860 edition the phrases "O adhesiveness! O the pensive aching to be together—you know not why and I know not why" occur, although "O adhesiveness!" is placed at the end of the preceding line in the printed version. This change gives somewhat less emphasis to the phrase, although it is still clear that the "pensive aching" is in apposition with "adhesiveness." What is not entirely clear from the printed version is the reference of the next line, "O a word to clear one's path ahead endlessly!" back to "O adhesiveness!" The word in question is "adhesiveness," of course, and it is that which is to "clear one's path ahead." It is under that sign that Whitman and his reader/lover can "join hands and haste on." In the 1867 revisions the passage is considerably muddled by the omission of both "adhesiveness" and "pensive aching," as well as the characteristic change of "O my comrade!" into the stilted and artificial "O camerado close!" Without "adhesiveness" the reference to "a word" becomes meaningless. We can only speculate, of course, on the reasons for these changes. No doubt, as one critic[46] has suggested, the changes were prompted primarily by artistic considerations; certainly the stanza profits by some cutting of the repetitive "O"s and the vague and pompous "power, liberty, eternity." But at the same time it has lost its specific appeal to unity through adhesiveness. Perhaps Whitman thought the "word" would be understood by his readers without being specified. If so he erred. It has not been understood when stated, much less when implied.

Although Whitman did not use the words "adhesive" or "adhesiveness" in any poem after 1860, they clearly remained part of his vocabulary. In a notebook entry, apparently from 1870, Whitman wrote: "Depress the adhesive nature / It is in excess— making life a torment / All this diseased, feverish disproportionate *adhesiveness*." If evidence is still necessary, this should serve as final confirmation of the fact that Whitman did not use the term in its phrenological meaning—after all, why should he want to depress friendship?—but as a synonym for what we now call homosexuality. This same notebook has a number of entries which record Whitman's uncertainties and doubts about his relationship to Peter Doyle. It should be noted, however, that nowhere does Whitman question his own adhesive nature. He does not ask, "Am I adhesive?" but writes, "Depress the adhesive nature," for which we may read "repress." Whitman's uncertainty stemmed from his fear that his love for Doyle was not returned: "fancying what does not really exist in another, but is all the time in myself alone." Whitman concealed the fact that these diary entries referred to Doyle by writing first "P" and then substituting "16" or "164" (for "PD"). Clearly he was afraid that someone might see them and tried to conceal the evidence of his apparently unreciprocated love for another man. For the same reason, he changed the references to Doyle from "him" to "her" throughout these entries.[47] "Adhesiveness" was the word that Whitman used for the sexual attraction of one man for another, including his own for Peter Doyle.[48] Whatever his personal agonies (and certainly they were great) the attempt at self-repression was unsuccessful. The fact that later editions of *Leaves of Grass* continued to announce "adhesiveness" indicates that Whitman continued to believe in his cause, whatever personal suffering it brought and whether or not he found personal satisfaction in love. As he wrote in a line added to "Calamus" 39 in 1867: "I loved a certain person ardently and my love was not return'd, / Yet out of that I have written these songs."

In the absence of a word to express the central emotional fact of his life and the basis of his political and spiritual beliefs, Whitman turned to the language of phrenology. From its store of words he chose the one which came closest to satisfying his needs. But he transformed that word by his usage; from the word for friendship he made the word for manly love. He did this not so much to create a code—although that may have been one of its results[49]—but to give a name to a feeling which existed but had no name capable of expressing its emotional as well as sexual nature. The process of naming was essential to the process of identifying the concept, hence in some sense of creating it.[50] Whitman knew that such love existed, despite the absence of a name. But he also knew that as long as there was no name, there could be no concept and no understanding. What that name should be involved a crucial question of self-definition. By choosing "adhesiveness" Whitman could draw upon the phrenological idea of friendship, the word's inherent associations with fidelity and closeness, and possibly an associated political meaning (as in "adherent"), and then add his own meanings through the contexts in which he placed the word in his works. By thus drawing from the vocabulary of phrenology, he insisted upon an aspect of character and not merely a sexual act.

The opposition which Whitman posited, in *Democratic Vistas*, between adhesive and amative love (the latter phrase appearing to be etymologically a pleonasm, and only making sense when one realizes that Whitman means not amative but heterosexual) shows his allegiance to the traditional idea of two loves. That view is most clearly expressed in Plato's *Symposium*, where Pausanias distinguishes between Heavenly Aphrodite (Aphrodite Urania) and Common Aphrodite (Aphrodite Pandeumia). Those who are inspired by Heavenly Love "are attracted toward the male sex, and value it as being naturally the stronger and more intelligent . . . their intention is to form a lasting attachment and a partnership for life."[51] From this idea of "lasting attachment" Whitman may well have derived his idea of adhesiveness, sticking together, which otherwise seems somewhat at odds with his concept of "lovers, continual lovers." The passage from *The Symposium* was also the source, not long after Whitman wrote, of the word "Uranian," which came to identify an entire school of English verse.[52] Whitman's concept and that of the Uranians, however, must be distinguished. The Uranians almost always favored pederastic love (despite Pausanias' clear distinction between boy-love and the higher love of men, which he attributed to the influence of Urania) and in general saw themselves as a separate class. The Uranian poets frequently followed classical models. They sang the evanescent beauty of the male adolescent; they mourned the necessity of its passing; and they believed that the love of which they wrote was of a higher order than heterosexuality. Uranian love was fundamentally elitist and undemocratic; it affirmed the special as opposed to the common. Whitman's adhesiveness, although it may derive in part from the same Platonic text, is essentially different from Uranian love; and it is important to remember that Whitman never sought a Greek justification for his concept. It was firmly of America and the nineteenth century.

Whitman's most distinguished English follower, Edward Carpenter, used the phrase "intermediate sex,"[53] in light of which one can see the fundamental difference between him and Whitman. Carpenter's "intermediate sex" is basically a biological concept, and in the hands of the German sexologist and social reformer Magnus Hirschfeld it became explicitly physiological. It is a refinement of the concept of hermaphroditism. Even without appealing to biological anomalies, Carpenter's concept suggested a difference that was not primarily emotional or political but physical; its source seems to have been a desire to win social acceptance on the grounds of an innate difference. Carpenter, a socialist, rejected the elitism of the Uranians, but he kept the idea of a fundamental distinction between the intermediate sex and the "normal" individual. Whitman's adhesive lovers, however, were not biologically different from other men; they were not half men, half women (one can see how Carpenter's concept is similar to that advanced by proponents of transsexual surgery) but "manly" men, realizing their full potential for love and showing the way for other men to follow. Whitman believed not that adhesive men were a different class but that they represented the future development of all men.

Whitman's term has not survived; its meaning has been so clouded by time that it is necessary now to uncover its significance anew. But it was a first step in the search for a name to describe both the love and those who shared it. Of the several attempts made in the nineteenth century, only "homosexuality" caught on.[54] But that term was felt by homosexuals themselves to be too clinical, too restricted to sexuality. It seemed to allow no place for affection. And so words like "homophile" were used for a time, without gaining popular acceptance. Increasingly the word "gay," which seems to have acquired this meaning early in the twentieth century and to have entered the literature through Gertrude Stein,[55] has been accepted because of the desire of homosexuals for a word that is both nonclinical and nonsexual. Many people are unhappy with it, finding it perhaps as awkward as Whitman's "adhesiveness." But, like Whitman's term, it does not really matter what the word once meant; the point is what it has come to mean. For Whitman naming was an important stage of the process of self-avowal.

"Calamus"

Probably no body of poems, except perhaps Shakespeare's sonnets, has aroused as much controversy as Whitman's "Calamus." The reason for this is clear: readers' reactions to "Calamus" have depended on their responses not merely to the poetry but even more to the man they have found there. Since most readers have been heterosexual and have shared the prevailing American attitude that homosexuality represents not sexual choice but moral turpitude, they have found it impossible to react to these poems apart from their moral, or moralistic, responses to homosexuality. So, as with criticism of the sonnets, there have been two principal, apparently opposed, approaches. One has recognized that the poems are indeed depictions and even celebrations of love between men, and has condemned them for immorality and abnormality. The other has attempted to reconcile a distaste of homosexuality with a high regard for Whitman's poetry or his political and religious ideas; this approach has denied that the poems depict homosexuality, insisting that they be read metaphorically or as depictions of an ideal, i.e., asexual, friendship. Although these two approaches result in vastly different attitudes toward Whitman, their source is in a similar moral position and a shared assumption that homosexual content in a work of art invalidates the work.

The most hostile statement has been made by Mark Van Doren, who acknowledges Whitman's homosexuality and then asserts that this fact prevents any response by what he terms "the common reader" to "these simpering tales of men who hold hands, blush in one another's presence, long for one another, and ludicrously make eyes as they pass." Since Whitman's political and social views were repeatedly stated by him to be founded on the principle of "adhesiveness," Van Doren finds them invalid, for "manly love is neither more nor less than an abnormal and deficient love."[56] The classic "defense" of Whitman is given by James E. Miller, Jr., who concludes, "there exists no evidence that Whitman's ideal is grounded in abnormality." Miller suggests instead a religious reading of the poems, arguing that Whitman was making use of "the Christian concept of brotherly love."[57]

One of the most elaborate attempts to answer Van Doren's charges was made by Newton Arvin, who shared Whitman's political and social views and did not want to see them invalidated by a charge of abnormality. Arvin also shared Whitman's sexual preferences, although he was unwilling to say so in print,[58] and perhaps even believed, with Van Doren, that such sexuality was "deficient." Arvin accepts Whitman's homosexuality as given: "the fact of Whitman's homosexuality is one that cannot be denied by any informed and candid reader of the 'Calamus' poems, of his published letters, and of accounts by unbiased acquaintances: after a certain point the fact stares one unanswerably in the face." Arvin then goes on, however, to suggest that homosexuality, although a fact, is not a terribly important one: it "is only one of the eccentricities or pathologies that may give a particular bias to a writer's work." Finally, Arvin accepts the Freudian view of a degree of latent homosexuality in everyone but argues that, when it is dominant, "the normal imagination is bound to feel that . . . something has gone tragically awry with the free, full, and balanced development of the social life and human personality."[59] He tries to counter his own argument by showing that Whitman is a more complete human being than most of his literary contemporaries, such as Bryant, Emerson, Poe, or Dickinson (he could well have added Thoreau and perhaps Hawthorne to his list). But Arvin betrays his own confusion and indecision in his argument. He is unwilling to say that Whitman's homosexuality was a source of political strength and a valid basis for his political belief in brotherhood; instead he retreats half-heartedly to the view that Whitman's homosexuality is a neurosis of which the reader should be tolerant. While one can sympathize with the inner conflicts that must have raged as Arvin wrote these pages, one must also recognize that his well-intentioned attempt to protect Whitman and defend him against Van Doren ultimately performs a major disservice, by removing the core of Whitman's thought and leaving a meaningless husk. Arvin's work is an excellent example of homosexual self-oppression (or perhaps one ought to say the agonizing internalization of destructive social mores); but it is also the first attempt by a modern critic to come to terms with Whitman's homosexuality.

Homosexual readers in Whitman's time had much less difficulty recognizing the major theme of "Calamus" and responding positively to it. In the United States Charles Warren Stoddard and Bayard Taylor wrote directly to Whitman, sending him their books and seeking his support for their own "Calamus" themes.[60] From England, Roden Noel wrote, "the proclamation of comradeship seems to me the grandest and most momentous fact in your work."[61] Edward Dowden exclaimed in the *Westminster Review*, "The chord of feeling which he strikes may be old—as old as David and Jonathan—but a fulness and peculiarity of tone are brought out, the like of which have not been heard before."[62] And George Saintsbury wrote in relatively open terms in *The Academy*, "he reiterates the expressions of Plato to Aster, of Socrates respecting Charmides, and in this respect fully justifies (making allowance for altered manners) Mr. Symonds' assertion of his essentially Greek character."[63]

The most enthusiastic response, as well as the best known, was that of John Addington Symonds, who began a correspondence that lasted almost twenty years. Much has been made of Whitman's final letter to Symonds, with its assertion that Whitman was the father of six illegitimate children. That letter was the

response of an aged, tired, and annoyed Whitman to the persistent
inquiries of Symonds; it would be a delightful tall tale were it
not that many people seem to have believed it (and that it was
cruel to the admittedly tiresome Symonds). But more important
is the fact that Whitman kept up a correspondence with Symonds
over all those years, in full knowledge of Symonds' reasons for
his admiration for, and sense of sympathy with, Whitman. Symonds' first letter to Whitman in 1871 mentioned only "Calamus"
of all the sections of *Leaves of Grass* (citing the highly erotic "Scented Herbage of My Breast") and enclosed a poem of Symonds',
"some echo, faint & feeble, of your Calamus."[64] His second letter
was more direct, addressing Whitman as "my Master!" and con-
fessing, "I have pored for continuous hours over the pages of Calamus (as I used to pore over the pages of Plato), longing to hear
you speak, *burning* for a revelation of your more developed meaning, panting to ask—is this what you would indicate? Are then
the free men of your lands really so pure & loving & noble & generous & sincere?"[65] When Whitman did not respond to his hint,
"tell me more about the Love of Friends," Symonds wrote again,
sending his "study of Greek friendship." Although Whitman
never offered Symonds the direct confirmation he sought, neither
did he offer any denial until the end of his life, and so encouraged
Symonds in his conviction that the two shared a belief in the positive value of "Greek friendship," or homosexuality.

Despite the enthusiastic reception given "Calamus" by readers who immediately sensed the possibility of community, so absent from the lives of many nineteenth-century homosexuals, academic critics in the United States have generally been negative
in their responses. Indeed, the only major American critic to write
honestly of Whitman's homosexuality has been Malcolm Cowley,
a poet and not an academic. Although himself heterosexual, Cowley had the rare ability to look at Whitman's poetry honestly and to
speak openly of what he saw. In Cowley's view Whitman first expressed his homosexuality "obliquely, in language that could be
easily understood only by others of his own type," but by 1860
the "impulse to reveal himself" had become strong enough that he
abandoned indirect language.[66] Certainly there is growing frankness and directness in Whitman's treatment of homosexuality in
the first three editions of *Leaves of Grass*, although, as we have
seen, his first use of "adhesive" came in 1856, and he included
passages directly depicting homosexual activity in the 1855 edi-

tion. And Cowley is mistaken if he thinks that "adhesive" was a code word, understood by "others of his own type" (at least I know of no evidence that this is so and no use of the term by anyone else). But the major argument of Cowley's essay is surely correct: Whitman came fairly early (before 1855, although the exact date is unimportant) to an awareness and acceptance of himself as a homosexual—as we would say, he "came out"—although there were times at which he despaired of achieving love, given his nature and the social domination of heterosexuality. No one has followed the example of Cowley and provided a full reading of "Calamus" as the account of Whitman's "coming out," of his emerging self-awareness and his acceptance of this new self and the roles it offered him.

The process of "coming out" is not identical with the first homosexual experience, or even with the first mature homosexual experience. Indeed, many people are predominantly homosexual in their sex lives without ever "coming out," i.e., without ever coming to a full awareness of themselves as homosexuals. In other words, there is a distinction between the noun "homosexual" (or "gay") and the adjective "homosexual"; it is entirely possible to "do" it without "being" it. In distinguishing between doing and being, I deliberately employ an existentialist vocabulary. In the deepest sense, a person becomes a homosexual not when he or she has sexual relations with another person of the same sex but when he or she accepts homosexuality as an element of self-definition. The prison bully who rapes his young cellmate, the boy scout who proposes a "circle jerk," the choirmaster who proposes to take his young charges swimming, the college students who "get drunk" and then "can't remember" what they did, the Italian gigolo offering to fuck his rich American clients—none of them may be considered to "be" homosexual, although each is engaging in some form of homosexual activity. But their homosexuality is not "authentic," to use Sartre's term, because it is not grounded in self-recognition.

Whitman, on the other hand, was, as Cowley wrote, "completely aware of his own nature"[67] and saw it not as an anomaly or, in Arvin's term, an "eccentricity," but as the source of his art, the center of his book, and the foundation of his political theory. Prior to Whitman there were homosexual acts but no homosexuals. Whitman coincides with and defines a radical change in historical consciousness: the self-conscious awareness of homosexuality as an identity. "Calamus" is the heart of *Leaves of Grass*, as well as the root; it is Whitman's book of self-proclamation and self-definition. This does not imply, of course, that it is to be taken as direct autobiographical statement. Like any autobiography, it is fictional, an artful rearrangement of life in order to present oneself in a particular light. "Calamus" does not describe an affair with a particular young man, nor does it deal with an emotional crisis that we may presume to have really occurred. Instead it offers a dramatized version of Whitman's acceptance of himself as a homosexual and his realization of the consequences of that acceptance.

The first poem of the "Calamus" sequence announces the poet's purpose and indicates a major change of heart. Textual evidence presented by Fredson Bowers[68] indicates that the manuscript version of the poem (the Valentine MS in the Barrett collection) was prepared in 1859. However, since that manuscript differs substantially from the version printed in 1860, it is clear that Whitman undertook major revisions of this poem in late 1859 or early 1860 and that he did so with an eye to preparing the introductory poem of this section and to introducing his major symbol, the calamus. (The earlier manuscripts, as Bowers shows, were organized around the central symbol of the live oak, and the first poem of that projected section became number 14 in 1860.)

The original manuscript is of a short, simple six-line poem:

> Long I was held by the life that exhibits itself,
> By what is done in the houses or streets, or in company,
> The usual adjustments and pleasures—the things which all
>   conform to and which the writers celebrate;
> But now I know a life which does not exhibit itself, yet
>   contains all the rest,
> And now, escaping, I celebrate that concealed but substan-
>   tial life,
> I celebrate the need of the love of comrades. —

Only the equivalent of about two lines have been salvaged for the 1860 text (in the final text, parts of lines 3, 11, and 18 are derived from the original text). The calamus symbol is not present nor even implied in the manuscript. Instead, there is an account of what we may term a "conversion." The poet looks back from his new life upon an earlier life, prior to his conversion, and contrasts the two lives. The contrast is strongly established: the first three lines of the manuscript form a single independent clause concerning the past and controlled by the opening words, "Long I was held," while the last three lines, introduced by the sharp transition of "but now," form another independent clause in the present tense with its strong verbs "I know" and "I celebrate."

The sense of contrast is heightened by the opposition between the two lives depicted: in line 1, "the life that exhibits itself," and in line 4, "a life which does not exhibit itself." By that first life the poet was "held," but now he is "escaping" to the second life, which is "concealed but substantial." The first life is the more public life; it represents what is done openly and consists of "the usual adjustments and pleasures—the things which all conform to and which the writers celebrate." Whitman's choice of language is precise: the pleasures of the earlier life are "usual," but not by any means universal. Still, despite their lack of universality, "all conform to" them. In artistic life as in real life, no options are presented: "the writers celebrate" only these usual pleasures. Whitman alone, in the terms of the poem, breaks the tyranny of this conformity, by daring to "celebrate the need of the love of comrades." The poem presents the poet after conversion, looking back at the world of conformity which he has rejected, and contemplates the nature of that conversion. The Whitman of the first three lines is still a "sinner," held by the unregenerate life; the Whitman of the last three lines is a "new man," born again. It is a remarkable achievement to have appropriated the conventional language of the conversion experience for the purposes of a wholly secular conversion, one which, moreover, would have seemed to most religious readers a conversion to the deadliest sinfulness. Whitman represents perhaps the ultimate secularization of the Great Awakening and the transformation of the language of religious enthusiasm into the language of physical and psychological awareness. He has come to "testify," to "bear witness" to his own experience and to celebrate the new life.

Although in the version published in 1860 the opposition between two lives and the nature of the conversion experience are less apparent, the conversion remains the emotional core of the poem, without which it cannot be read properly. In the published text the prior life is present in line 3 ("the life that exhibits itself") and line 4 ("all the standards hitherto published"). The transition comes in line 6, beginning "Clear to me now," which announces the conversion and its consequence—withdrawal from

the conventional world. This line contrasts with the earlier lines
by its "standards not yet published." As in the manuscript poem,
Whitman sees himself as the first to announce homosexual love.
He repeats this elsewhere in the "Calamus" poems and had already
implied it in the letter to Emerson ("as to manly friendship, everywhere observed in The States, there is not the first breath of it
to be observed in print").[69] This has led Edwin H. Miller to criti-
cize him for ignoring "Cooper, Melville, and Thoreau, to cite only
three examples"[70] and for claiming too much significance for himself. Of the three names Miller gives, however, Whitman was
probably unfamiliar with Melville and almost certainly did not
know Thoreau's only homosexual work,[71] the poem "Sympathy,"
a Platonic consolation. Although critics since Leslie Fiedler[72] have
read Cooper as a homosexual (repressed or not), it is unlikely that
Whitman would have seen him in that light. The point remains
that with the exception of *Moby-Dick*[73] there was in the 1850s
no literary tradition of homosexuality in America[74] available to
him, and so Whitman was quite justified in seeing himself as
called upon to establish "new standards."

Whitman added to his earlier version the image presented
in the first two lines:

In paths untrodden,
In the growth by margins of pond-waters

This figure introduces a spatial element to the contrast already
established between two points in time: the new space, like the
new time, announces Whitman's conversion. The new man is to
inhabit a new world. The "untrodden" paths represent Whitman
not only as the pioneer but also as the "first man," as Adam.
Whitman's dramatization of his conversion demands that he see
himself as radically new, going alone into virgin land, whatever
his knowledge of other authors. While Whitman makes use of
the pioneer and explorer metaphor, it is significant that he does
not situate himself in a western landscape. In Whitman space is
not a territory to be conquered (as is characteristic of male heterosexual literature)[75] but a place "by margins" to be explored, a
"secluded spot" which is not a territory beyond but alongside.
Instead of an extension in length, as in the metaphor of conquest,
there is a broadening, an extension in width to include what was
once seen as "marginal."

The new territory of "In paths untrodden" is an aspect of the

self, not of the other. In the myth of the explorer (which is perhaps
the quintessential male heterosexual myth) place is always outside, different, and alien to the self. But the place chosen by
Whitman is isolated, suitable for meditation and self-exploration.
Like Thoreau, Whitman must escape "the clank of the world";
but unlike Thoreau he learns not survival but self-expression.
Whitman needs to withdraw from the world and its sounds and
enter into silence, in the Quaker manner. In that silence he can
find his own voice, as the "inner light" shines forth through his
personal revelation. In lines 8 to 10, Whitman sees a greater frankness as the result of this strategic withdrawal: "no longer abashed,"
"I can respond as I would not dare elsewhere." The words he will
utter, the songs he will sing, come from the spiritual world and
are channeled through him; he is an Aeolian harp on which the
Spirit plays. Whitman conveys his mystical experience in traditional terms: he is "talked to here by tongues aromatic." But the
"tongues," the Pentecostal voices, merge with the reeds or calamus and hence with the male genitals. If "the scent of these arm-
pits" is "aroma finer than prayer," how much holier must be the
incense of the pubis? Here as elsewhere in Whitman the sexual
and the mystical are thoroughly intertwined; the spiritual speaks
through the physical without, however, transcending or negating
it.

The setting of this first poem of the "Calamus" cycle is reminiscent of one of the most famous of homosexual poems, Virgil's
Second Eclogue, and the resemblances are sufficient to suggest
that Whitman had Virgil in mind as he prepared the 1860 version of his text. In the eclogue Corydon withdraws from the world
into a dark wooded undergrowth to sing his songs of unrequited
love for Alexis:

> Formosum pastor Corydon ardebat Alexim
> delicias domini, nec, quid speraret, habebat.
> tantum inter denses, umbrosa cacumina, fagos
> adsidue veniebat. ibi haec incondita solus
> montibus et silvis studio iactabat inani.

(ll. 1–5)

The opening of "In paths untrodden" echoes this scene, one of the
best known in pastoral literature. Whitman, like Corydon, withdraws from the world to find solitude in dark places and to draw
forth his art from his experience of impossible love (a theme made

more explicit in the 1867 revisions of "Calamus" 39, "Sometimes with One I Love"). Like Virgil, Whitman uses the song of the abandoned lover as the type of all music and turns his suffering into a beautiful hymn in praise of love. (He returned to this theme in "Lilacs" and "Out of the Cradle.") Nor is setting the only point of similarity between "Calamus" and Virgil's eclogue: Whitman's repeated use of the figure of gathering scented flowers as a love-offering (especially in "These I singing in spring") almost certainly has its source in Corydon's offerings:

> et vos, o lauri, carpam et te, proxima myrte,
> sic positae quoniam suaves miscetis odores.
>
> (ll. 54–55)

Unlike most Victorian classicists, Whitman does not attempt to recreate the Roman poet's landscape; instead he transforms it into a self-consciously American scene. In place of laurel and myrtle, we have maple, wild orange, chestnut, and aromatic cedar. The plants of Whitman's pastoral are real not literary, American not Roman; but their use as a love-token imitates one of the greatest homosexual love poems—a rare example of literary borrowing in Whitman.[76]

While Whitman almost certainly took his images from Virgil, the complex of imagistic associations may be traced further back, to Theocritus. It is even possible that Whitman's "Calamus" derives from Theocritus' Idyll 13, with its scene of the spring in which Hylas is drowned:

> Soon, by a hollow, Hylas saw a spring in the rushes,
> deep among dark celandine, green maiden-hair, a crop
> of bushy parsley, with wild marsh grass all around
>   (translated by Anthony Holden in Greek Pastoral Poetry,
>   Harmondsworth, 1974)

In Theocritus the landscape seems to symbolize the "dark" nature of the female genitals and the threat they pose to homosexual love. In Virgil there is no sense of threat, merely lost love. In Whitman the hidden place among the rushes becomes a refuge and a love-nest. Thus a single set of images is transformed from a symbol of death into a symbol of life.

Whitman's conversion in "In paths untrodden" leads him to resolve "to sing no songs to-day but those of manly attach-

ment." The "to-day" may be taken as referring to the poems of
the "Calamus" sequence, but in a larger sense all of Whitman's
work may be said to date from this point, the moment of rebirth
which begins his new life (Symonds always dated his life from his
first homosexual experience). Henceforth Whitman's sense of mission will inform all of his work, whether or not it is present as
an explicit theme. It is precisely as a sign of rebirth that one is
to understand line 15: "Afternoon, this delicious Ninth Month,
in my forty-first year." The precision of this reference has led many
to assume that Whitman is simply providing a point in actual
time for the composition of the poem, i.e., September 1859. It
is of course possible that Whitman indeed composed (i.e., revised
or rewrote) the poem in that month; but surely it is evident that
the primary function of such precise dating here is to provide not
realistic detail but symbolic fact. (Whether Whitman simply recognized the symbolism of an actual event or invented his fact to
suit his symbolism we can, of course, never know.) The Quaker
phrasing of "Ninth Month" calls attention to the symbolism of
birth and gestation (Whitman first used the Quaker terms in the
1860 edition of "Song of Myself"), heightened by the associated
phrases "bequeathing" and "forty-*first* year" (my emphasis). Whatever Whitman has been before, he is now reborn, and his new
life as the Calamus poet must be dated from the moment of this
spiritual rebirth. He does not, however, speak merely for himself
but "for all who are, or have been, young men." In other words,
Whitman accepts the responsibility of speaking for those who cannot speak. This is an important example of Whitman's use of the
first person to create a *representative* self. At forty-one, he is hardly
a young man, but he has been one; and by telling "the secret
of my nights and days," he acts on behalf of all, disclosing what
has been hidden. Again it is significant that Whitman does not
suggest that he has discovered homosexuality at this point but that
he has decided at this point to speak of his sexuality, to reveal
his "secret." The moment of Whitman's birth as Calamus poet
is not the moment of first sexual encounter but of first honesty
and revelation. By speaking he becomes himself.

The last lines of "In paths untrodden" announce the dual
mission that Whitman undertakes:

To tell the secret of my nights and days,
To celebrate the need of comrades.

The second of these lines is even clearer in manuscript: "I cele-brate the need of the love of comrades." Critics have, by and large, made more of the telling than of the celebrating, that is, they have considered the poem as a revelation but not as a celebration. In fact, it is surprising how often critics, even those who claim to like Whitman, find "Calamus" a dreary, neurotic, depressing section, when it is precisely the opposite. The reason for this mis-reading (in the old-fashioned, not Bloomian, sense) is their own view of homosexuality as guilt-ridden and neurotic. Thus Edwin H. Miller finds "fear more than joy" and attributes this to the poems' source in "maladjustments";[77] despite a more fashionable jargon, his position is essentially the same as Van Doren's. The poems cannot be good or happy because they are founded in sick-ness. Even more astounding is a comment by J. Albert Robbins, who finds "Calamus" "a forboding dirge, brooding, agonising, solitary and death-ridden."[78] "Calamus" is, on the contrary, a sequence of great joy. It is not a mindless celebration, oblivious to the inevitability of death, the possible failure of love, or ulti-mate human isolation. But it is a celebration: in poem after poem Whitman celebrates, calmly but with deep joy, the pleasure of being together with a lover, and again and again asserts that this pleasure exceeds fame or worldly success. He proposes love, specif-ically love between men, as a response to, and triumph over, iso-lation and death.

Another charge frequently repeated and particularly relevant to "In paths untrodden" is that of evasion. Because of its pastoral theme, it is argued that "'Calamus' is an act of simplification, an evasive gesture, a retreat from nineteenth-century, and human, complexity."[79] Again there is a clear misreading of Whitman's intention and accomplishment. As I have suggested, Whitman consciously used a pastoral model in Virgil's Second Eclogue,[80] but he did so in order to invoke a tradition of poetry in which the love of men played a major and honorable part. It is doubtful that he knew of any other. But even while using that model, Whit-man adapted it to his own purposes and to the American land-scape. The reader is invited not to return to a Roman pasture (as in the First Eclogue, which Whitman does not call upon) but to recognize that love between men can exist and may be the source of art. It is of course true that, in general, social questions are not addressed in "Calamus"; but then, why must a sequence of love poems address social issues? What is important is that the love celebrated in "Calamus" is the basis for Whitman's program of social change, set forth in "Passage to India" or *Democratic Vistas*. Whitman does not retreat from the world. He does indicate that self-examination requires a temporary period of sequestration, following which he returns to the world, strengthened by his recognition of the need for the bonds of friendship and love. The speaker of "Calamus" is no Ahab, as has been suggested;[81] he is, rather, an Ishmael, who must learn from the simpler man, Queequeg, the lesson of manly love which will enable him to survive in the world of Ahab. Whitman, like Melville, is suggesting that only when men accept their innate homosexuality can there be any hope for real change and a final victory over the aggression, acquisitiveness, and death-drive which, he believes, are rooted in heterosexuality. This is indeed a revolutionary idea; no wonder, then, that some critics have been so alarmed that they have been unable to address it.

Whitman continues the account of his conversion and recognition of his mission in the second of the "Calamus" poems, but adds a new element—death. Whitman's understanding of death is expressed in a horticultural and a phallic metaphor. The horticultural "perennial roots" represent the essential self, contracted into the smallest space possible as an act of self-preservation, yet conserving the potential for rebirth. As a flowering plant is cut back in winter so that it may conserve its energy and bloom again in spring, so the "underground" self, the root, is enabled to survive and "emerge again." The phallic "scented herbage of my breast" is, by extension, the pubis. The blooming again, "out from where you retired," proclaims a new erection. As in "Song of Myself," reerection equals resurrection; death is merely the "little death." For Whitman, the essential awareness of renewal is phallic; the fear of impotence may be conquered through the realization that the phallus can indeed rise again. Death then need no longer be frightening; it is no more than a temporary impotence, a period of natural hibernation, from which will come new life. The phallic and the vegetative, as in mythology,[82] are intricately woven together throughout this poem. One plants the seed, waters the earth: these are the phallic processes of spring; one cuts back the plant, covers it over, and waits through the long winter: these are the phallic processes of winter and death. The new life is the flower of the sex, the "blossoms of my blood" (cf. Genet's *Miracle of the Rose*).

There is an element of inner conflict evident in the poem, especially in lines 9 and 10. Here Whitman has confronted his phallic needs ("O burning and throbbing," followed in the manuscript by a phrase he later omitted, making the sexual context even clearer, "O these hungering desires!"), which provoke uncertainty and doubt:

> O I do not know what you mean, there underneath your-
> selves—you are not happiness,
> You are often more bitter than I can bear—you burn and
> sting me

Such lines are cited as examples of Whitman's guilt-ridden nature. Yet they comprise only two lines out of forty-one, and are quickly followed by, "Yet you are very beautiful to me." It must be remembered that the medical views of Whitman's day, as well as the religious views, condemned not only homosexuality but also masturbation (onanism) and warned of the dangers of madness and death; it is not surprising then that sexual desires should bring about guilt and conflict, especially when there appeared to be no possibility of fulfilling those desires. The paradox confronted in this section of the poem is that desire in itself is painful since unfulfilled, yet the fulfillment of desire brings death and the absence of desire. The cycle of life and death is the cycle of the penis. The price of avoiding death is perpetual erection and perpetual unfulfillment. One must die (Elizabethan pun intended) in order to live and die again.

At the center of the poem (lines 18 to 21) Whitman addresses his "timid leaves" with a series of calls for self-revelation: "Do not fold yourselves," "Do not remain down there so ashamed," "Grow up taller." The call is for physical rebirth, a spring of the year, as well as a new phallic arousal and erection, and, finally, for an unfolding and release of the repressed self. The structure of the poem reflects a conversion, the first half expressing doubt, a groping search for understanding, conveyed through symbols, and the second announcing a new poetic program that will resolve those doubts. With new self-awareness the poet rejects the use of symbolism and its inherent indirectness (lines 22 to 24). The past is cast off—"I have long enough stifled and choked"—as the poet refuses the world of shame and concealment which previously had seemed the only life possible for a homosexual. The "emblematic and capricious blades" have served their purpose, in enabling the poet to move from a generalized view of natural cycles of rebirth to a specifically phallic one, but they have also involved indirection. The new life will refuse all such strategies and replace them with direct statement:

> I will escape from the sham that was proposed to me,
> I will sound myself and comrades only—I will never again
>   utter a call, only their call

Deliberate rejection of the "sham" is the crucial stage in the poet's regeneration; for he recognizes the duplicity of the lives of most homosexuals, who pretend to be something they are not. Who before Whitman had said, "I am a homosexual and I shall live like one and write like one?" The gesture is difficult enough today;[83] it required extraordinary courage in 1859.

Whitman attached considerable importance to his phrasing here, as one can see from the manuscripts. First he wrote "mask" where the later version reads "sham"; then he substituted "the costume, the play" before finally settling on "sham." Each of these alternatives suggests how fully Whitman felt the pressures of conventional life and how dishonest he knew that life to be for himself. It is probably true, as many have charged, that Whitman in later life partially replaced the mask that he so bravely removed here. Anyone sensitive to the pressures of the time and to the burdens of Whitman's old age (as well as, alas, to Whitman's desire for acceptance) ought not, however, condemn this too loudly. Whitman did not repudiate the honesty of his text,[84] however dishonest he may have chosen to be in his life (and we really do not know much about his life or how dishonest his friends were). In any case it is disturbing to read that Whitman was "evasive" and "duplicitous"[85] from a critic who condemns homosexuality as a maladjustment. "Scented Herbage of My Breast" is a strong statement of Whitman's determination to establish a new life based on reality and not appearance.

The contrast between reality and appearance is the basis of the last section of the poem, lines 29 to 41. Whitman adopts a Platonic vocabulary to suggest that what appears as life, "what I was calling life," is in fact merely the "shifting forms of life," "the mask of materials." Behind that material life lies another, spiritual life, what he calls "the real reality." As always in such discussions, the language seems somewhat confused, but it remains clear that the life of the spirit is seen as greater than the life of the material body. Life is merely a "show of appearance," while death is an eternal life to which we shall have access when we penetrate behind the curtain (to pursue the theatrical metaphor) and see things as they are, not as they seem. The paradigm for the transition to the spiritual life is the poet's recognition of his own sexuality; the spirit of death is imagined as a composite Death/Love angel, modeled on the Greek figure of Hermes. (Later, in the 1876 Preface, Whitman would return to the figure of Hermes, the "beautiful and perfect young man,"[86] his beloved psychopomp.) Unfortunately the poem, in its 1860 version, is somewhat muddled. Whitman makes explicit the Platonic sources of his thought, but in line 30 he drops "and manly love" after "O Death," thereby losing much of the *Liebestod* associations. It is clear that Whitman had difficulty working out his meanings in this poem, and readers have consequently had trouble understanding the relationship between love and death. In one sense the poem is a *memento mori*, a reminder of the vanity of human existence. The death of the flesh leads to despair, unless one can see it as part of a larger cycle which leads ultimately to reunion and reconciliation. "All life tends toward death," as Freud declared. Long before Freud, Whitman believed that the attempt to deny death through procreation was but a sign of man's imprisonment in the world that is a shadow of reality.

It seems certain that Whitman was familiar with Plato at least from the time of his revisions of this poem.[87] The manuscript version shows no use of Platonic language (it is possible of course that Whitman already knew Plato but had not made use of him at this point), whereas the printed text introduces the terms "essential," "forms," "masks of materials," and "show of appearance." All are used in the second half of the poem, as Whitman extends his conversion from appearance of heterosexuality to reality of homosexuality into a conversion from the appearance of life to the reality of death. It is here that the poem is weakest and most derivative, because, I suspect, Whitman is ill at ease with his material. There is every sign that his Platonism is newly acquired and incompletely digested. It is certain, however, that Whitman found something very sympathetic in Plato's idea of a spiritual essence behind appearances and of death as a passage to union with pure spirit. Such ideas permeate all Transcendentalist thought, of course, but are rarely as explicit as in Whitman. The Platonic view had particular meaning for Whitman because of the association in Plato of death with the restoration of the original whole; only in death could the two lovers finally achieve their deepest wish to be reunited and merge into one. For Plato man remained incomplete and even his most perfect love unsatisfied, as long as he remained separated in the physical world from his other, spiritual half.[88] The idea of the individual as half of a self, wandering the world in search of its other half and completion, underlies all of the "Calamus" poems. Whitman's poems have often been misread as cries of anguish from an individual expressing his personal loneliness and isolation. While such personal feeling may underlie the poems, it does not explain their mythic power, which comes from a belief that the yearning for completion is universal and that it can only be consummated in death. (On this point, Poe and Whitman are strikingly similar, of course, since both are Platonists—Poe derived from an original hermaphroditic self and Whitman from an original male self, in terms of Plato's myth.) It was Plato who gave Whitman his conviction of the possibility of fulfillment in death through the promise of union with the perfect lover.

The third of the "Calamus" poems is a warning to the reader, one of several in this sequence which begin by playing upon the identity of the author and his book ("Whoever you are holding me now in hand") and conclude by denying that identity ("For it is not for what I have put into it that I have written this book, / Nor is it by reading it you will acquire it"). The placement of this poem is crucial, for it immediately precedes (in 1860) "These I singing in spring," the first poem to introduce directly the symbol of the calamus root. One of its functions (not unlike Crane's "Poster," the first of his "Voyages") is to prepare the reader for what is to follow. Whitman adopts the persona of Christ in order to suggest his own role as moral teacher and to remind the reader of the difficulty of following such a gospel. As elsewhere, Whitman deliberately echoes the words of Jesus: "You would have to give up all else—I alone would expect to be your God, sole and exclusive." The claim is not, again, blasphemous; Whitman was not a Christian. It is rather a realistic account of the difficulties implicit in a commitment to a program of social change as wide-reaching as that of homosexual liberation. Whitman is aware that he will have readers who do not share that goal, who have gotten this far in Leaves of Grass without grasping his meaning, and that there will be others who, although they might claim to share that goal, are unwilling to make the personal sacrifices necessary for its realization. "The whole past theory of your life, and all conformity to the lives around you, would have to be abandoned." Whitman thus speaks as a social revolutionary, who must warn his followers of the extent of the commitment that will be required of them. No one can in good faith claim to desire such significant change, yet expect it to come about without effort. Whitman warns his reader that he will have to give up his "conformity," abandon his "past theory." Those who are unwilling to make this commitment should "put me down, and depart on your way."

But for others who are willing to make the necessary commitment, there will be a sign of brotherhood: a kiss on the lips, "the comrade's long-dwelling kiss, or the new husband's kiss." While this kiss recalls the Christian Kiss of Peace, it also transforms it from a ritual to a personal gesture. At first it can take place only stealthily ("first watching lest any person, for miles around, approach unawares"); can one doubt the caution that must have been necessary before two men kissed each other on the lips in 1859? Whitman depicts with magnificent accuracy the first tentative steps toward a recognition of one's homosexuality, the furtiveness that is a result of almost unbearable social pressure, and the growing confidence that comes once that first step has been taken. So in the following stanza there is not merely a kiss, but Whitman (or his book) is thrust "beneath your clothing, / Where I may feel the throbs of your heart, or rest upon your hip." Only such personal signs can be the evidence of brotherhood and the mark of discipleship. In the new religion of a long-delayed brotherly love, there can be no real conversions through reading, only through experience. It is not by talking about love but by living it that one accepts Whitman's message; it is not "by reading it you will acquire it." As Whitman said repeatedly, his book is only a means toward transformation, which the kiss itself accomplishes. With that warning, Whitman asks all who are not prepared to continue his journey of love to "depart on your way." From now on the only readers will be lovers.

These lovers are addressed in the fourth poem, "These I singing in spring." Here the poet is identified with the regenerative powers of spring, and his role as chthonic spirit is made evident. He springs forth from the earth and passes among all men, offering them gifts of life and love. The passage of the poet from the garden to the pondside and into the forest is deliberate, for it is the passage from domesticity into the more primitive, less regulated world of Pan. The flowers of the garden are hardly suitable as a token of comradeship: they are too domestic, too "feminine," too cultivated. As he moves on into the forest, a crowd of followers forms: "a silent troop gathers about me," acknowledging his role as god of the new life. Those who gather about are "friends, dead or alive" (in the manuscript, "friends, lovers, comrades dead or alive"). "Friends" refers not to the poet's personal friends but to all who ever have been friends. His mission encompasses not merely the living but also the dead and joins together in a community of feeling all who have shared the love of men. As in a dream they come together, gathered around the poet who will redeem them. Whitman evokes these spirits to place the love of which he speaks in a historical context and to suggest a beginning of continuity and community. He creates a continuum with the past that offers promise for the future. As he passes through the forest he looks for a token, "a name," thus alluding to his own poetic process; for in line 16, he offers "out of my pocket, some moss which I pulled off a live-oak in Florida." As we know, Whitman's original name for this section was "Live-Oak with Moss," a symbol which he kept for "Calamus" 20, "I saw in Louisiana a live-oak growing." Eventually Whitman rejected that symbol for the section as a whole, along, he suggests, with other possible symbols, and chose instead the calamus, because he found it in the pond where "I last saw him that tenderly loves me—and returns again, never to separate from me." The calamus gains its special significance from its association with the poet's own experience; it means far more to him than any other symbol, for it alone is grounded in personal love.

Whether the experience referred to is a fictional one invented for dramatic reasons (to justify the symbol) or an actual experience in Whitman's life, there is no evidence of the "crisis" often posited in Whitman criticism. In Whitman's own terms, he chooses the calamus because it was at the pondside that he saw "him that tenderly loves me"; and it is out of that experience of love that he draws his principal symbol, which he will reserve for those capable of sharing such a love. There is no evidence whatever at this point of suffering because of this experience. Rather, the text suggests that the experience provided a greater specificity to Whitman's vision. The central symbol is no longer one of generalized relationship (as with the live oak with moss) but one that is specifically sexual, that has its origins in personal experience, and that has broad consequences for the poet's life and art.

One of the first signs of the broad consequences of the love symbolized by the calamus appears in the first line of the following poem, "States!" (Most of the poem eventually was deleted from *Leaves of Grass*.) This poem is Whitman's first statement of his political creed, that only love could achieve the democracy and national unity which he desired as America's heritage. As he puts it most simply, "Affection shall solve every one of the problems of freedom." Like E. M. Forster, who learned so much from him, Whitman endorsed personal relations as a means to social change. Whitman's vision seems to me not naive but radical. He proposes that the aggressive impulse of man is rooted in competitiveness, the basic form of which is the search for a bride to provide property both now and in the future. Men can only be forced to kill each other by a distortion of their impulse to love one another, in which that love is directed toward women and the acquisition of power. If that love were returned to its source, if men saw each other as potential lovers rather than potential rivals, they would perhaps no longer be willing to kill each other. Whitman suggests that the ultimate revolution is that accomplished by the individual who refuses to hate, who turns aside a blow with a kiss. Instead of self-seeking, there will be sacrifice for others; instead of American coldness and fear of physical contact, there will be warmth and the affection of kiss and touch. For these ideas Whitman drew upon classical models, including the sacrificial death of the Greek hero for his lover, as in the story of Achilles and Patroclus.

But, more significantly, he drew upon Quakerism. He had been profoundly influenced by Quaker thought, with its deep belief in the power of love. For the Quaker, love is not *a* solution, it is the *only* solution. Whitman drew upon the Quaker language of love and carried it to its ultimate conclusion. He restored to love its primary meaning of physical expression of affection, but in so doing he in no way diminished the radical social and political dimensions of the Quaker concepts. Whitman's service in the war as a nurse was fully in accord with Quaker principles and not unlike the conscientious-objector service performed in hospitals and elsewhere by later Quakers. Quakers have always believed that no problem can be solved without love.

From this political statement Whitman moves to a more personal one, in "Not heaving from my ribbed breast only." As we have seen, this is the only poem in the "Calamus" series to use the word "adhesiveness." The poem enumerates the physical manifestations of adhesiveness—erotic dreams, pounding heart, unfulfilled desire—but does so only to deny that adhesiveness is more necessary there than in his poems. Each of the long catalog of "symptoms" begins with "Not" or "Nor" until the shift in the middle of the last line when the poet calls out, "O adhesiveness! O pulse of my life!" Far from seeing his adhesiveness as mere physical symptom, then, he transforms it into the life-giving spirit. As he could not live without his heart, so he cannot live without his sexual nature, and so (in the final line) his poems cannot exist without a recognition of that sexual nature. What appeared to be mere physical torment or illness is now revealed to be essential to his identity and his art.

The seventh and eighth poems of the sequence are each structured according to a contrast between two states of consciousness of which the second, grounded in the new recognition of love, reflects back upon and answers the first. In "Of the terrible question of appearances," Whitman returns to his Platonism, this time without full assurance. What, he asks, if his belief in a continuation of life after death is "a beautiful fable only"? He records a state of total mental confusion, as he tries to grapple with the problems of appearance and reality. In line 10 the poem shifts, by the assertion that these vexing questions "are curiously answered by my lovers." The last five lines bear witness to a new state of mind, which does not provide philosophical answers but makes even the questions seem irrelevant. Whitman suggests that such intellectual riddles have meaning only for those who lack personal satisfaction, that a concern for the next world betrays a certain unconcern for this one. Thus it is personal love—"When he whom I love travels with me, or sits a long while holding me by the hand"—which resolves the doubts that have tormented the poet. He no longer looks to eternity for satisfaction, since he has found it here and now; with this satisfaction the world seems to vanish and the lovers are alone in an eternity of their own. The poem is an interesting presentation of the theory of sublimation, in which sexual desire is translated into intellectual curiosity and intellectual curiosity resolved by sexual satisfaction.

A similar contrast between two states of mind is presented in "Long I thought that knowledge alone would suffice me." Here the subject is not philosophy but a more autobiographical statement of the poet's interests and ambitions. There is a sharp contrast between the past, indicated by the "then" of lines 2, 3, and 4, and the firm opening of line 5, "But now take notice." As in several of the poems already discussed, Whitman establishes his point of view after a conversion experience and structures the poem by means of a contrast between the unregenerate and the regenerate selves. It is not, of course, that there is anything evil about the life presented in the opening lines here; it is merely that the heroic life, or the life of the national poet, now seems a vain ambition compared to the life of love. What once appeared interesting and pleasurable is now "empty and tasteless." The earlier life had been one of service to others or to an abstract goal; the new life is to be one of self-sufficiency. Certainly there is egotism here, but it is egotism *à deux*. The statement expresses the frame of mind of a person who has just fallen in love. In the passionate world of the first discovery of love all else vanishes; nothing seems important but love, for which one is prepared to die. This is the paradigmatic Western love story. For Whitman it is a stage in the development of consciousness that is being dramatized in "Calamus." At the same time there remains a fundamental truth in Whitman's assertion. Being in love does cast all other activity in a different light; and while the passionate commitment of the first days or even years may not be sustained in its original intensity, Whitman believes that the discovery of personal love will infuse all of life. When he declares, "I heed knowledge, and the grandeur of The States, and the example of heroes, no more," one hears echoes of Virgil, Marvell, Marlowe, and Shakespeare; has any love poet doubted the all-consuming passion of love?—"It is enough for us that we are together."

Not, of course, that love is always an experience of happiness; passion also brings suffering. This is the subject of "Hours continuing long, sore and heavy-hearted." The suffering of the poet is double, because of his sense of himself as "different" and because of his feeling of abandonment. Depicting the end of a love affair, the poet is anguished by the realization that his suffering is not shared: "for the one I cannot content myself without, soon I saw him content himself without me." Time passes, but his pain does not abate, and there is not even the consolation that the other is suffering as well. The pain seems cruelly personal; has anyone else ever known such pain? The feeling is common to rejected lovers (think of Swann suffering as he spies on Odette, or Tonio peeking in at the dance); but it gains particular intensity for the homosexual who wonders if anyone can possibly share his anguish (Isherwood's *A Single Man* presents this sensation in very moving terms). "Is there even one other like me?" he asks. Unable to speak of his pain or to share it with others who will understand, his isolation is complete. Every mention of his lover's name, even the most casual, brings renewed pain and the wish that at least the lover shared such pain, for if he suffered, it would mean that he too had loved.

But the suffering of the ninth "Calamus" poem is ultimately a measure of the depth of his love and the extent to which that love can inform his whole life. In this way the poem leads to the next, "You bards of ages hence!" with its famous injunction, "Publish my name and hang up my picture as that of the tenderest lover." Again there is a contrast between the political poet and the personal. Whitman, who has just displayed his capacity for tenderness through his suffering, asks to be remembered in this way and not as the "rough" of "Song of Myself." In order to understand the impact of this poem, it is necessary to place it in its historical context. Men in midnineteenth-century America did not cry, suffer, and languish for love; these reactions were deemed "feminine." Men were the aggressors in love; women waited and suffered. Against this orthodoxy of strict sexual delineation Whitman affirms his "feminine" qualities. He argues that love between men implicitly challenges traditional Western ideas of male superiority and of male hardness and female softness. The homosexual, more than other men, can experience the world from the perspective of a woman. He knows the impotence of unreturned love, the inability to speak out, the need to bear everything quietly. To call oneself the "tenderest lover" is to accept one's femininity or, more accurately, to challenge all social prescriptions of behavior according to gender. Whitman's ideal is nonactive, nonproductive; his joy is in companionship, in being, not doing. He recalls his "happiest days" in the past, "wandering hand in hand," "saunter[ing]." To wander, to saunter, is to move without purpose, to find one's satisfaction in the moment rather than the future. These views go directly against nineteenth-century (and American) ideals of progress, directed activity, and work. The organization of patriarchal society, psychoanalysis argues, rests upon the suppression of nonprocreative sexual behavior.[89] Competition between men ensures the maximization of productiv-

ity, while love between men represents a radical resistance to unnecessary productivity. If men walk arm and arm in the streets,
they are not busy in the factory or begetting children. Hence their
danger to society; and it is precisely thus, as an opponent of dominant social values, as an exponent of the "feminine" in culture,
that Whitman asks to be remembered.

Similarly, in the splendid "When I heard at the close of
day," [90] Whitman consciously rejects the usual masculine standards of success. Fame—"How my name had been received with
plaudits in the capitol"—is nothing compared to the immediate
and sensual pleasures of love and companionship. In this poem as
in so many Romantic texts, the superficial delights of the world
are contrasted with the real delights of the soul, which can be
experienced only in nature. But what Whitman adds to his reading of Wordsworth or Emerson is his idea of love. In more traditional Romantic texts the poet is alone with nature, as in Whitman's fifth line, a lyrical evocation of man in nature: "When I
wandered alone over the beach, and, undressing, bathed, laughing
with the cool waters, and saw the sun rise." In Whitman there is
communion and a sense of oneness with the universe, but this
oneness emerges from the experience of personal love. "And when
I thought how my dear friend, my lover, was on his way coming,
O then I was happy"; through the coming of his friend Whitman
experiences a sense of harmony with the natural world. There is a
structural affinity between this poem and Shakespeare's Sonnet
29, "When, in disgrace with fortune and men's eyes." There it
is the thought of the lover which brings the soul forth "like the
lark at break of day arising." As in "Hours continuing long" the
absence of his lover called his whole world into darkness, so in
"When I heard" the presence of the lover calls the whole world
into "morning light." The dominant symbols of the poem are
dawn and sunrise, and the power of that light extends even into
the darkness of the night the lovers spend together, under "autumn moonbeams." [91] The autumn moon is the moon of love and
marriage; and so it is appropriate that under its light the two
men lie together, their union consecrated by nature. The poem
emphasizes physical contact—"sleeping by me under the same
cover," "his face was inclined toward me," "his arm lay lightly
around my breast"—which provides a happiness which recalls the
poem's first line, when "still it was not a happy night"; but now
"that night I was happy."

The following poem, like the earlier warning, is addressed

to the would-be follower and suggests that love is not always satis-
factory. Characteristically it casts the relationship between poet
and reader in terms of lover and beloved:

> Do you think it so easy to have me become your lover?
> Do you think the friendship of me would be unalloyed satis-
> faction?
> Do you suppose I am trusty and faithful?

Again one is invited to read on only if one is prepared to take
the poet as a man and not an ideal, to accept the imperfections
of human love. Clearly many of Whitman's disciples ought to have
read this poem more carefully. But it is a brief interlude before
Whitman returns to his principal symbol, again asking those who
are not prepared to accept Whitman's terms to "depart." "Calamus" offers no immediate satisfactions, but hard work.

"Calamus taste" presents the nature of that work through
its extended horticultural metaphor. The offerings of the poet are
"frost-mellowed berries, and Third-Month twigs." We are in
blackberry winter, the very first, or potentially false, spring. If
the twigs of March bloom too soon, they will die before reaching
fruition. So it is with Whitman's "Calamus" mission: if it is offered to a hostile world, it will die without bearing fruit. It cannot
succeed without the promise of the spring. What Whitman offers
are "love-buds," as yet unopened, which will open if tended and
warmed:

> If you bring the warmth of the sun to them, they will open,
>   and bring form, color, perfume, to you,
> If you become the aliment and the wet, they will become
>   flowers, fruits, tall branches and trees

It is Whitman's readers who can turn the potential of his love-
offering into reality. To speak of the possibility of homosexual
love is to propose a first timid bud of March; whether that bud
will bloom depends upon the reception it finds. Throughout "Calamus" Whitman insists on the need for his work to be fulfilled
by his readers. They are asked not to be passive admirers but to
become gardeners of love, watering, feeding, and providing
warmth so that what Whitman first offers may eventually be accomplished. He knew that "Calamus" would not be enough to
bring forth the love of men, but he hoped that it might be a root
planted, waiting for spring in order to bloom. As with Whitman's

earlier use of a horticultural metaphor, here too the phallus is implied. The flaccid penis is a "love-bud" whose blooming depends upon the warmth and encouragement of others.

The next two poems insist that the poet's work cannot be understood apart from his sexual nature. "Not heat flames up and consumes" repeats the terms of "Not heaving from my ribbed breast only" and is similar to it in structure. The ebb of the sea, the flame of fire, are not accidental but essential. The poet likewise is ruled by his essential nature: in a series of analogies, he burns like a flame, ebbs like the sea, is blown about by the air— all in search of love and friendship. As in the earlier poem, his sexuality is as fundamental as the flow of his blood: "O drops of me!" One recalls that medical theories once held that "bad blood" had to be released in order to cure illness. Thus Whitman's blood, his adhesive "pulse," is spilled, released from his body and transferred to the page. Yet, although Whitman alludes to the theories of the "leech," he also alters them; he does not eliminate the blood, but frees it: "drip, bleeding drops, / From wounds made to free you whence you were prisoned." By ridding himself of his "humor" he turns it into public testimony of his sexuality: the "cure" becomes an act of self-declaration. The "confession drops" are not to be confined to this poem nor to a few poems but are to "stain every song I sing." The last four lines illustrate Whitman's reversal, as that which was shameful becomes proud:

> Let them know your scarlet heat—let them glisten,
> Saturate them with yourself, all ashamed and wet,
> Glow upon all I have written or shall write, bleeding drops,
> Let it all be seen in your light, blushing drops.

It should be noted that the "drops," although literally drops of blood, also suggest drops of semen, in such phrases as "all ashamed and wet." (It is helpful to recall that nineteenth-century medical theory held that blood was converted into semen in the testes and that the loss of semen was as dangerous as the loss of blood.) Whitman converts the fear of masturbation into pride, insisting that all his work be interpreted in the light of his "shameful" sexuality. In an age when masturbation was believed to lead to insanity and the punishment for masturbation was castration, it was an act of considerable courage to write of art through the metaphor of masturbation as often as Whitman did.

There is a constant ebb and flow through "Calamus." Each

section of honesty and forthrightness is followed by one or more of hesitation and warning. To have written the first book in two thousand years in praise of homosexual love required a fortitude that must, even in Whitman, have occasionally wavered. Thus the announcement of his sexual nature is followed by a brief hesitation, "O conscience-struck! O self-convicted!" No doubt Whitman passed through periods in which he accepted the prevailing social attitudes toward homosexuality and masturbation (the two were considered synonymous); "Calamus," as a dramatization of the poet's acceptance of his homosexual self, includes portrayals of such moments of doubt and even despair. What is far more striking is Whitman's ability, without any external support, to overcome such despair. In each case he realizes that his sexuality is his nature and that it must be given expression. Whether it is right or wrong becomes absurd once he recognizes that it simply is: "as if it could cease transpiring from me until it must cease." If his love is "wrong-doing," still it must be. Like Twain's Huck, Whitman learns that natural inclinations are often at odds with social definitions of good and evil.

The following poem recounts a dream of the death of a lover. Again the poem is a *memento mori*, in which Whitman reflects upon his life and those of others and alters his system of values. The first half of the poem (lines 1 to 7) recounts the dream, the search for the body of the beloved—"but he was not in that place"— and the realization that the houses of the living are really houses of the dead. As in the Platonic poems, Whitman here maintains that death itself is no worse than a living death not, however, through belief in an extension of life but through conviction that the majority of men are already dead, as they lack the ability to love. Upon awakening he rejoices in the existence of love here and now and accepts death without fear. In the second half of the poem he thus rejects Christian superstitions about death and burial practices which reflect a deep fear of death. He accepts cremation and dispersion of the body for himself and his lover, asking that memorials be "put up indifferently." Whitman's response to the Victorian cult of the dead illustrates his recognition of the ways in which that society stifled life. For Whitman, death frightens above all those who have been too timid to live, and so their cities and even places of amusement become enormous cemeteries in which ghosts move numbly. Whitman deliberately echoes the language of the Bible and the death of Jesus in his search for his lover, reminding his readers that their own religion taught that the dead god is to be found not in the tomb but among the living. Whitman denies the Christian concept of personal rebirth and offers instead a return to the elements, the sea or the winds. He suggests that the Christian emphasis on the person leads to fear and the denial of the self. Hard as it is to accept the death of a lover, Whitman argues that one must, and must see what appears to be personal tragedy as part of a larger plan of the universe.

It is a logical progression from the dream of the death of the lover to the following poem, "City of my walks and joys!" (later called "City of Orgies"). For this poem celebrates not a personal attachment, as many of the "Calamus" poems do, but a series of brief encounters. From realizing that the lover will eventually die and that those who refuse the sensual pleasures of the city are already dead comes a desire to celebrate the transitory. This is not, I think, to deny the importance of the quest for an ideal lover, but to suggest that there is no necessary conflict between the search for the ideal lover and the enjoyment of brief, passing moments of love. At the same time it does seem likely that Whitman's concept of the ideal lover was influenced to some extent by his reading of Plato and remains more a poetic fiction than a felt desire. The notion of the ideal companion as the other half of an incomplete self gave a kind of legitimacy to homosexual love and placed it alongside the western tradition of idealized heterosexual love (one true love, eternal devotion, two blending into one, and so forth). But Whitman seems also to have delighted in a promiscuous sexuality that celebrated moments of sensual awareness in which a democratic unity was ratified by a sexual response to a passing stranger. Whitman's treatment of this theme appropriately places emphasis on the response of the eyes: "frequent and swift flash of eyes offering me love." Through visual recognition and response the homosexual might recognize other homosexuals without being observed by others around. Deprived of the usual rituals of courtship, the male homosexual has substituted a ritual of eye contact which is still familiar (compare Crane's "eyes at search or rest" from "Recitative"). Such contact offers not only the possibility of sexual encounter but also an affirmation of community. The city remains distant and foreign—a "pageant," "tableau," or "spectacle"—until the response of eyes removes the poet from his situation as spectator and brings him on stage. At this moment the boundaries of self and world dissolve.

From that moment of brief encounter we move quite naturally to the kiss of the nineteenth poem, "Mind you the timid models of the rest, the majority?" The first stanza of this poem repeats the structure of the other conversion poems. Those who conform to heterosexual patterns are assured that the poet too once followed such "timid models," but now he has "adopted models" for himself. Again Whitman expresses the need to construct a model for the homosexual who has been offered no model other than that of the majority, who conform to the ways of the world. But Whitman hears "another drummer" (the point of view is strikingly Thoreauvian) and thereby gains courage for the act of the second stanza, where the poet views his aging self with ironic distance, not, like Prufrock, to confirm his timidity, but rather to emerge triumphantly from it with a gesture of love. Lines 6 and 7 present the kisses of two men, each time in a public situation, on the street and on the ship's deck. Their kisses are specifically those of "American comrades," for they are not hidden or genteel; instead they are signs of a "robust love" that is as democratic as the potential of America, and as uncultivated. Their love is not that of the salon nor even the European kiss on the cheek. It is a kiss on the lips of "two natural and nonchalant persons." In this way, Whitman asserts a relationship between men in which their "manliness" is retained. He deliberately works against the social assumption that the homosexual is an effeminate man and against the Greek model in which the lovers' inequality is enforced by the difference in their ages. While some of Whitman's concepts (particularly his idea of the "élève") derive directly from Greek homosexuality, the major thrust of the "Calamus" poems is toward a democratic partnership of men.

The twentieth poem of the sequence comes from the original group of poems and retains its central symbol of live oak with moss. The relationship between the trees and the moss is a "token" of "manly love." But the tree itself remains "solitary." It seems to represent a self-sufficiency that the poet himself must have found inadequate. He concludes with a sense of his own distance from this symbol: "I know very well I could not." It is clear that the calamus root offered far greater symbolic possibilities for Whitman. The live oak, even when twined about with moss, remains a symbol of independence. For Whitman's purposes the potential of the root was far more suitable than the achievement of the tree. From the root could spring many branches, each apparently independent of its source; from the tree only a dependent parasite could hang. A symbol implying such dependence would be inappropriate to Whitman's theme of interrelatedness, as the following poem, "Music always round me," suggests. While this poem has no immediately apparent relationship to the major theme of "Calamus," it is not inconsistent with it. It is a celebration of diversity and of the unity to be achieved through the harmonious merging of diverse elements. Whitman's analogy for this is musical, as the various voices—soprano, tenor, and base [*sic*]—and the various instruments—flute and violins—play together in harmony to create an operatic whole. While such praise of "parts" suggests Whitman's own mosaic and symphonic form, it also offers an implicit justification for the acceptance of sexual diversity. The homosexual, by analogy, is not opposed to the heterosexual; he is merely playing a variation upon a theme.[92]

Two effective poems now recapitulate the theme, as Whitman plays his own variations, of the encounter with a "passing stranger." In the first, there is a mystic sense of prior meeting, as if the two have known each other all their lives. Whitman evokes the way in which a sudden encounter can give the impression (or illusion—"as of a dream") of full and deep knowledge. In part the poem is based upon the Platonic idea of halves, so that the two partners are literally part of each other. This sense of destiny leads the poet to his final assurance that they are "to meet . . . again." But there is another source, probably equally important in Whitman's experience, in a mystical sense of prior experience (*déjà vu*). If such an encounter can occur between two passing strangers, it can also occur between those who have never met and will never meet but who nonetheless feel themselves to be in communion. Whitman constructs his own community in his imagination, through his conviction that there "are other men in other lands, yearning and thoughtful." Their desires create a bond between them and the poet which is stronger than the limitations imposed by nationality or distance. Whitman carries his claim to be the poet of national unity through adhesiveness one step further, in suggesting that adhesiveness can become a force for world brotherhood, as all men become "brethren and lovers." One can see in this poem the germ of ideas later to be worked out in "Passage to India."

Certainly Whitman was aware of the response he would receive if many of his fellow citizens understood the full import of these poems. Consequently, in "I hear it is charged against me," he

responds implicitly to charges that he will "destroy institutions."
It is unlikely that Whitman was responding to actual charges in
this poem: those came later (for one thing, there were not many
readers of the first two editions). It is more likely that, anticipating
such charges, he is suggesting a comparison between himself and
Socrates. Whitman, however, does not view the charges tragically
but rather with ironic distance. He denies that he wishes either
to establish or to disestablish institutions: "What indeed have I
in common with them?" He then turns humorously, in the last
two lines, to his own institution, the "dear love of comrades."
It has no "edifices, or rules, or trustees, or any argument." By
implication one thinks of the "academies" so dear to nineteenth-
century America, how they strayed from the Socratic ideal in their
establishment of "rules" in the place of dialogue and "trustees"
in the place of lovers. Whitman need not destroy institutions; they
will fall of their own accord, once the "love of comrades" is restored
to its proper place in daily life.

If Whitman was thinking of such classical models, he never
sought to restore America to a pseudo-Greek landscape, unlike so
many of the homosexual literary figures of the late nineteenth century, especially in England. After all, Whitman lived in the midst
of a highly classicized America, which he attempted to recall to
its native destiny. His work was a constant plea against the growing domination of Genteel values, to which he opposed the phys-
icality and "vulgarity" of American life. As the Gilded Age began, Whitman still spoke for the values of Jacksonian America,
one of which, he believed, was male comradeship. (It is in part
to such ideas that one may trace Whitman's apparently ambivalent
attitude toward women. He believed in the equality of women,
but also felt strongly that it could not be achieved apart from the
destruction of those values that were increasingly being identified
as feminine.[93] Insofar as women stood for propriety and sexual
repression, domesticity and gentility, Whitman stood against
them and in favor of men. One senses the same conflict in Crane.)[94]
To express the idea that American life should reflect the American
landscape, he appealed to the theory of spiritual correspondence,
articulated most clearly by Baudelaire, but part of a tradition already well known through the Transcendentalists, particularly
Emerson.[95] According to this theory the external world "corresponds" to the spiritual world, so that man is able to perceive
spiritual truths through physical objects. The theory, obviously

grounded in Platonism, was naturally congenial to Whitman. Thus for him "the spiritual corresponding" of the prairie-grass (another kind of grass—calamus is a kind of marsh-grass) was the "copious and close companionship of men." Each quality of the wheat provides a quality for friendship: the wheat grows close together, in the open, in the sun, erect; and so men must press together, take their love out of doors, stand up with pride and phallic energy ("sweet and lusty flesh, clear of taint, choice and chary of its love-power"). The love of men in America is to be "of earth-born passion, simple, never constrained," growing as free and as wide as the wheat.

With this evocation of the land and the wheat, we move nicely to another lyrical "picture," of "we two boys together clinging." That Whitman, who was forty-one, chose to depict himself as a boy has led to some merriment at his expense. It does not seem to me justified, however, to imagine that Whitman really thought of himself as a boy in years. Rather, I think that he recognized, perhaps unconsciously, that the social role he chose for himself was one of permanent boyhood, as boys were allowed a kind of freedom denied to adults in Victorian America. Considering the decline of the boy from Huck Finn to Penrod, it is not surprising that many critics find such an image sentimental, but it is also, at least potentially, political. Boys neither make war nor work in factories; they represent play (girls in Victorian America, of course, are not allowed even that much freedom). They are active, but their activity is play-acting: "sailing, soldiering, thieving, threatening." We are placed in the world of Tom Sawyer, in order to establish the outlawry of boyhood and then introduce the forbidden but always implied subject: boys making love to each other. (It is interesting to note that in the revisions for this poem Whitman changed the first-person singular of the manuscript draft to the dramatic "we two" of the published poem.) There is a bravado to this poem that makes it less appealing than some of the other, gentler poems, but it has its origin in a desire to show manly love as a part of ordinary behavior.

After this boisterous interlude we move to a much more serious poem, "O Love!" Like most of the later poems in the sequence, this poem presents few difficulties. Whitman seems to have exhausted the problems arising from his homosexual identity; the poems now are largely lyrical, often composed of a single, straightforward statement. The subject is again the opposition between a living death and a new life, structured around the imagery of conversion and rebirth. The "corpses of me" are the old selves, shed like so many serpent's skins, as the poet strips away his social self and discovers the living body beneath the grave-clothes. Whitman accepts the idea of constant change and renewal, not mourning the past but delighting in the present. This "living! always living" is embodied in the style characteristic of these poems. Their brevity, sharpness of outline, and "imagist" qualities reflect the state of constant flux, in which only a single, brief image can be seized. Whitman's own hurried, sometimes careless style is appropriate to his desire always to live in the present, always to move on. It is also for this reason that he wanted the edition of *Leaves of Grass* he had just completed to be the only one; the past was remodeled and reborn in the present. His decision has been unfortunate for his reputation, as it preserved the weakest works of his old age and concealed the greater accomplishments of earlier years; but it was entirely consistent with his aesthetic views.

The acceptance of life in its transitory glory contributes to Whitman's denial of worldly fame and political success, to which he opposes the pleasures of love. So, in the twenty-eighth poem, "When I peruse the conquered fame of heroes," he contrasts the "fame of heroes" or "victories of mighty generals" and "the brotherhood of lovers," through the opposition of the two clauses, "When I peruse" and "But when I read." Even the two verbs seem appropriately chosen to illustrate the difference between a sophisticated, erudite usage and a simple, homely one. Whitman asserts that fame and victory cannot make him envious but that love can. It may well be that he is referring to some actual reading of his own; he had probably read of the Sacred Band of Thebes, the army of lovers whose valor was based upon the lovers' sacrifice and devotion for one another. The specific allusion seems likely because of the military references of the first line, but it is not in any case necessary. The point is a simple one: that love and fidelity are the highest rewards of life, the only ones which could inspire "the bitterest envy."

After this general statement, the reader is given a precise illustration, in "One flitting glimpse." The style of this poem, as has been observed,[96] may be usefully compared to Dutch genre painting. It is a "caught" moment, viewed not directly but "through an interstice," thereby creating the impression of real life observed, of the absence of art. Many such poems can also be compared to the apparent simultaneity of photography, although it should be noted that the "snapshot" style which this resembles was not possible in the 1850s because of the time-exposures required. What Whitman's technique shares with photography is a desire to create an illusion of artlessness and spontaneity, to oppose the meaningful moment to the ponderous generality. The poet is himself in his own range of vision, but "unremarked." He is the artist as unobtrusive observer, the recorder of life within rather than the observer from without. He will be no Miles Coverdale, but a participant in the life of "workmen and drivers." At the same time, in the manner of the Dutch painters, the ordinariness of the scene is redeemed and transformed by a luminosity that seems to come from within, a light that is an outward sign of a spiritual emanation. In the midst of a scene of apparent chaos, "amid the noises," there is a moment of silent harmony, a spiritual union which is specifically nonverbal. That moment of meeting and the love that it implies shed grace on the ordinary and "smutty" and transform them into the holy. For Whitman that holiness is always of the world, and rooted in personal affection. The spiritual light is the halo of love.

Two brief and simple poems follow. The first, "A promise and gift to California," restates the poet's "American" theme, through an analogy between a notion of manifest destiny toward westward expansion ("These States tend inland, and toward the Western Sea") and the poet's own obligation to express his "inland," or American, spirit. Without denying a European heritage, he nonetheless expresses an obligation to go with the land and to develop a new aesthetic in the new world, including "robust American love." The following poem, "What ship, puzzled at sea," gives us two models of leadership: the poet offers himself in the first stanza as a ship's pilot and in the second as an artillery commander, raising the siege. In both cases it is suggested that the endeavor to achieve the goals of "Calamus" will require the help of a strong leader, which Whitman proposes through his poetic example. Neither of these poems particularly advances the development of themes, and it is hard to imagine that the section would suffer by their excision.

The thirty-second poem, "What think you I take my pen in hand to record?" is much more significant. Again worldly goals and love are opposed, and it is suggested that the passionate kiss of two friends is a more appropriate subject for the poet than the battleship or the city. The last three lines form a simple lyrical image, similar to those we have already seen. But here the relationship between the image and an aesthetic statement is clear. Whitman deliberately renounces the functions of the epic poet to accept those of the lyricist. This is in some sense to embrace "minor" art and, by doing so, to reverse the usual standards of judgment. It has traditionally been thought that "great" art must have political or social aims and that only "minor" art could concern itself with feelings. By renouncing the art of the world for the art of personal experience, Whitman is making a choice similar to that made by many female artists. A woman can, of course, adopt the standards of "male" art. But many women have insisted on the validity of a "female" art, which explicitly rejects politics and war as the subjects suitable for art. One can see this rejection most clearly in the ironic lines of Anne Bradstreet in her "Prologue." These lines have often been misread as an indication of her poetic "modesty,"[97] whereas in fact they represent a deliberate undercutting of male values. Later, one can see Virginia Woolf make the same choice.[98] As long as art is popularly presumed to be an expression of the values of the dominant class (male heterosexuals), then the artist will be obliged to deal with those values in his or her work (one can, of course, deal with them negatively, as, say, Stendhal does, but even such Romantic treatments must be set against a traditional epic background). What begins to occur in the work of women and homosexuals is a questioning of those values, by the simple decision to abandon them. Whitman's "Calamus" poems are revolutionary, because no one (since Virgil at least) had written, "He loves him"; instead they had written, "He loves her" and "He kills him." Whitman "takes pen in hand to record," performs the traditional epic gesture, but then undercuts it by recording a kiss between two men, inappropriate as subject both because it is two men and because those men are "simple" and of no historical significance. In Woolf's terms, Whitman records "moments of being." Throughout his work he performs this subversive role with regard to the epic. While a poem such as "Song of Myself" has the scope of an epic and some of the external form, it is in fact an antiepic, for it celebrates only the self and not "arms and the man." The hero is within, not without, and the drama is one not of the founding of a city but of the establishment of a self. Whitman turns the form of the epic against itself.[99] Similarly, in "Passage to India" the end of the quest of the epic hero becomes not land but love; India is finally a place of the mind. Thus Whitman works constantly against the western tradition, in which the quest for spiritual values becomes a framework on which to hang the "real" story, of the adventures of the search for the Grail. For him the adventures are of no value unless they lead to spiritual development. Instead of men at war we constantly have men in love. For this very reason, of course, his style must be episodic rather than linear.

A similar point is made in "No labor-saving machine." Here the contrast is not with the functions of the epic poet but with those of the man of the world, who will leave a "wealthy bequest" or "deed of courage." Of course Whitman was aware that he would leave behind a book (although the more aware he was of that, the more his work declined); but he is deliberately taking a position against permanence, against the usual standards of success. For that reason he does not deny his work, but opposes his "carols" to a book; he wants to leave behind—"vibrating through the air" —something which has become part of the popular imagination, which will serve, not social or political advancement, but merely "comrades and lovers." His heritage is, as he put it earlier, outside of all institutions.

Whitman realized that his mission would not be accomplished easily. He recognized the utopian quality of his thought and expressed it directly in "I dreamed in a dream." By setting the ideal commonwealth in a dream, Whitman emphasized the distance that it was necessary to travel before its realization as well as the visionary quality of his ideal. The "city invincible to the attacks of the whole of the rest of the earth" is the City of God, the New Jerusalem, the City on a Hill. It represents earthly perfection and appropriates the language of Christian eschatology for the expression of a consciously secular goal, one that was indeed "sinful" by the lights of most Christians. By so doing, Whitman reminds the Christian reader how far his commonwealth is from realizing the (supposed) Christian goal of brotherly love. The City of Friends may be taken to be Philadelphia, which is both the Quaker City and the City of Brotherly Love, but Whitman's context makes it clear how far such an actual city falls short of the ideal, how far Christianity has betrayed its own potential. Whitman saw the irony in a Society of Friends which did not recognize love between friends, and he urges a revitalization of the Gospel, an infusion of "robust love" into Christian love. D. H. Lawrence, a follower of Whitman, would elaborate this idea in his fantasy, "The Man Who Died." The difference between Whitman's vision here and Lawrence's is the specifically phallic consciousness of Lawrence (even to the pun on "cock") and the more idyllic vision of Whitman. Although there are many passages in praise of the phallus and of sexuality in *Leaves of Grass*, "Calamus" is devoted almost exclusively to the celebration of being together; the lovers kiss and embrace, they sleep together, but they are not depicted in actual sexual acts (as in "Song of Myself"). "Calamus" is largely a sequence of artistic and psychological significance, in which the learning of affection has primary place. Whitman never denies the importance of sexuality, but he seems to suggest that men need to learn to touch each other even more than to fuck each other. As I have suggested earlier, fucking a man does not necessarily require a rethinking of oneself; touching a man does. Whitman specifies in his manuscript that men are to love each other "tenderly" and to walk "hand in hand."

Whitman's dream, although utopian, is not manifestly impossible. For it is based not on a transformation of men but on a realization of their potential. In "To you of New England" Whitman expresses his view that "the germs" (following the basic horticultural metaphor) "are in all men." He thus anticipates the theories of psychoanalysis, which, early in the twentieth century, suggested that all human beings are bisexual but that their homosexual impulses are arrested by social pressures. Whitman is not asking for understanding or tolerance for a minority. His position is much more radical: that all men are potentially homosexual and will be fulfilled only when their homosexual impulses are recognized and given expression. As in *Democratic Vistas*, he sees this latent homosexuality as the potential foundation of national and international unity and the essential condition for harmony among men. He ascribes divisiveness to the imposition of heterosexuality upon otherwise homosexual men, resulting in the frustration of their desires and the transformation of those desires (sublimation) into aggression. To express this view, he salvaged a line from the manuscript of "Proto-Leaf" ("Starting from Paumanok") and placed it here, to suggest that his utopian vision need not await the end of time but might find a suitable home in the present. For it was to be in America above all that homosexuality should find its expression, as homosexuality was implied in the entire history of American experience; as he put it in the manuscript, "I believe the main purport of America is to be found in a new ideal of manly friendship, more ardent, more general." This became, in the 1860 text, "a superb friendship, exalté, previously unknown." America's prophetic destiny was to be realized through the establishment of the "new ideal"; since homosexuality is universal, America would again become a beacon for the world. Whitman would write, in *Democratic Vistas*, "I say democracy infers such loving comradeship, as its most inevitable twin or counterpart, without which it will be incomplete, in vain, and incapable of perpetuating itself."[100] Whitman seems to have believed, like Melville in *Typee*, that heterosexuality was the sexual expression of capitalism and of a society based on property. Homosexuality was for him the sexual expression of community, and would follow necessarily in a true socialist society.

From such an extended political and social statement, Whitman returns to the personal, in "Earth! my likeness!" a poem which records poignantly Whitman's own awareness of the distance between his ideal conception and its realization, even in his own life. The poem is structured around an analogy between the earth, with its deceptively calm exterior and its volcanic interior, and the poet's self, likewise appearing calm but actually burning within (the "smouldering fires" of "Proto-Leaf"). This inner disturbance is "fierce and terrible" because it is the love between the poet and an athlete. The situation is chosen in part for its echoes of the past: the poet and the athlete inevitably recall Pindar's Olympian odes, rather than evoke any actual experience of the poet's. But that very echo operates ironically, as the frankness of physical celebration which was possible for Pindar is no longer possible. As Whitman puts it, "I dare not tell it in words— not even in these songs." To write the songs of homosexual love and still to feel constrained to self-censorship is the terrible burden of the poet, which may in part derive from inner doubts, but also, in large part, from societal attitudes. Friendship was sanctioned by a long literary tradition well known in Transcendental America. Love and sexual desire between men were much less known, and deliberately rejected by those who did know. By confining himself to "friendship" Whitman stayed barely within the bounds of the permissible. It is perhaps also for this reason that he changed "an athlete loves me,—and I him" of the manuscript to "an athlete is enamoured of me—and I of him." To be *en amour* seemed a shade safer than to *aimer*.

After the confession of secret desires, Whitman returns to his celebration of companionship. But that companionship is now informed by what he has not told us. Declaring what one will not say is often a more effective strategy than saying it; thus omission, when stated, becomes a statement in itself. The nonconfession of "Earth! my likeness!" informs the concluding songs. The following poem, "A leaf for hand in hand," again celebrates "natural persons," "boatmen and mechanics," among whom Whitman will carry his message, transforming homosexuality from a sign of élite decadence (as in, say, Beckford or Walpole) into an attribute of democracy. The shift from the love of women to the love of men is a shift, Whitman suggests in "Primeval my love," from primeval or earthbound love to "ethereal" love of men. While the idea that homosexuality represents an advance over heterosexuality is common to most of these songs, the terms in which it is expressed here seem to contradict Whitman's democratic credo. As so often, Whitman has returned to vaguely Platonic language, seeking thereby to justify his call for manly love. The "disembodied" lover is certainly derived from Diotima's account in *The Symposium* of the ascending stages of love, in which at the highest stage the lover "instead of a beauty tainted by human flesh and colour and a mass of perishable rubbish, is able to apprehend divine beauty when it exists apart and alone."[101] As usual, Whitman is at his weakest when he calls upon such sources, for they accord ill with his declared political and social intentions, not to mention his insistence upon an "embodied" love. Still we must recognize that Plato's *Symposium* represented for Whitman one of the very few literary texts to have discussed the love of men. It was natural that he should call upon it for support and adopt some of its models. But Whitman's strength and his contribution to the development of a homosexual literary tradition certainly lie not in his adaptations of Plato but in his naive American enthusiasm and consequent willingness to celebrate love between men in a direct and nonallegorized way.

Another Platonic model is called upon in "That shadow, my likeness," as Whitman returns to his distinction between the real life of the spirit and the life of the world, which only appears to be real. Here, as in the early poems of "Calamus," the Whitman who lives in the conventional world is opposed to the Whitman of the love poems. Unlike those earlier poems, however, there is no distinction in time between a prior self and a present self.

Instead, by implication, the two selves coexist, but the "real" Whitman exists only "among my lovers, and carolling my songs." Again the language is close to that of existentialism, for the "authentic" Whitman is the Whitman of "Calamus," the self-defined; while the socially defined Whitman that "goes to and fro, seeking a livelihood," remains inauthentic. It remains true even now that many homosexuals live lives of such duplicity, and likewise know their social selves to be a lie, because of the need to earn a livelihood. Whitman's language may be Platonic, but he describes an actual problem of life in nineteenth-century America.

Of the last group of poems three celebrate love, while two deal with the relationship of love to art. "Sometimes with one I love" suggests the importance of love as the basis of Whitman's art (an idea developed most fully in "Out of the Cradle"): "Doubtless I could not have perceived the universe, or written one of my poems, if I had not freely given myself to comrades, to love." Love becomes essential to art, in this formulation, because art requires self-definition and self-expression. Had Whitman not given himself "to comrades," he would not have developed the perception of self which underlies a work so self-examining as his. It will be remarked that this original formulation is quite different from the one finally adopted in the Blue Book revisions:

> (I loved a certain person ardently and my love was not re-
> turn'd,
> Yet out of that I have written these songs.)

The revised version picks up the idea of "return" for love and substitutes an artistic return for a more direct return of love itself (thus anticipating the Freudian view of sublimation); but it substitutes a more specific vision of unreturned love for an earlier expression of love freely given. The second version appears to be more personal and may reflect a greater ability, with the passage of time, to understand the origins of the "Calamus" sequence. In either case the poem suggests strongly the need to love, regardless of the return that one may receive for one's love. "Here my last words, and the most baffling" alludes again to the need to conceal, yet paradoxically states that even this concealed version "exposes" most. Whitman's prediction is striking: the "Calamus" leaves are "the frailest leaves of me, and yet my strongest-lasting." Their frailty is revealed by the attacks they have provoked and by Whitman's own difficulties with this section. But their ability to last, too, is demonstrated by the fact that poets of the twentieth century have found in them a source of strength as they have sought their own poetic and sexual identities, and the links between the two. While for some, sexual choice remains "irrelevant," for others it is at least as important as nationality, religion, class, or any other factor that determines one's self. Whitman recognized that even as he "shaded down" his thoughts in this section, they acted toward his exposure. To speak of such love is to reveal it, as Whitman knew when he undertook "Calamus" as an act of self-definition.

Recognition occurs, of course, despite the "indirections," just as two men may meet and fall in love despite the absence of a socially sanctioned form to express that love. Even in a time when total frankness is impossible, a system of signs can establish communication. Such signs, in "Among the men and women," pass unnoticed by others, yet lead to a bond of friendship that is total, that allows for no closer bond, not even those to family, and that is founded not upon the inequality of heterosexuality but upon equality. And so the second stanza opens bravely, "Lover and perfect equal!" It is their love that makes men equal. For Whitman it was the equality of men that made any relationship between them more democratic than any heterosexual relationship, which must be founded upon inherent inequalities of power and status. Such a meeting of men could occur easily, as in "O you whom I often and silently come where you are," and could be based upon the simple pleasure of being together, through the recognition of a kind of animal magnetism—"the subtle electric fire that is playing within me."

Along with the relationships of equality, there is also the pederastic model, again derived from Plato and described in "To the young man." Whitman's "élève" is derived from the classical ideal of the pupil, learning from his older lover until he himself can become a master with his own pupils. The use of the French term may represent here, as it often does, Whitman's desire to add color to his language. But it may also reflect the search for a word to express a very special relationship, one for which the ordinary English "pupil" is inadequate. I suspect that Whitman said "élève" for much the same reason he said "adhesiveness" or "camerado": to find a new word to express a new meaning. Whitman's theory of learning as presented in this poem (nicely anticipating the more humorous version presented by Ionesco in *La Leçon*)

seems to connect learning and love. In any case, it is clear that
learning is insufficient without a willingness to put the learning
into practice, that one cannot be a disciple, or "élève," of Whitman without sharing, as he put it in the manuscript, "the blood
of friendship, hot and red" (this became merely "blood like mine"
in the printed text). The only sign that one has learned Whitman's
"lesson" is a willingness to love and be loved. Whitman returned
to the relationship between pedagogy and pederasty in the one
poem added later (in 1871) to "Calamus," "The Base of All Meta-
physics." Here Whitman suggests that the basis of philosophy
is the love of beauty, as Plato put it, and that the beautiful is
best incarnated in a young man:

> Yet underneath Socrates clearly see, and underneath the
>   divine I see,
> The dear love of man for his comrade, the attraction of friend
>   to friend

Whitman was certainly right about Platonism, of course, although the fact was rarely admitted at his time, and he may even
have been right about Christianity. But he vitiated his own statement, by continuing, as he would never have done in 1860, in a
descent, from the honest statement quoted above through a series
of increasing vagueness: "Of the well-married husband and wife,
of children and parents, / Of city for city and land for land."

If Whitman begins his "Calamus" with self-declaration, he
concludes with an injunction. He has asked the reader to follow
him through the presentation of the "secret"; he has revealed the
pleasures and pains of life as a homosexual in nineteenth-century
America. He has also offered a program for the future. Now it
remains for the reader to fulfill that program. Whitman's address
in the last poem is to the future—"To one a century hence, or
any number of centuries hence"—in recognition that the goals
he has set cannot be fulfilled in his own lifetime. His poems were
themselves roots, as he suggested in "Calamus taste," which
would require loving care in order to bloom. The burden falls
upon the reader as the author departs. The work written, the author vanished, the dialogue is between text and reader. It is the
reader who will "realize" (fulfill, make real) the poems. Whitman
offers that reader the assurance of his support and encouragement:
"Be it as if I were with you. Be not too certain but I am now
with you." The final lines return playfully to the tension of appear-

ance and reality. Is the author alive "now" when he writes, or "then" when he is read? Is the author finally ever there? If the poems have succeeded, they have not merely evoked a poet. They will have used the persona of the poet to spur the imagination of the reader. Is Whitman the man present in his poems? We shall never know. Whitman the man is deliberately elusive, reminding us of his view that the end of art is to transform reality, through its action upon the reader.

Whitman's final dramatization of self is as an evanescent spirit, much like the figure of "Sleepers." This is not to suggest that he is coy or deceptive, but to realize that his "exposure" has been a strategy, the results of which can only be seen in the future. The historical Whitman is of no literary interest. He can vanish and leave behind the spiritual Whitman, the eternal lover, the risen god of male love. Whitman predicted that of all his poems, "Calamus" would be "the last to be fully understood." But he did not doubt that such understanding would come.

2. The Academic Tradition

IN ORDER TO PLACE the achievement of Whitman in a proper context, and to understand why a younger poet such as Crane would turn to him with such respect, we must look briefly at alternate ways of expressing male friendship in nineteenth-century poetry, i.e., the Academic or Genteel tradition. It is not, by any means, that the subject of male friendship, even ardent friendship, or of the attraction of male beauty was absent from this tradition. On the contrary, the Genteel poetry of the day is suffused with the thin light of the Arcadian dawn. In some ways, male friendship is a particularly apt subject for the Genteel poet. The women of that tradition are bloodless and unreal; they exist only as Muse or as mother. Real emotional relationships exist only between men. They, too, are thoroughly spiritualized, so that there is none of the phallic imagery or the depiction of sexual acts which one finds in Whitman. For the Genteel poets the most passionate emotional experience is likely to be rendered as an idyllic afternoon on the grass, a deep look into a friend's eyes, or an understanding of brotherhood, rather vaguely defined. To some extent one can attribute the existence of such intense male relationships to the fact that only highly spiritual relationships were permitted with women. But one can also reverse the argument and suggest that the peculiarly ethereal women of such a literary tradition had their origin in an unspoken (and to some extent unrecognized) homosexuality which rendered a conventional tribute to women, but came alive only when released from this obligation and permitted to express its own nature.

The use of the word "homosexuality" with regard to this tradition must be more delicate than with Whitman. While it is possible (although, I think, unlikely) that Whitman never actually engaged in genital sex with another man, it is at the same time certain that he was fully and consciously aware of himself as a homosexual (with an adhesive nature, as he would have put it)

and that he built his poetic and political ideas around that awareness. In the case of the Genteel poets, however, the matter is far
less clear. One of the figures to be discussed here, Taylor, was
certainly conscious of his own sexual nature, at least during a large
part of his career. But several others, including a number of Taylor's friends, may not have been aware of their own sexuality.
There is no evidence (unless it is hidden away in some forgotten
archive) to indicate whether these men expressed their sexuality
directly, or whether its only expression was through their art.
What we know of their correspondence would suggest that their
relationships with other men were extremely warm and involved
both deep affection and physical contact. In the end, therefore, I
do not believe that it matters very much whether or not they par-
ticipated in genital sex with other men. I think it will be seen
from their work that their central emotional direction was toward
men. For the purposes of this study, then, they may be considered
as homosexual poets.

One can only speculate on the consequences for their personal
lives of the discrepancy between an apparent public heterosexuality and a private homosexuality (expressed publicly in indirect
ways). It seems likely that the emotional price for such concealment was high, although the tensions created by the need for a
constant disguise may also have been the source of a certain artistic
strength. I do not believe, however, that it is generally true that
repression is artistically valuable. One has heard it said too often
that "Yes, they suffered, but look what it did for their art." That
statement can only be made by someone unaware of the destructive nature of prejudice and intolerance and the resultant internalization of societal oppression. Furthermore, I think it will be seen
that the authors considered here did not in fact produce great art,
that their art was far inferior to the (admittedly uneven) work of
Whitman, the "unrepressed." The strategies adopted by these authors contribute to a weakening of focus and a fatal indirection.
The Genteel tradition in America failed for a number of reasons;
it would certainly be simplistic to blame its failure entirely on
the repression of homosexuality. But it must be admitted that one
reason for the particularly bitter reaction against "official" art in
the twentieth century has been a feeling, albeit often unsubstanti-
ated, that it is dishonest and unmanly. In a strange way, the philis-
tines have been right, although for the wrong reasons. What
caused the flabbiness and "femininity" of American official art of
this period was not that the authors were homosexual but that they

refused (or were unable) to recognize this fact. The reaction, unfortunately, has resulted in a mindless celebration of "male" virtues, a tradition which passes through Hemingway to Mailer and Dickey.

Those who, like myself, believe that, for all his strength, Whitman offers several almost insuperable obstacles, must regret the failure of the Genteel tradition and the subsequent rise of a cult of masculinity. Whitman's courage, audacity, and extraordinary insights are beyond doubt. He created lines and even poems of unquestionable beauty. One is grateful for his carnality, after the frigidity and bloodlessness of Thoreau, Emerson, or even Hawthorne. But there is also an enormous crudity about Whitman, a magnificent tastelessness that in the end leaves the reader weary. Given the suffocating, hot-house atmosphere of mid Victorian America, the overstatement and vulgarity of Whitman were probably necessary and even salutary. But there has existed in America no literary tradition that has successfully combined the frank sexuality and direct confrontation of the social and political issues of sexuality, which are the contribution of Whitman, with a real strength and purity of language, no works that could become essential parts of the literary imagination. This has happened in other places—with Shakespeare's sonnets, for instance, or with George in Germany or Gide in France.

It is perhaps unfair to ask of the American Genteel writers that they be more than they were—American Victorians. Yet out of that same world in England came a Tennyson, a Swinburne, a Pater, even a Wilde. One cannot help feeling that there is a sad story here. In part the explanation lies in the "feminization" of American culture; women bought and read the books of poetry, and so an artist who yearned for a popular audience as Taylor did increasingly came to reflect feminine values. And in part the explanation also lies in the often-discussed aridity of American culture. The Genteel writers seem to have been by and large *déchus*, like the progressives discussed by Hofstadter.[1] For them the central myth was the Fall, because it seemed to replicate their own fall from childhood innocence and from affluence. Their Arcadian dream was of a return to young manhood, when friendship had been uninterrupted by marriage and family. Many regarded the death of a young friend as the central symbolic fact of their lives. But when they sought modes of expression for their values, they could find none that had taken root in American soil. The dilemma of which James spoke in *Hawthorne* is felt only by the Genteel

writer for whom such things matter. It did not arrest the development of a Melville or a Twain. But the Genteel writer could not
sail on a ship, or even a raft, without turning it into Jason's ship.
Even then their allusions had no mythic resonance; they remained
faint echoes of larger things. They ultimately settled for decora-
tion, having no foundation on which to build.

Fitz-Greene Halleck

The first writer to be discussed here, as well as the earliest, is
Fitz-Greene Halleck. Although Halleck lived on until the beginning of the last quarter of the century, and probably knew Whitman at Pfaff's, his years of creativity were much earlier, from 1817
to 1827. He is completely forgotten by now, although widely
celebrated during his lifetime. In the battle over literary national-
ism which raged in the years of Irving and Cooper, Halleck took
the "wrong" side. He considered himself to be writing English literature, not American. This has undoubtedly contributed to the
decline of his critical fortunes, although his name still has a vaguely familiar ring, if only because of Poe's famous review.[2] Halleck
was a competent craftsman and a man of some sensitivity. He early
abandoned a literary career, however, and retired to live at home
in Guilford with his sister. He never married.

The central emotional fact of Halleck's life was clearly his
friendship with the poet Joseph Rodman Drake. This gave rise to
their literary collaboration, in the "Croaker" poems. The phe-
nomenon of joint authorship is an interesting one, although little
studied since it is so rare among authors of any standing. One is
hard put to think of another example since Beaumont and Fletcher
(unless, of course, one considers Eliot and Pound joint authors
of *The Waste Land*—but that is a much more complicated matter).
Drake and Halleck seem to have completely merged their personal
and artistic lives during the short time they had together, and
they are still thought of as a unit. In a study written during Halleck's lifetime, a biographer declared, "The two poets maintained
a friendship only severed by death," and continued:

> When the young physician was married . . . it was Halleck
> who officiated as groomsman; when he went abroad with his
> young wife, it was to his brother-poet that he addressed sev-
> eral poetical epistles; when his daughter and only child was

born, she was christened Halleck; when the pulsations of his gentle heart were daily growing feebler, it was his faithful and attached friend "Fitz" who, with more than a brother's love, soothed his dying pillow . . .[3]

The early death of Drake not only brought to an end their literary collaboration; it also appears to have cast a pall upon Halleck from which he never really recovered.

His testament to Drake is contained in his elegy, "On the Death of Joseph Rodman Drake," his longest-lasting literary work. It is reputed to have been written the day of Drake's death in 1820. It records Halleck's inability to transform his grief into "thoughts nor words." He wishes to transform personal suffering into public tribute but finds he cannot:

When hearts whose truth was proven
    Like thine, are laid in earth,
There should a wreath be woven
    To tell the world their worth;

And I who woke each morrow,
    To clasp thy hand in mine,
Who shared thy joy and sorrow.
    Whose weal and woe were thine,—

It should be mine to braid it
    Around thy faded brow,
But I've in vain essayed it,
    And feel I cannot now.

While memory bids me weep thee,
    Nor thoughts nor words are free;
The grief is fixed too deeply
    That mourns a man like thee.[4]

Ironically, Halleck's record of his inability to create a public tribute to his friend has become the very tribute by which Drake is still remembered.

It is of course impossible to deduce anything from the existence of this elegy, other than that Drake and Halleck were friends and that Halleck mourned his friend's death. Still, it must be remembered that the elegy has often served as a form for the expression of otherwise unspeakable emotions. Love that cannot be expressed by one man for another becomes permissible as soon as one of them is dead. "In Memoriam," Tennyson's tribute to Hallam, remains the most remarkable modern example of the use of this form to record the depth of personal love. Whatever the facts of Halleck's relationship to Drake, the poem testifies to its emotional intensity and is supported by the testimony of a contemporary biographer of Halleck: he speaks of Drake, "to whom he was deeply attached, and at whose bedside during the summer he had watched with more than a brother's love." The same writer records the opinion of Miss Mitford, for what it is worth, that the elegy is "a true and manly record of a true and manly friendship."[5] Halleck, in any case, apparently did not change his mind; he refused to write a memoir of his friend, and merely recalled "the days of sunny weather," the days with Drake, "he the most / Honored and loved, and early lost."[6] Clearly the memory of this early love marked the rest of Halleck's life.

Before meeting Drake, he had already shown a certain propensity toward male friendship. When he was nineteen, he was "intimate" (in the words of his biographer) with a "handsome young Cuban," Carlos Menie. He wrote a number of poems to Carlos, recalling his "pleasing forms" which recur to him in dreams:

> Oft in the stillness of the night,
>   When slumbers close mine eyes,
> Your image bursts upon my sight;
>   I gaze in glad surprise!

He wonders if Carlos shares such feelings, and reassures himself that his love is returned:

> Ah, yes! that gentle heart I know,
>   At friendship's touch it beats;
> I feel the sympathetic glow,
>   My breast the throb repeats.

> Then let us cherish well the flame
>   Of friendship and of love;
> Let peaceful virtue be our aim,
>   Our hopes be placed above.[7]

The second stanza cited above indicates the "Platonizing" which is apparently operating here. After "the flame / Of friendship and of love" there is a shift to "peaceful virtue," which does not seem to follow from the implied passion of the first two lines. It is as if there were a deliberate check upon the emotions, a resolve to confine this love to the realm of virtue, not to be expressed on earth physically, but rather in an afterlife spiritually. Thus one can observe in Halleck's lines the first traces of what would later be called the Uranian attitude: the assumption that love between men was purer and more spiritual than heterosexual love. In Halleck, however, one senses a tension, a deliberate refusal of passion, a renunciation not unlike that of Anne Bradstreet in "Lines upon the Burning of My House." Friendship appears to be seen as a sentiment of youth, something necessarily, if reluctantly, put away with adulthood; and so Halleck asks to be remembered by Carlos, "Let the remembrance oft intrude / Of friendship and of me," just as he assures Carlos of the permanence of his affection, despite their separation: "within my heart / Your memory firm shall dwell."

Halleck sought justification, apparently, for his feelings of personal affection and found it in the most likely source for an American at the beginning of the nineteenth century, the Bible (although Wilson, his biographer, turned to a classical source and called Drake and Halleck "the 'Damon and Pythias' of American poets"[8]—it is not clear what he meant by that). One of Halleck's youthful exercises was a "Lamentation of David over Saul and Jonathan." Halleck justified his choice of subject by his subtitle "paraphrased from 2 Samuel i 1–19," but the choice of this particular episode out of all those available is striking. One may attribute part of the cause to Halleck's place in a sentimental tradition: he marks an early attempt in American letters to introduce the conventions of European studies in sensibility. Thus he chooses from an acceptable New England text—the Bible—but chooses an episode for its sentiment rather than its religious meaning. It is still significant that Halleck's Wertherism found its expression in despair over a dead male lover and not over a distant and unavailable woman.

In addition, although the episode has Biblical sanction, Halleck clearly enlarged upon David's feelings for his "loved companion" and transformed the original story into a study in sensibility, of mourning for "a wound that time can never heal":

A mutual flame our bosoms fired,
A mutual love our breasts inspired,
Our pleasures and our cares the same;

We felt sweet friendship's hallowed flame,
Purer than that which warms our hearts
When pierced by the fatal darts
    That flashed from beauty's eye.
Affection twined our souls around,
And virtuous love our union bound
    With every sacred tie.[9]

As in the poem to Carlos, Halleck insists upon the purity of his sentiment. Here that is reinforced by the comparison between the two loves. Friendship has a "hallowed flame" and establishes a "sacred tie"; whereas "beauty" (i.e., love of women) brings only "fatal darts." Halleck's embellishments upon his source indicate his own feelings, and the beginning of a clearly defined distinction between the love of men, pure, holy, and virtuous, and the love of women, impure and destructive. The sources of this distinction, which would play a large role in the Genteel thought of the nineteenth century, lie not so much in misogyny as in a sublimated homosexuality. Male friendship, in the terms already established by Plato, is purer than love for women, precisely because it is not expressed in physical love and does not lead to procreation. An age which prefers sentiment to fulfilled passion would naturally turn toward the "purer" love of men. The friendships of youth remain timeless, fixed in eternal youth by memory and by the preservation of art. Sensibility thus gave an added force to what was almost certainly a personal desire for male friendships; but, while it permitted such friendships to flourish and even to be celebrated, in terms that would now seem excessive, without offending even the most genteel of readers, it also forced friendship to remain "platonic," confined to the nonphysical expression of affection, and determined the development of an attitude toward homosexuality that was both highly spiritualized and implicitly elitist. The Genteel tradition would give rise to an attitude that homosexuality was the province of superior beings, who nonetheless purchased their superiority at the price of physical expression.

Bayard Taylor and His Circle

When the memorial to Fitz-Greene Halleck was unveiled at Guilford, it was Bayard Taylor who delivered the address. The choice was not surprising: Taylor was considered at the time one of the greatest American poets, if not the greatest. But it is also possible that Taylor recognized other, more personal affinities between himself and Halleck. The address itself gives no indication, but Taylor's tribute to Halleck does establish a connection, admittedly tenuous, between Halleck, the first poet of friendship in America, and the flourishing of what can almost be called a school in the 1860s and 1870s. Taylor's tribute is in any case an interesting document because of its emphasis on the barrenness of American life and the consequences of that lack of tradition and social order for American literature. One wonders if James, ten years later, did not recall Taylor's words: "The destiny that placed us on this soil robbed us of the magic of tradition, the wealth of romance, the suggestions of history, the sentiment of inherited homes and customs. . . ."[10] But Taylor, unlike James, believed that the period of intellectual desiccation was over, brought to an end by the development of a national and realistic literature.

So at least he thought in 1869. His early works display something quite different. Taylor had established his reputation as a travel writer, whose reports from abroad fed a growing appetite for the exotic and the romantic. He provided landscapes of the Far North, the Orient, the Middle East, Africa, always with an atmosphere of adventure and romance. In his homely fashion he did for American literature what French painters such as Delacroix were doing, namely, offering the new bourgeoisie dreams of travel and excitement, ways of spending their new affluence and of countering the boredom of everyday life. For Taylor travel fulfilled a moral purpose as well, by extending the options open to a man in mid nineteenth-century America and permitting the expression of ideas that were inconceivable at home. (Taylor's own background was rural Pennsylvania Quaker, a milieu that he found stifling and repressive, to judge by his fiction—his Quakers seem indistinguishable from the neighboring Amish.) Taylor's travel narrative permitted him to describe Turkish baths, hashish smoking, dancing girls, drunken brawls, and pretty Arab boys without fear of censorship; he was merely reporting exotic customs. The travel books thus served a function not unlike some early forms of pornography: under the guise of science they offered erotic titillation.

Taylor's poetry often made use of similar strategies. His most successful book was his *Poems of the Orient* (1854), with its "To a Persian Boy," subtitled "In the Bazaar at Smyrna." [11] The poem draws upon its Persian setting, but also upon a tradition of Persian love poetry, often addressed to boys (thus line 12 cites Hafiz). In other words, the poet indicates that his tribute to the beauty of a boy is a mere literary exercise, prompted by the scene. This strategy allows the poem to communicate on two levels: appearing as a minor literary exercise to some readers, while at the same time conveying to other readers Taylor's attraction for "the wonder of thy beauty." Still, in this very early poem (first published in 1851) Taylor does not concentrate on the boy's beauty but uses the poem as a means of communicating his taste for the East, in terms that suggest a moral contrast with America: "From under thy dark lashes shone on me / The rich, voluptuous soul of Eastern land." It is precisely the voluptuousness, the frank sensuality of the East, which appeals. Taylor's own travels may well have served as a means for him to experience such voluptuousness at first hand. Like his friend Herman Melville, Taylor may have felt that true pleasure, particularly pleasure between men, could be found only in another land, where the burden of rigid moral codes was less heavy.

In another poem, "Hylas," [12] Taylor adopted a different strategy. Here the convention is Greek, not Persian, but the method is the same. Taylor is able to express a sensual response to a young man by imitating a classical legend. Since the story of Hylas is told by Theocritus, Taylor can justify his loving portrayal of the boy by reference to the homosexual content of Theocritus' works and the conventions of Greek romance. He can thus appear to be merely the translator, as it were, and so enjoy the sensuality without fully avowing it. Within the poem itself, the strategy of the poet is one we might call the "Leander" strategy, in honor of its most famous use by Marlowe. In his delightful, unfinished poem Marlowe diverts the reader's attention from the story itself, the love of the youth Leander for the priestess Hero, to a subplot involving the rape of Leander by Neptune, who mistakes him for Ganymede. The subplot is far more interesting than the plot itself, coming much closer to Marlowe's own sexuality, but it is still contained within an acceptably heterosexual frame. (Something of the same tension between heterosexual plot and homosexual subplot may be observed in Marlowe's plays as well, to a much smaller degree in Shakespeare's plays, and, more recently, in most of Forster's novels, such as *The Longest Journey* or *A Passage to India*.) In the case of the story of Hylas, the original legend is itself largely homosexual, concerned with the love of Hercules for Hylas and Hylas' drowning at the hands of nymphs. But it also offers an occasion for the celebration of male beauty.

So Taylor suspends his narrative long enough to linger over the form of young Hylas:

> Naked, save one light robe that from his shoulder
> Hung to his knee, the youthful flush revealing
> Of warm, white limbs, half-nerved with coming manhood,
> Yet fair and smooth with tenderness of beauty.

Taylor places Hylas exactly at the point preferred by the Greeks, the brief moment of flowering before the first signs of manhood (in Greek pederasty, the younger lover lost his charm the moment he began to grow a beard):

> manhood's blossom
> Not yet had sprouted on his chin, but freshly
> Curved the fair cheek, and full the red lips, parting,
> Like a loose bow, that just has launched its arrow.
> His large blue eyes, with joy dilate and beamy,
> Were clear as the unshadowed Grecian heaven;
> Dewy and sleek his dimpled shoulders rounded
> To the white arms and whiter breast between them.
> Downward, the supple lines had less of softness:
> His back was like a god's; his loins were moulded
> As if some pulse of power began to waken.

There is considerable power in these lines, with their evocation of the barely confined erotic strength of the youth. Taylor's language is, as usual, highly uneven. His simile for the lips is, if extravagant, effective and sensual, while his image for the eyes, "dilate and beamy," can only be called awkward. But the last line cited above, with its strong iambic beat and effective use of short, heavy words and the repeated "p," conveys well the effect he is seeking. In such moments his verse almost seems to come alive, to awaken from its lethargy.

Taylor's most recent critic has argued that this poem is "about nothing important; it has no reverberating echoes or suggestions of larger meaning. It comes close to being 'pure poetry,' for it is unrelated to anything else, including human experience." [13] While one can understand the reasons for such a statement and even see a certain truth in it, it is a half truth which has its origin in the critic's inability to imagine what Taylor was trying to do in the poem. He apparently does not see that the story of the death-nymphs and their victory over the body of the beautiful boy is a major element in the mythology of homosexuality. This story has remained one of the most important myths for homosexuals[14] because it offers an "explanation" for the transformation of the young lover into a heterosexual and hence his loss. Read mythically, the story says: Hercules loves Hylas until the day that Hylas is about to become a man; at that point he becomes attractive to women, who seduce him and thereby kill him; Hercules is left mourning for a lost love. The myth blames women for the destruction of homosexual love, as in the story of Orpheus or, more recently, in Eliot's "Prufrock." It also suggests homosexuality as a lost ideal, a state once enjoyed but now vanished, which one can recapture only in the imagination. Such a reading of the myth clearly underlies Taylor's adoption of it. Taylor's "Hylas" is indeed related to human experience; it is deeply related to Taylor's understanding of himself as a homosexual. His choice of the Hylas myth as a poetic subject is part of an attempt at self-definition and also part of an attempt to situate himself in a poetic tradition which will justify his own emotional life. The failure of the poem comes from Taylor's inability fully to avow his real subject: the love of Hercules for Hylas and his own for young men. In Marlowe wit and humor carry the day. For the sentimental Taylor there can be no such baroque pleasures. His language is luxuriant but finally vague; unable to depict directly the body of love, it wanders off into repeated similes.

Taylor's next major work was his *Poet's Journal*, published in 1862. It is a strange collection of narrative and lyric poems, founded on the relationship between two brothers. (The theme of two brothers in love was used often by Taylor, e.g., in his extraordinary story, "Twin-Love." The use of brothers appears to be a dodge, allowing for an expression of affection which would otherwise be unthinkable. Note in particular that the brothers in the story are called David and Jonathan!) Although one of the brothers is depicted with a wife, she plays almost no role in the narrative, except to serve as a model of domestic bliss (and to bear a child). Philip awaits Ernest's return, since he has missed feeling "upon my lips the brother-kiss / That shames not manhood."[15] Such references make it plain that Taylor was aware of the possible censure of his readers—and imply that the kiss he imagines is not so brotherly. Taylor feels obliged to insist upon the innocence of the kiss, and by so doing reminds us that there are kisses between men which might "shame" manhood. The emotional relationship between Philip and Ernest is highly charged, especially when Ernest reflects that he is asked to "bless" Philip's marriage:

> Go, hide your shameless happiness,
>   The demon cries, within my breast;
> Think not that I the bond can bless,
>   Which seeing, I am twice unblest.[16]

The situation must have been one familiar to such writers as Taylor. Since their homosexuality was publicly unacknowledged, their beloved young men must often have asked them to bless their marriages. The situation is familiar to homosexual literature at least since Shakespeare, but it was given particular importance in the late nineteenth century: one thinks of Hopkins trying to write an epithalamium for his brother and wandering off to dream of boys in "mansex fine" swimming naked, or of poor Housman writing his epithalamium for his beloved Mo as: "Friend and comrade yield you o'er / To her that hardly loves you more."

One particularly striking section is entitled "Love Returned" and plays upon the ambiguity suggested by the title, whether a god or a sentiment is being evoked. Throughout the poem it seems clear that a real young man is being described—"He was a boy when first we met"—although Taylor protects himself by allowing for the possibility that it is the god of love he is discussing. Lines such as this, however, seem clear in their meaning:

> on his candid brow was set
> The sweetness of a chaste desire.
> But in his veins the pulses beat
> Of passion waiting for its wing.[17]

Taylor thus plays on the tension between an apparent innocence and an innate sensuality, waiting for expression. The poem then turns to the development of a mature love, which has passed through the summer fires of passion and settled for a world of greater repose. Whether the poem refers to an actual friendship in Taylor's life is not entirely clear, although it seems likely (the poem was advertised as autobiography). Several of Taylor's friends were extremely close to him and seem possibly to have been the objects of his love, particularly George Henry Boker and Richard Henry Stoddard. The letters to Boker, especially, are so effusive and romantic that one cannot help wondering if their friendship was not the basis for such poems. (If it was, that might help explain the mysterious dark lady of Boker's sonnets, hidden away during his lifetime: Is it possible that she was actually Bayard Taylor?) In any case it is clear that the three figures of the poem—man, wife, and brother—can be reduced to two, the wife playing only the most marginal of roles.

Although Taylor continued in the 1860s to write a few poems and travel narratives, his primary work was in prose fiction. Here he worked in a realistic mode, emphasizing character portrayal and local color. His novel *Joseph and His Friend* (1870) is an amazingly frank portrayal of homosexual love and a plea for understanding of homosexuals. Although Joseph and his friend Philip both marry, Joseph's marriage is a disaster, as his wife is out to steal his money, and Philip's marriage a mere sop to convention occurring in the last few pages. The emotional and physical intensity of the work comes from its portrayal of the relationship between the two men. Philip is a self-conscious spokesman for the expression of homosexual love, explaining that "there are needs which most men have, and go all their lives hungering for, because they expect them to be supplied in a particular form." [18] Joseph argues for the realization of these needs through a change in "form," that is, through the exploration of the love of men. He seeks justice for "the men—and the women—who cannot shape themselves according the common-place pattern of society,—who are born with instincts, needs, knowledge, and rights—ay, rights—of their own!" [19] The novel is not merely a political argument in favor of rights for homosexuals; it is also a depiction, although in highly romantic terms, of the realization of love between two men. Taylor's language is lush, melodramatic, and sentimental, but it was an act of considerable courage to write:

> They took each other's hands. The day was fading, but only the twitter of nesting birds was heard in the boughs above them. Each gave way to the impulse of his manly love, rarer, alas! but as tender and true as the love of women, and they drew nearer and kissed each other. As they walked back and parted on the highway, each felt that life was not wholly unkind, and that happiness was not yet impossible. [20]

Within the framework of a thoroughly Genteel novel, Taylor creates a world that seems astonishingly close to "Calamus."

In fact, Taylor's relationship with Whitman is an interesting subject for speculation. Unfortunately we do not know enough to establish all the facts in the case. We do know, however, that in 1866 Taylor wrote to Whitman, sending a copy of his *Picture of St. John* and praising Whitman for his "deep and tender reverence for Man—your unwearied, affectionate practical fraternity." In his second letter, after Whitman had responded, sending him *Leaves of Grass* and discussing their projected meeting on December 27, Taylor was even more explicit, praising "that tender and noble love of man for man which once certainly existed, but now almost seems to have gone out of the experience of the race." Taylor was aware, of course, that their views on poetry were vastly different: "We should differ rather in regard to form than substance, I suspect. There is not one word of your large and beautiful sympathy for men, which I cannot take into my own heart. . . ."[21] Although we know that the planned meeting did take place, we have no record of what transpired. Did a difference over "form" prevent an understanding on "substance"? Or did the two poets in fact interpret "substance" differently? Or did they in fact get along well, and did their disagreements arise later?

All we know is that in 1876 Taylor began a series of articles in the *Tribune* attacking Whitman. It may be that Taylor was prompted to this largely by the activities of O'Connor and others of Whitman's disciples. It may even be that Taylor was jealous of Whitman's increasing fame. Or it may be that Taylor now objected to the sexual frankness of Whitman. A Whitman scholar has written recently, "Taylor was attempting to still, if not actually exorcise, that portion of his nature which responded so enthusiastically to Whitman's celebration of the body."[22] He implies that Taylor sought to suppress his own homosexuality through an attack on Whitman. While this is not impossible, there is no evidence to support the theory, which does not seem consistent with the strong advocacy of homosexuality and homosexual rights in *Joseph and His Friend*. Nor does it accord with the publication in the same year, 1876, of Taylor's children's book, *Boys of Other Countries*, with its rapturous account of twelve-year-old Lars, the post-boy, with whom he shares a bed on reindeer skin. As they "lay close together, warming each other," Taylor "dreamed of gathering peaches on a warm August day."[23] Of course Taylor did not expect his readers to notice anything unusual in this passage, but it illustrates a continuing preoccupation with male sexuality in his work and also illustrates, in an extreme manner, how almost any text could be "diverted" for a brief moment of erotic pleasure. It seems unlikely that the man who wrote that could have disapproved of Whitman's homosexuality; it seems more likely to have been his manners that offended.

The world of the Orient was an important element in Taylor's development and self-definition. As he put it in "L'Envoi" to *Poems of the Orient*,

> I found among those Children of the Sun
>   The cipher of my nature,—the release
> Of baffled powers, which else had never won
>   That free fulfillment, whose reward is peace.[24]

The theme of the northerner discovering a land of warmth, beauty, and love is a familiar one, of course, and one that very often has homosexual meaning; it is probably nowhere better expressed than in Mann's "Death in Venice," but Mann was himself drawing upon von Platen, and one could equally well cite Lawrence, Forster, von Gloeden, Gide, and many others, in all of whom there is a link between the ancient gods and an older, darker civilization which remained in touch with the primitive sources of sensuality. For Taylor his journeys to the East provided a "cipher," a way to an understanding of his own nature and the realization of his own sexuality. In this surprisingly confessional poem, Taylor associates the East with freedom and release, indicating that he might never have realized his own nature had he not experienced this exotic, sensual world. In the first stage of his development these experiences led to a dream of the recovery of lost innocence, a pastoral reverie:

> The Poet said: I will here abide,
>   In the Sun's unclouded door;
> Here are the wells of all delight
>   On the lost Arcadian shore.[25]

By 1870 Taylor was no longer satisfied with such dreams. *Joseph and His Friend* makes use of the pastoral ideal, only to reject it. Joseph finally discovers Philip's valley of bliss, with groves, orchards, and flowers. But he also recognizes that it is a mere dream, unless the men who go there have changed their own attitudes. The pastoral dream leads finally, not to California, but to the self:

> we will only go there on one of these idle epicurean journeys of which we dream . . . not to seek a refuge from the perver-

sions of the world! For I have learned another thing, Philip: the freedom we craved is not a thing to be found in this or that place. Unless we bring it with us, we shall not find it.[26]

Bayard Taylor enjoyed an immense advantage over Fitz-Greene Halleck. By the 1850s and 1860s a considerable literary community had developed in New York and Boston, providing friendship and support. These writers spoke for Genteel values and would be firmly opposed by Twain and others. But they provided the second important literary community in the United States, the first being the Transcendentalists. The Genteel writers shared a regard for friendship, which they practiced in their lives and celebrated in their art. Around Bayard Taylor were several writers clearly on close personal terms with him, whose work displays a sharing of literary ideas and a frequent interchange of gestures of support and homage. Bayard Taylor appears to have been at the center of a homosexual literary circle which flourished for a period of about twenty years, despite the fact that most of the authors concerned were married and all enjoyed considerable reputations with the literary public. None of them was, however, nearly as frank, or as concerned with homosexual definition, as Taylor.

In 1852 Richard Henry Stoddard dedicated his *Poems* "to my friend, Bayard Taylor, whom I admire as a poet, and love as a man." In the same volume he published his sonnet "To B. T.," which included his invitation, "let us join our hands, / And knit our souls in Friendship's holy bands."[27] While the image of hands could refer merely to a handshake, it is immediately followed by an image of the union of souls expressed in terms reminiscent of matrimony: "holy bands" inevitably recalls "holy bonds." Stoddard is establishing a model for friendship (which he Platonically capitalizes) that will be parallel to, and perhaps even superior to, the love of man for woman. This same volume includes his "Arcadian Idyl,"[28] which imagines an encounter between Lycidas and Theocritus. The apparent purpose of the poem is to contrast two poetic styles, a Miltonic or Latinate and a Greek, but it does so by contrasting two friends who represent Taylor and Stoddard himself.

Most of the poem is a dramatic monologue spoken by Lycidas (Taylor). He casts the difference between himself and Theocritus (Stoddard) largely in terms of a contrast between Apollo and Pan. Lycidas is the spirit of Pan, earth-bound, delicate, gentle, soft, compared to a fawn or a dove; while Theocritus is the spirit of

Apollo, stern, rugged, and wild, an eagle to Lycidas' nightingale. Lycidas calls himself "Pleasure's Poet," while Theocritus is a worshipper of Wisdom. It is interesting that these distinctions are not presented merely in poetic terms but are also part of the discrimination of friendship. Stoddard seems to have used the amusing conceit of a meeting between Lycidas and Theocritus as an occasion for contemplating the nature of friendship. The monologue suggests the attraction of opposites—"We love in others what we lack ourselves"—and locates the model for such a complementary love in the relationship of Hercules and Hylas. Lycidas declares, "I have a friend as different from myself, / As Hercules from Hylas, his delight." Lycidas chooses an example drawn from Theocritus to illustrate the two poets' loving relationship (the use of "delight" leaves almost no doubt that Stoddard meant this as a conventional homosexual reference—it recalls the Virgilian "delicias"). Yet Hercules-Theocritus-Stoddard "will wed his love ere Summer dies," while Hylas-Lycidas-Taylor "must live a pensive bachelor."

It seems odd that Stoddard chose to write a poem largely from his friend's point of view, although the poem seems to suggest a necessary balance between the two values. The values represent a full expression of the socially defined notions of masculinity and femininity—lover and beloved, eagle and dove, wisdom and pleasure, wild and gentle, rugged and delicate. The idyl would appear to suggest that Stoddard and Taylor saw their own relationship in terms drawn from the language of heterosexual love. Unlike Whitman, who expressed his ideal as two boys together, the love of comrades as equals, both "manly," Taylor and Stoddard seem to have adopted a much more conventional language, which never questioned basic issues of sexual definition. Even in his remarkably political novel, Taylor establishes a male couple based on respective strength and weakness. And in another novel (*Hannah Thurston*) Taylor expressed his opposition to women's rights, an opposition founded on the fear that the emancipation of women would bring about a decline in femininity. Taylor was thus consistently the spokesman for feminine values, even in his own relationships with other men. Taylor clearly accepted the terms set by Stoddard in the "Arcadian Idyl," since the dedicatory "Proem" to his *Poems of the Orient*, addressed to Stoddard, declared that Apollo "is your God, but mine is shaggy Pan."[29]

Most of Stoddard's love poems are addressed to an unnamed and sexually undifferentiated beloved. It is possible, of course, that they are addressed to a woman. But it seems likely that this

anonymity was enforced by the fact that they were addressed to
boys or men. After all, even if Stoddard had wished to conceal
a female lover from his wife, he could still have written his poems
to a woman. That homosexuals can make their love poetry universal by concealing the beloved is a frequent supposition: it has been
expressed as a desirable goal by Auden. But the strategy is likely
to result in indirectness and lack of focus. And it is not clear how
universal it actually makes the poem, since a heterosexual love poet
would ordinarily identify his beloved as a woman. Stoddard, however, conceals his beloved behind "thee." One poem in particular,
although confined to an anonymous "beloved," seems to express
the secret nature of homosexual love and to suggest that Stoddard,
unlike Taylor, was unwilling to let the world know of his emotional life:

> Beloved, since they watch us,
>   For all we meet are spies,
> And we can have no messengers,
>   Except our loving eyes,
>
> I check my fiery feelings,
>   The words I must not speak
> Content to see,—I dare not pluck,—
>   The roses of thy cheek![30]

Whatever the sex of the beloved, Stoddard gives an interesting
account of the repression of forbidden love.

Taylor was not Stoddard's only close friend. Another was Edmund Clarence Stedman, the poet and anthologist. Stoddard's
sonnet to Stedman[31] is another link in the chain of relationships
that drew these poets together. Stoddard addressed his own sonnet to Stedman "with Shakespeare's sonnets," and so we are to
imagine that the poem actually accompanied a gift of the book
(as well it may have). Stoddard implies a comparison between his
own poem to Stedman and Shakespeare's to his young friend, in
order to regret that Stoddard and Stedman do not live in the
"antique days" when such "sugared sonnets to his strange-sweet
friend" were possible. Shakespeare's sonnets, Stoddard declares,
record "fancies like these, where love and friendship blend . . . in
amorous phrase." These love poems are remembered "with praise,"
and so Stoddard and Stedman, had they lived then, could perhaps
have competed successfully in the composition of such love poems:

"we would have won the bays." In the end, the poem turns to a world-weariness—"many a man has lived an age too late!"—which conceals the real subject of the poem: the inability in 1870 to write poems of love for another man, as Shakespeare had done. Stoddard thus gains legitimacy for his own expression of affection for Stedman by an allusion to Shakespeare, casting his love poem in an honorable tradition. At the same time he expresses the frustration that he must feel at the need to conceal the real nature of his love behind the strategy of literary allusion. Shakespeare's sonnets were a reminder that men could love other men and create great art out of that love. This misfortune of Stoddard's life was that his recognition of these possibilities did not give him the courage to follow in Shakespeare's tradition, but only led him feebly to lament his fate.

Stedman had earlier dedicated his *The Blameless Prince and Other Poems*[32] to Stoddard, and had included in it his "Hylas," which he called a translation. He also included his sonnet to Bayard Taylor. But, although his choice of Hylas as a subject links him to Taylor and Stoddard, and his dedications to them indicate personal friendship, there is no clear treatment of male love in Stedman. Taylor appears to have been unusual in his frankness and his commitment. Although he had friends with whom he could undoubtedly share his views and express his desires, his own example does not seem to have led to any significant development of homosexual literature. The relative openness of the 1850s gave way to the discretion and blandness of the 1870s.

George Santayana

There is a sort of indifference to time, as there is a sort of silence, which goes with veritable sympathy. It springs from clear possession of that which is, from sureness about it. Those who are jealous, jealous of time, of rivals, of accidents, care for something vague that escapes them now, and that would always escape them; they are haunted souls, hunting for they know not what. Not so those who know what they love and rest in it, asking for nothing more. If circumstances had led Bayley and me to go through life together, we should have stuck to each other against any incidental danger or enemy. . . .[33]

So George Santayana wrote, recalling his "sudden, isolated, brief attachment," one of several which occurred during his years at Harvard. It is a remarkable tribute to the power of friendship and to the assurance that comes from loving and being loved. Bayley became, of course, "my first, perhaps my fundamental, model for *The Last Puritan*." The other friend of this period, recalled in the same passage from Santayana's autobiography, *Persons and Places*, is Warwick Potter, the "W. P." of the sonnets. Santayana has relatively little to say about Potter in his autobiography. He records that he "was particularly open to new impressions, plastic, immensely amused, a little passive and feminine," and sums it up: "He was civilized."[34] But these recollections were written fifty years after Santayana had recorded his first and lasting tribute to his friendship in the sequence of four sonnets.

These sonnets are strikingly similar to Housman's poems of the same period (there is no question of Housman's having influenced Santayana: Housman's poems appeared in 1896, Santayana's in 1894). They are a moving tribute to a young man whose early death is the occasion for a meditation upon time and art. One might easily modify Poe's statement and declare that there is no more poetic subject than the death of a beautiful young man. For Santayana, Warwick Potter's death provides a permanent model of the transformation of body into spirit. He becomes a token of all mortality, a reminder to the poet of the vanity of all worldly things, and a promise of reunion after death.

The first of the four sonnets[35] introduces the guiding metaphor of a journey by sea, in terms of which Potter becomes a helmsman, keeping a straight course, and the dead become his "mates" and "partners." Potter's death is seen as "holy," since "your virgin body gave its gentle breath / Untainted to the gods." The virginity of Potter is essential to Santayana's image of him, since it raises their love out of the merely worldly and into the eternal. Santayana's terms of reference are, of course, Platonic, and Potter is his figure for the embodiment of Spiritual Beauty. Santayana considered the physical world a means to the discovery of a deeper, spiritual world. By dying young, Potter remains "untainted," his beauty undiminished, his goodness untested by time. And, by his death, he offers Santayana a permanent erotic figure, a beloved to whom he can remain always faithful. He is an idealized figure of male beauty who by dying in his youth is protected from the ravages of time and, being dead, can offer no carnal temptation to the poet.

The second sonnet turns to Santayana's sense of loss. The octet neatly balances the sestet, the first lamenting what "hath passed away," the second recording the gifts left behind. The poet is consoled by the knowledge of the friendship, and its memory: "For these once mine, my life is rich with these." In the third sonnet, Santayana seeks understanding; the philosopher asks why love was cut down so early. And his consolation comes from the thought that Potter's youth is not lost but preserved, that death has made love eternal: "God hath them still, for ever they avail, / Eternity hath borrowed that delight." There can be no regret for a love which is not destroyed but preserved intact. Only timeless love is permanent; there is union only in the tomb:

> There all my loves are gathered into one,
> Where change is not, nor parting any more,
> Nor revolution of the moon and sun.

(One is tempted to suggest that Rupert Brooke's delightful parody of Neoplatonism in "Tiare Tahiti" is based on a reading of this sonnet.) Potter's death becomes a sign, not of the loss of love, but of its perfection.

The final sonnet continues the contrast between time and eternity and celebrates death as a victory over time: "For time a sadder mask than death may spread / Over the face that ever should be young." (The idea is almost identical to that presented by Housman in "To An Athlete Dying Young.") Santayana picks up the tree metaphor of the second sonnet—"A tree made leafless by this wintry wind / Shall never don again its green array"—and transforms it:

> The bough that falls with all its trophies hung
> Falls not too soon, but lays its flower-crowned head
> Most royal in the dust, with no leaf shed
> Unhallowed or unchiselled or unsung.

The sentiments are those of Housman, but the language has the magnificence of Shakespeare. For all that the poem states that the death of a young man is a victory, its inner life records a poignant struggle to come to terms with what was apparently a very painful loss. From that time on Santayana expressed in all of his work a belief that love in the world was impossible, that love could be realized only in death, after a burning out of passion.

Santayana's principal sonnet sequence is presumed to be addressed to a woman, although no one has successfully identified her. A recent critic has identified Santayana's sister as the "Dark Lady" and suggested that the sonnets celebrate an incestuous love. The same critic dismisses any suggestion that Santayana may have been homosexual as "peripheral" (it is amusing to observe that incest is apparently thought preferable to homosexuality). Since Santayana has said that he was "unconscious" of his homosexuality while a student, she writes: "What seems more likely, is not that Santayana was saying he was a homosexual in this sense, which is the only real sense, since latent homosexuality is a very slippery concept indeed, considering its universality, but that he was simply trying to characterize an emotional life in which he was cut off from intimate relations with women and relied for affection and close relationship on his men friends."[36] She denies a homosexuality which is not acted out, and sees Santayana's emotional ties as the result of being "cut off" from women. Her view is characteristic of people who assume that anyone is heterosexual until there is proof, not of homosexual feelings, but of homosexual acts. The fact remains that Santayana was comparing himself to Housman and suggesting that although he shared Housman's sexuality, he was "unconscious" of it. In order to make such a statement, he must now, it would seem, be "conscious" of it.

In any case, Santayana was always less than totally frank in his accounts of himself. He did not wish his art to be diminished by being considered "merely" homosexual; he wished to make a universal statement on the nature of love. And it is unfortunately the case that homosexual sentiments are presumed to be particular and of no interest to the heterosexual. Santayana also sublimated a great deal of his sexuality into art. Since he saw no possibility for its realization in this world, he embraced a philosophy which would justify the transformation of the carnal into the spiritual. In that endeavor he had the support, of course, of Plato, at least as he and most nineteenth-century readers understood Plato.

Santayana's sense of himself as a Latin, or half Latin, was an important part of his self-definition. One might say that he felt incomplete, a permanent alien, too English for Spain, too Spanish for England or New England. His dual nature[37] made him an outsider and observer of life. There is a striking resemblance between Santayana's feeling about himself and Mann's portrait of a similar figure in *Tonio Kröger*. As with Tonio, it seems likely that part of what Santayana loved in Potter was his Englishness, a sense of moral rectitude and clarity, what one could call "blond" or "male" values. Santayana's artist and sensualist self sought completion through union with a more thoroughly northern figure. There was, perhaps, in Santayana as well as in Tonio something of the *bourgeois manqué*.

Sonnet 35[38] seems to give expression to such feelings. It is one of the "Dark Lady" sonnets, but seems to me to be addressed to Warwick Potter just as much as the four sonnets actually dedicated to him. The sonnet begins with a statement of the difference between the two lovers, who "needs must be divided in the tomb." The speaker of the poem "would die among the hills of Spain" while the beloved "will find scant room / Among thy kindred by the northern main." (It is not clear how the critic can reconcile these lines with her interpretation of the beloved as Santayana's sister.) The sestet resolves the problem posed by the lovers' separate burial through the realization that their love, since spiritual, will not be confined to the earth and its tombs. "Gallants" and "ladies" may lie together "in one cold grave, with mortal love inurned." But the speaker and his beloved triumph over their separation, since they burned with "love immortal." Unlike the gallants and ladies who are wed in the flesh, the "we" of the poem "were wedded without bond of lust" and so have already achieved union of soul. The sonnet expresses a Platonic belief that the love of men, because spiritual, is higher than the love of man for woman, which is confined to the senses. The pure spirituality of Santayana's love will permit him to triumph over death. His love has been of the realm of Aphrodite Urania and leads toward eternity. Santayana's concept is almost a gloss on *The Symposium*. He may have come to it through Michelangelo's sonnets, e.g., Sonnet 53 (in John Addington Symonds' translation):

> The love of that whereof I speak ascends:
> Woman is different far; the love of her
> But ill befits a heart manly and wise.
> The one love soars, the other earthward tends;
> The soul lights this, while that the senses stir;
> And still lust's arrow at base quarry flies.[39]

The ambiguity in Santayana's sonnets as to the identity of the beloved appears to have been deliberate. As he wrote in Sonnet 39, "The world will say, 'What mystic love is this? / What ghostly mistress? What angelic friend?'"[40] His choice of the terms "mistress" and "friend" indicates Santayana's conscious appeal to the example of Shakespeare's sonnets. However, although they provide a model for the expression of love for a young man, they also illustrate a worldliness and a delight in the erotic which are missing from Santayana's work. Santayana felt a certain amount of guilt over his "sinful" nature (he may not have been quite as "untainted" as Warwick), which sometimes expressed itself in an erotic vision of Christ:

> I sought on earth a garden of delight
>
> . . . .
>
> And though his arms, outstretched upon the tree,
> Were beautiful and pleaded my embrace,
> My sins were loth to look upon his face.

The mechanics of transferal operating in such a poem are not unlike those in Hopkins. And, as with Hopkins, there appears to have been a masochistic strain in Santayana which perhaps desired the beautiful god's punishment. As he put it in one of his most famous sonnets, "A perfect love is nourished by despair, / I am thy pupil in the school of pain." [41] While the Swinburnean tones are undoubtedly unintentional, they do reveal links between suffering and the erotic in Santayana's art.

His career reflects a preoccupation with pain, transformed into an aesthetic of restraint which is expressed as an attempt to provide a classic hardness of line and clarity of vision. He did nourish his love upon despair, and created out of renunciation an art of simplicity and rigor. To the soft dreaminess of the nineties he opposed a toughness of mind that was perhaps necessary; but that toughness was based on self-denial and mortification. Santayana, the last and probably the best of the poets of the Genteel Age, left in the end a legacy that was as vague as that of the earlier poets. He concealed the sources of his art in the belief that this would improve it, and he refused to allow himself to believe that he could ever recapture the love of his youth, symbolized by the figure of Warwick Potter. For Santayana the death of Potter was the loss of innocence, a sign of the expulsion from the garden of youthful delights. The rest of his career was a gaze backward, an enduring tribute to the permanence, not of love, but of its impossibility and loss.

3. Hart Crane

Early Poems and White Buildings

Hart Crane's early work was marked by the influence of the two strains we have traced in American homosexual poetry. Himself a midwesterner, he looked for a poetry that could express a particularly American identity, as was to be found in the work of Whitman and his successors. But Crane was also a product of the fin-de-siècle mood, with its emphasis on hopeless love and the alienation of the artist. Crane's homosexuality gave added force to the search, in his life and in his poetry, for a love that could transform the physical into the spiritual. Throughout his career he was an ardent Platonist, seeking a return to the unity of body and soul.

The sources of Crane's Platonism cannot be traced exclusively to his homosexuality. Certainly his association with Christian Science, in which his mother believed, was an important contributing factor. Christian Science opposes an unreal world of sensations to a real world of essences, and asserts the power of the essential world to triumph over the pain of the sensational world. While Crane was not conventionally religious, he made use of conventional religious imagery in many of his poems (from "C 33" to "The Broken Tower") and repeatedly asserted the primacy of the visionary over the real, most notably in the concluding lines of "For the Marriage of Faustus and Helen." He was, in a sense, a Christian Scientist *malgré lui*, deriving from that philosophy an essentialism which accorded well with his belief in the redemptive powers of love. Love was for Crane a spiritual experience, one which, although rooted in the physical act, found its supreme value in its ability to transport the lover into a visionary and timeless world.

Crane's Platonism, unlike Santayana's, did not lead him to believe that the highest form of love was one without physical expression. But he did believe that the highest form of love moved from physical expression to a state of pure transcendence: "the pure possession, the inclusive cloud / Whose heart is fire." As he put it in a letter to his friend Wilbur Underwood in 1920, using the same word ("inclusive") that he would employ in "Possessions" almost four years later: "Something beautiful can be found or can 'occur' once in awhile, and so unexpectedly. Not the brief and limited sensual thing alone, but something infinitely more thrilling and inclusive."[1] In the same letter Crane spoke of the effect of his new love in religious terms: "I believe in, or have found God again." Crane's restless sexual adventuring thus may be seen as part of his search for God.

At the same time he was constantly struck by the discrepancy between the ideal love of which he wrote and the real love (and sex) which he encountered in his life. Crane was, as he put it in a poem to his lover Emil Opffer which is related to the "Voyages" cycle, "the terrible puppet of my dreams."[2] Every bit as much as Poe, Crane was possessed by the memory of an ideal love once glimpsed and then lost forever. Again like Poe, Crane believed that the poem could recreate the lost state of vision by "an elevating excitement of the Soul."[3] Crane's poems mount in ecstasy as they attempt to recapture the moment of spiritual union, or look back in sorrow at its inevitable loss.

Crane had inherited a tradition which held that homosexuality offered a higher, purer form of love but that the price paid for that love must be a renunciation of physical passion as well as a sense of exile from "normal" society. This view of homosexual love coincided with his Platonism, filtered in part through the spiritual idealism of Christian Science and in part through the literary examples of Shelley and Poe. Crane could well say with Poe,

> From childhood's hour I have not been
> As others were—I have not seen
> As others saw—I could not bring
> My passions from a common spring—[4]

Crane's early poetry in particular emphasized this view of the artist as lonely exile. It was, after all, a position characteristic of the poets of the nineties who were Crane's first literary models. The example of Laforgue offered a way out of this self-pity, but that path led inexorably to Eliot and what Crane saw as his pessimism. In any case, was he to mock his own sexuality? For Crane the dilemma was double, since for him the plight of the homosexual in a heterosexual society and the plight of the artist in a materialistic society were conjoined. The solution must also be double: it must resolve Crane's anxieties about his artistic vocation and its relationship to the more democratic mission of expressing the potential of his own society, as well as his anxieties about his homosexual identity. As we shall see, only Whitman was able to provide a solution to this dilemma, for only Whitman affirmed his homosexuality as a source not of alienation but of brotherhood. Although Crane seems to have read Whitman almost from the beginning of his career, however, the major influence of Whitman did not become apparent until about 1926. Prior to that time Crane was struggling to come to terms with the conflicting (as he thought) claims of love and lust.

Crane's first published poem, "C 33," gives a good indication of the attitudes of the young poet. His choice of subject is striking. The title denotes, of course, Oscar Wilde's cell number at Reading Gaol, and thus captures the double subject that so occupied Crane's imagination: the alienation of the artist and the persecution of the homosexual. It is interesting to compare Crane's poem to another poem on the subject by a major homosexual poet, Housman's "Oh who is that young sinner with the handcuffs on his wrists?" [5] Housman, whose poetry is generally written in a mood of longing for the "land of lost content," the remembered world of friendship with his beloved Mo, was roused to anger by Wilde's fate, and in his poem denounced the society which condemned Wilde for a quirk of fate—"the colour of his hair" (i.e., his homosexuality). Housman is not interested in the fact that Wilde is an artist, and views his homosexuality as a merely physical attribute. Crane, on the other hand, sees Wilde as the type of the artist, destroyed by a philistine society, yet redeemed by that experience. It is likely though not certain, that Crane had read the passages from *De Profundis* that were published in 1905 (the complete text was not published until 1949), [6] since he seized upon the principal theme which Wilde elaborates there: that suffering acts as a cathartic force, bringing final understanding and love.

Crane's treatment emphasizes the contrast between Wilde and the world, seeing in Wilde a force of rejuvenation. Although the world is an "empty heart" and a "desert," he can bring the "thorny tree" to bloom. The images of the heart and the rose recall Wilde's fairy tale, "The Nightingale and the Rose," [7] which was probably somewhere in Crane's mind as he wrote this poem. In the tale the Rose-Tree tells the Nightingale, "If you want a red rose, you must build it out of music by moonlight, and stain it with your own heart's-blood." Wilde's tale is a tribute to the sacrificial act of perfect love, and Crane accurately sees Wilde in the Christ-like attitude which he increasingly adopted. For Crane, Wilde's "far truths" contrast with the "searing sophistry" of the world; he offers a truth—of love—which passes unrecognized. But by suffering for that love, by his imprisonment, he testifies to its intensity. Wilde is not praised as a great poet—in fact he is seen as providing "song of minor, broken strain"—but he acts on behalf of a great truth. By so doing he reflects new light upon the "gold head" of "Materna," the sorrowing Madonna who watches over her children and finally gathers them up into her bosom.

Crane's effort here is not an accomplished or mature work. It reads like a rough draft rather than a finished poem (especially since its structure is close to that of a sonnet, but of only thirteen lines). Nonetheless, it is important as an indication of the young poet's beginnings. There is a clear sense of identification between the poet and Wilde. Although the call to the Mother Goddess is not justified by the internal logic of the poem, Crane perhaps felt it justified by Wilde's devotion to his mother, or, more likely, by his devotion to his own mother, Grace Hart Crane. It is even possible that it is Wilde himself who is seen as the maternal figure here. The poem concludes with a striking image of loneliness—"you who hear the lamp whisper thru night"—which testifies to Crane's growing strength as a poet as well as his sense of himself as the homosexual artist dying a sacrificial death for his art/love.[8]

Two other poems from Crane's very early career deserve discussion at this point because of the ways they introduce themes and images which become central to his later, better-known work. "Modern Craft" is a surprisingly successful poem, with few weaknesses. Here the goddess figure is seen not as succoring mother but as whore/bitch, anticipating the transformation that Crane would accomplish in "Three Songs." In "Modern Craft" the unnamed woman is an early flapper, displaying her newfound sexual freedom. Crane sees her as a distant figure, a moon goddess shedding a cold, virginal light. She is the virgin as temptress and castrator. The first of Crane's four quatrains shows her unresponsiveness:

> Though I have touched her flesh of moons,
> Still she sits gestureless and mute

and bemoans her "innocence dissolute." The second quatrain presents her as an up-to-date woman of fashion. The images chosen illustrate the fear which she arouses and the sense of distance the poet feels. Her "tiger-lilies" give her a frighteningly feline aspect, and when she "bolts herself within a jewelled belt" the inner half-rhyme suggests that it is her chastity (appropriate to the moon goddess, of course) which is being locked in. While she appears aggressively virginal, she is also somewhat shopworn, as the third line suggests—"Too many palms have grazed her shoulders"—with its pun on "palms."

It is in the third quatrain that the poem takes a significant new direction. The hostile tone of the first two quatrains is replaced by an attitude of sympathy. The transition is obtained through the figure of Ophelia, whose name is the first word of the last stanza. Ophelia is a victim of love, whom "sank in love and choked with flowers," a representative of the fate that the modern vamp is attempting to avoid. Unlike Ophelia, for whom passion leads only to death, "this burns and is not burnt." There may be a weakness in the poem at this point, as the reference of "this" is not totally clear. It would appear to refer back to the woman who is the subject of the poem, whose passion, since never completed, never consumes. At the same time "this" appears to refer forward to "my modern love," in which case it is the poet's love which is contrasted with that of Ophelia. It should be noted, however, that such ambiguities of reference are not necessarily signs of immaturity in Crane; even in his best poems he frequently makes deliberate use of such devices. Here, then, the woman of the poem avoids the fate of lovers by remaining cool and distant; although she may "burn," it will not be with a fire that consumes. Parts of this figure were retained by Crane in "Three Songs." Surely she reappears in the "nameless Woman of the South" with her "rehearsed hair—docile, alas, from many arms," an apparent rewriting of "too many palms have grazed her shoulders." And the passion which "is not burnt" recurs in the "burnt match" of "The Tunnel." In both places it is informed by its source, the flame "ever still / Burning, yet ever inconsumable" of Shelley's "Epipsychidion."

The image of burning leads Crane to his striking final statement: "My modern love were / Charred at a stake in younger times than ours." The "modern love" of this figure contrasts with the "modern craft" of the title. The carefully prepared woman is a creature of craft, while the poet sees himself as a creature of love, undesigning and undesigned. At the same time he recognizes the forbidden nature of his love: it would have been consumed by fire, since he would have been burnt at the stake as a sodomist in "younger times." (Reportedly, about a quarter of those burnt by the Inquisition were executed for sodomy.)[9] The reason for the poet's reluctance to reveal his "modern love" is clear—as clear as the reason for the woman to protect herself against men. It is interesting that Crane evidently was aware of a connection between the situation of women and the situation of homosexuals, and expressed it in a poem by what he would later come to call the logic of metaphor, or what we might here simply term free association. The logic proceeds more or less like this: the modern virgin "bolts" herself in against men, too many of whom have touched her, so that she will not end up like Ophelia, another victim of men; thus she will not be "burnt" by her burning, which then reminds the poet of quite another kind of burning, which he would have suffered for his love.

"Modern Craft" is a harsh view of love in the modern world, but one which also suggests the possibility of survival. A much more tender view is given in "Carrier Letter." The difference in tone of the two poems may be attributed to the difference in subject: "Modern Craft" concerns the nature of love in general and the influence of social attitudes upon sexuality, while "Carrier Letter" concerns a personal experience of love. Like so many homosexuals, Crane appears to have found it easier to express the love that he found in his own life (at least for brief intervals) than to see what place love might have in a larger social context.

"Carrier Letter" is a simple poem of eight lines, phrased as a message to an absent lover. The first stanza laments the departure of the lover, while the second finds consolation in that which "endures." There is a significant contrast between the nighttime world of love and the daytime world of loneliness and separation: "with the day, distance again expands / Between us." This contrast is an important recurring theme in Crane's work. Night is the time of love, dream, and poetry, while day is the time of work, reality, and fact. In "The Visible the Untrue" Crane mourns the departures of a later lover, Emil Opffer: "It is always the day, the farewell day unkind." And "The Harbor Dawn" plays upon the competing claims of day and night, as the speaker resists the "siren" call of day and makes love one last time "before day claims our eyes."

The second stanza begins "Yet" (anticipating the beginning of "Voyages" II: "—And yet") and provides a victory over time and space, which together had seemed to conquer the poet's love. The poet entrusts his love to the carrier pigeon, who will presumably carry the message of love back to the beloved; so the poet constructs a model of art as the perpetuation of love. The pigeon, since it is called a "dove" whose "wings" clung about my heart," is a symbol of the Spirit. Its visit to the poet becomes a descent of the Holy Ghost, a spiritual visitation as well as a token of survival: it is the dove that will sight land and signal to the inhabitants of the Ark that they have weathered the storm. Like the gulls of *The Bridge*, the dove serves Crane as a "carrier" of his love, a token of its success, and a bridge between separated lovers. The poem's final symbol, "the blue stone / Set in the tryst-ring," serves a similar purpose. Its color promises fidelity and spirituality, while its setting in the tryst-ring promises the lovers that they will survive their separation and will return to each other. Crane's symbolic use of blue appears to have been consistent throughout his career; twice in *The Bridge* he uses blue in a similar way: in "Ave Maria" the poet cries to the Virgin, "Assure us through thy mantle's ageless blue," and in "Indiana" the mother begs her son, "Oh, hold me in those eyes' engaging blue." "Carrier Letter" is an early statement of Crane's faith in the possibility of an enduring and returned love.

Crane's mature work is marked as well by the same two emotions: a strong, almost obsessive belief in the miraculous powers of love, and a sense of despair brought on by the impossibility of experiencing that love. For Crane this sense of impossibility was grounded not only in a Platonic idealism which held that any actual love must be inferior to its ideal form, but also in the conviction that his homosexuality set him apart from other lovers and prevented him from achieving a full spiritual relationship. There were moments, of course, when he was able to overcome these doubts, most triumphantly in the "Voyages" poems. There his own happiness in the relationship with Emil Opffer could lead him to believe in the capacity of love to endure and even prevail over time. But in the majority of his poems Crane was tormented by the belief that he was split apart by his sexuality, that it was virtually impossible to reconcile the spiritual self of the poet and the physical self (the "ape" of "Recitative") of the unfulfilled lover. Such self-hatred was common in homosexuals of Crane's time, who could find no way of fulfilling their desires without violating the image of the ideal, spiritual relationship which had been constructed for homosexual love. This was the "trap" of Platonism. Homosexuality was "higher" than heterosexuality because more spiritual and less physical; the assertion of a homosexual identity was then at odds with the fulfillment of homosexual desire. Crane's feelings of guilt were increased, moreover, by the realization that his closest friends were unsympathetic to his homosexuality. He was unable to share with them the emotional realities of his life, lest they condemn him as a pervert.[10] He was likely to find sexual satisfaction only with men lacking in intellect or sensibility (the homosexual equivalent of the Victorian nun/whore dilemma), since experience had taught him that men (and women) of intelligence would condemn homosexuality. Crane's homosexuality was for him a "secret vice" even when he proclaimed it loudest. Only with Emil Opffer[11] was he able to find a love which brought both spiritual and sexual satisfaction; out of that relationship "Voyages" and *The Bridge* were born.

Crane had only about eight years of creativity as a mature poet (if we except his final poem, "The Broken Tower," written in Mexico). These years show extraordinary development and shifts in emotional state. The first few years (roughly 1919 to early 1922) are marked by the influence of the Decadent poets of England and France; and some of the poems of these years are characterized by a tone of self-pity alleviated by ironic self-mockery. The Pierrot tone dominates; Crane views himself as the impossible lover, "beauty's fool" as he put it in "The Bridge of Estador." During the last half of this period Crane was influenced in part by his friendship with Wilbur Underwood and by Underwood's work, largely translations or imitations of French verse which had appeared a decade earlier.[12] The next years (1922 to 1924) were years of struggle and frequent despair. Crane was involved in the literary feuds of New York, he was attempting to find a job which would allow him the freedom he needed to continue to write, and he was subject to the pressures and exhilarations of life in New York. The poetry of these years is frequently tortured and obscure, as Crane sought his own poetic voice. Its treatment of sexuality is bleak; although New York undoubtedly brought an expansion of the possibilities of sexual encounter, it brought Crane no closer to love than he had been in Cleveland or Akron. The poems reflect a growing conviction of the impossibility of reconciling mind and body. In 1923 Crane fell in love with Slater Brown, a love necessarily confined to spiritual affection, since Brown's "physical propensities," as Crane put it, went in the "opposite direction." [13] While he was in love with Brown, he was still seeking sexual satisfaction in the bars and with sailors. The poems of these years agonize over an inner division which Crane clearly found intolerable. This period ended in 1924, when Crane fell in love with Emil Opffer, and at last found a love which both was reciprocated and combined physical affection with spiritual friendship. Its power is reflected in "Voyages" and in major sections of *The Bridge*. His love for Opffer cannot be the sole source of *The Bridge*, of course—Crane had already begun work on "Atlantis" in 1923— but it did reinforce in Crane all that wanted to believe in the power of love as a redemptive and catalytic force which could transform man from animal into spirit. From 1924 to 1926 Crane was infused with the energy of love, that energy which set his greatest poems in motion. Before he had finished his most ambitious project (*The Bridge*), however, the energy ran out, and Crane was never able to recover it.

"My Grandmother's Love Letters" offers an excellent illustration of the Crane of the first period. The poem shows certain influences from the Symbolists Crane had been reading, yet is at the same time a strong and independent poem. Music which serves as a bridge to the past is a characteristic Symbolist device, one that in Proust, for example, recurs as Vinteuil's sonata. In Crane's poem, however, the assumption that music or poetry can communicate emotion and establish links between persons separated in time and space (as in Hugo's "Si mes vers avaient des ailes") is undercut by an ironic conclusion. The rain, the atmospheric element of the poem, is transformed from a "loose girdle," an envelope of reverie, into a sign of impossibility and loss, as the Pierrot-poet recognizes his failure: "And the rain continues on the roof / With such a sound of gentle pitying laughter." The influence of Verlaine on this poem of 1919 is striking. One hears clear echoes of the fifth "Ariette oubliée," with its "piano que baise une main frêle," and, of course, the famous third "Ariette," "Il pleure dans mon coeur / Comme il pleut sur la ville." What Crane has learned from Verlaine and his English imitators is a continuity between self and world, in which the external becomes a sign of the internal.

The poem is an interior monologue, in which the poet reflects upon a past love, and the difficulty of establishing a connection between his present emotions and those which he ascribes to his grandmother and her lover. In the second stanza the fragility of the physical letters is a sign of the evanescence of their spiritual content. Like the snow to which they are compared, they will not survive examination but will vanish the moment they are possessed. It is a poem, then, of auras, as the first lines suggest: "There are no stars to-night / But those of memory." Like a musical note lingering on (or perfume, in one of Verlaine's metaphors), the stars linger in the mind long after they have disappeared. The first two stanzas demonstrate Crane's mastery of the langorous tone of world-weariness associated with fin-de-siècle verse. But in the central stanzas, he adumbrates a change in mood which is then achieved in the final stanzas. The first indication of danger comes in the third stanza, as Crane introduces the metaphor of the tight-rope walker, whose "steps must be gentle" as he walks along the "invisible white hair." Crane here makes use of the image of the bridge in a primitive form. There is no other image—except perhaps the voyage—of such great meaning for Crane. For him the bridge symbolized the perfection of love; to cross the bridge was to realize one's love both physically and spiritually. In "My Grandmother's Love Letters" Crane expresses his desire to be loved and his fear that love could not survive the passage of time. The letters represent what Crane would later term the "imaged Word," a physical representation of a spiritual truth, in which he placed all his hope for the survival, and even the victory, of love.

One must then wonder why, at this point, Crane did not feel such confidence in the word. The questions of the fifth stanza, with their inner rhymes of self-doubt ("long enough," "strong enough"), suggest an answer. For Crane imagines himself not as the sender of the letters, his grandmother's lover, but as their recipient, his grandmother:

> Is the silence strong enough
> To carry back the music to its source
> And back to you again
> As though to her?

There is a failure to communicate experience. Crane cannot read the letters as his grandmother must have read them, for he does not have her memory, her "loose girdle," which permits the past to survive alongside and inform the present. If Crane wishes to understand his grandmother's love letters, however, he also wants her to understand his:

> Yet I would lead my grandmother by the hand
> Through much of what she would not understand;
> And so I stumble.

The fall of the aerialist (to pursue Crane's metaphor) is due not to his failure to understand her love but to her (presumed) failure to understand his.[14] The comparison between two loves, his grandmother's and his own, collapses because of this failure of understanding. Even though he realizes that she, too, has loved, Crane does not believe that his grandmother would be capable of understanding what earlier he has called "my modern love." It is Crane's homosexuality which serves as the barrier, for although he can understand a love letter from a man to a woman, he does not believe that that woman could understand a love letter from a man to him. Thus the ironic twist—as well as the self-pity—of the final lines is due to Crane's conviction that his love placed him beyond the bounds of human communication. He had plenty of literary justification for the image of himself as Pierrot, the thwarted lover; but for Crane that image took on a particular burden, since his suffering, like his love, could not be shared with others. The "laughter" of the rain is a sign of the mocking of the world, from which Crane would always feel at least partly an exile. The bridge of love which he repeatedly sought to build was to be his link to the past, his bond to the human community. One of the bitter facts of Crane's career is that this greatest of modern love poets was unable to acknowledge the nature of his love. Singing the praises of love, he still believed that his love, because of the form it took, confirmed his isolation and separated him from the love known by the rest of the world.

In a poem which Crane apparently never completed to his satisfaction, "The Bridge of Estador," he spoke of those who "are twisted with the love / Of things irreconcilable." The image of being twisted by love suggests that a source of the poem is *Winesburg, Ohio*, where the characters are all rendered "grotesque" by their attempts to love. Parts of the poem are related to the earlier "Episode of Hands" (to which we shall return in the following section), particularly the third stanza, with its recognition of sudden beauty revealed in the most unlikely of situations. Behind these lines lies Crane's homosexuality, which enabled him finally to *see* a hand, rather than praise it for its abstract qualities, and which makes him "twisted." He has known love ("the Gods that danced before you / When your fingers spread among stars"), and that love will remain in his memory, even if it is never reenacted.

Crane, as was his custom, mined the poem for material which he could use elsewhere. The first part of "Faustus and Helen" incorporates the line, "twisted with the love / Of things irreconcilable," as "There is the world dimensional for those untwisted by the love of things irreconcilable." The world of "Faustus and Helen" draws from the mythology of heterosexual love. Those who are "untwisted by the love of things irreconcilable" inhabit a "dimensional" world, one whose boundaries are familiar. The dilemma reflected in this poem is that Crane, who saw his own love as "irreconcilable," was nonetheless working within a literary tradition which embodied love as Helen or Venus rather than Hyacinth or Ganymede. The poet turns to Helen, finding identity with her in the passion that ultimately consumes and in the death which brings freedom: "I meet you, therefore, in that eventual flame / You found in final chains, no captive then." Like the Helen of his imagination, Crane's "love of things irreconcilable" led him to believe that only in the *Liebestod*, in the passage of love beyond the "dimensional" world, could he achieve the freedom he yearned for, release from "the body of the world."

The final lines of "The Bridge of Estador,"

The everlasting eyes of Pierrot,
    Or, of Gargantua, the laughter.

would also recur, in "Praise for an Urn," with "Or" changed to "And." By the time the lines appeared in "Praise for an Urn" Crane had apparently divested them of their erotic content, since he reassured Wilbur Underwood that his friendship for Ernest Nelson, for whom the poem is an elegy, "is, or was, entirely 'platonic.'"[15] Crane, however, should hardly have been surprised that Underwood thought the poem reflected a love between the poet and his friend. For one thing, line 6 speaks of "the white coverlet and pillow" (of course, these could be the clothing of Nelson's sick-bed). More interesting is a letter from Crane to Underwood in January 1921, referring to a love affair: "I am still under the 'halo' influence. Your poems are particularly appropriate to the subject. The head and eyes of Pierrot,—a beautiful grace with a certain sadness, and every movement of the body a poem. Mon Dieu! How I shall hate to depart." [16] Here we can see the development of the Pierrot image in Crane's mind: from its source in French decadence, via Underwood and his imitations of the French, to a figure for a beloved boy, to a sign of impossible love in a mundane (and heterosexual) world, and finally to a sign of the plight of the artist in a philistine society, dying unrecognized. Crane's imagination enabled him to transform a banal figure to serve a variety of purposes so that each informs the others. Crane rises above the maudlin dangers of this poem through the beneficent influence of Donne, who is the source of Crane's rapidly developing wit. [17] At the same time Crane brings with him the inheritance not merely of Nelson's death as an unacknowledged artist but also of Wilde, Verlaine, and his other early heroes, whose fate as artists was intensified by their fate as homosexuals.

Crane's years in New York modified his ironic stance. They appear to have brought an increase in sexual tension as well as an increase in self-rejection. Crane, for all that he seems to have had an active sex life, was never satisfied that the sexual encounter before him (or behind him) was "pure" or "whole" enough. There seems to have been something of the Don Juan in his relentless search for the perfect and unobtainable love. "Possessions" is the poem which gives clearest expression to Crane's desire to join Helen, to achieve a perfection of passion which is beyond passion. The speaker of "Possessions" confronts the deadly repetition of "cruising," the obsessive searching of the city streets for a sexual partner. Lust is a "fixed stone," a heavy burden reflecting no light. Although the speaker has his "key, ready to hand," still the doors of the self do not open:

> —sifting
> One moment in sacrifice (the direct)
> Through a thousand nights the flesh
> Assaults outright for bolts that linger
> Hidden

The assaults of the flesh do not penetrate the soul, and the wandering poet/lover feels himself crushed under the burden of his lust.

He hesitates, Prufrock-like, his life composed of "trembling tabulation." Crane has written what is probably the first poem of the modern urban homosexual in search of sex, his hesitations the result of fear and self-oppression. He desires and yet he fears; he will go and yet he hesitates. Whitman's poems of random sexual encounter are quite different; for Whitman, the two men who pass in the street have a moment of instant recognition and love, while for Crane there is only fear, "wounded by apprehensions out of speech."

"Tossed on these horns" (of dilemma), the poet is impaled, not in the fulfillment of passion, but in unfulfilled desire. His fate becomes representative of modern man ("the city's stubborn lives"), who lives in a "waste land" of his own making (Eliot's poem appeared a year before Crane's). He is consumed by "rage and partial appetites," and yearns for relief through apocalypse,[18] for "the pure possession, the inclusive cloud / Whose heart is fire." Only the appearance of God in a fiery cloud will release him from his tormented existence. The poem thus conjoins two themes which were central for Crane: the desire for an all-consuming love, and the desire for a moment of visionary perception. Both are in fact aspects of the same desire, a yearning to escape the ordinary routines of a life which he had come to hate. And both also express Crane's identification of the origins of art with the descent of Eros. When finally the purgative storm should come, bringing with it a "white wind" of purification, the world of darkness and despair would give way to "bright stones wherein our smiling plays." It is one of Crane's darkest poems, yet it also expresses Crane's belief that only by passage through such despair could one arrive reborn at the state of pure spirituality. Crane never advocated escape from this world (although he often escaped personally to such private paradises as Woodstock or the Isle of Pines) but insisted, with Blake, on passage "thro' the Gates of Wrath."

Over and over again Crane dreamed of the descent of the Spirit in a fiery chariot, which he identified with a response to his own smile. The return of love would bring instant hope: in "The Wine Menagerie," "my blood dreams a receptive smile / Where new purities are snared," and in "Recitative" he offers a "much-exacting fragment smile" which awaits "one critical sign." Crane, again, identified the external world with the internal, and sympathetically assigned to the city around him the despair he found within himself. But he could just as easily transform that despair into joy if only his smile were returned. As he put it to Wilbur Underwood, "hell may be turned into Paradise with the proper company."[19]

"Recitative" proposes an early form of the solution for Crane, through its introduction of the metaphor of the bridge. The poem makes use of the image of the divided self—"Janus-faced," "twin shadowed halves" seeking reunion. Seeing a reflection of himself in a glass, the poet turns to comment on the agonies of man's inner divisions. He appears to identify his quest for sexual union with the Platonic theme of the quest for reunion of the divided self, so that the meeting of two men as lovers becomes a restoration of lost twinship. Only the discovery of this other "half" can restore the speaker's lost unity. Thus he asks of his lover a total commitment to breach the "nameless gulf" between them, to "leave the tower" of the individual self by means of the bridge of love: "The bridge swings over salvage, beyond wharves" (I hear a pun on salvation in "salvage"). This poem is an important stage in the development of Crane toward *The Bridge*. In the last half of his major poem one can see the same progression: from the tower of "Quaker Hill" to the passage through hell of "The Tunnel," and finally to the reemergence of a new, harmonious self in "Atlantis"—this last section (significantly) introduced by a quotation from *The Symposium*. The bridge is a bond between the self and the world and between two individuals; crossing the bridge makes possible the reconciliation of opposites and the restoration of harmony. Thus the speaker in "Recitative" calls upon his "shadow" to accept the love which is proffered him and to respond by crossing the bridge. Only then can the distortion of the image in the glass be corrected; only then can that which is "cleft" be joined again. The "single stride" of the last stanza in "Recitative" is a triumphant coming together, in which what was once separate is now perceived to be whole. The "darkness" of lust "falls away," and the lovers can now "walk through time with equal pride."

The poem which Crane chose to introduce *White Buildings* is an expression of his commitment to passion and his belief that only by passing through experience could one achieve what is here called "the bright logic" and a "constant harmony." "Legend" depicts the poet as passionate Romantic, seeking a consummate love-death. He bravely announces, "I am not ready for repentence; / Nor to match regrets." Likening himself to the moth drawn toward the flame, he asserts that the value of experience can be learned only by living it, that only pain can sanctify love. In a world of death, represented by the snow ("white falling flakes"— an image of living death as opposed to passion which was drawn almost certainly from Joyce's "The Dead"), "kisses are,— / The only worth all granting." This was Crane's usual response to the depressions of the city, a belief that total immersion in the "destructive element" of passion would yield up something of meaning. As he put it in a letter, "How I am stalked by lust these dog days! And how many 'shadowy' temptations beset me at every turn! Were I free from my family responsibilities [this was written while Crane was in Cleveland] I would give myself to passion to the final cinder. After all—that and poetry are the only things life holds for me." [20] The flame, as we have seen, represents three things for Crane: the descent of the Spirit, the descent of Eros, and the descent of the Muse. Only by the "lavish heart" can the meaning of existence be learned. Crane turns to a religious figure, the "bleeding eidolon," to assert his belief that true passion can never reject pain, for that way lie mediocrity and fear. The bleeding heart, symbol of Christ's sacrificial love, becomes a token of Crane's own sacrificial love for the world. As R. W. B. Lewis has pointed out, Crane saw that the "real obstacle to creativity" was the "bleak piety" of "the decayed and distorted Protestant conscience." [21] He set as the emblematic poem for his first collection a proud assertion of his own passionate self-sacrifice in the name of a finer art, a statement of his belief that the "perfect cry" of great poetry could come only from experience, a "spending" of self that for Crane necessarily included the expression of his own sexuality.

A similar expression of the necessity to "push off" (in Melville's terms) from the safety of land to explore one's own unconscious and erotic potential is given by Crane in his magnificent "Voyages." Crane placed this sequence of poems immediately following "At Melville's Tomb" in *White Buildings*, thus suggesting his indebtedness to Melville. Much of that indebtedness is verbal, [22] but there is another element which has not been recognized sufficiently: Crane saw in Melville a model for the expression of love between men. He seems to have read *Moby-Dick* first in 1922, reporting to Underwood with delight, "the memorable and half-exciting suggestions of dear Queequeg." [23] Crane seems to have felt, accurately in my view, that Queequeg provides the moral vision of Melville's novel, offering an alternative to Ahab's lust for power in his own advocacy of pleasure in undirected sexuality. Queequeg represents an Eros liberated from phallic aggression, and thus free to engage in homosexual play (as in "A Squeeze of the Hand"). It is Queequeg's love which enables Ishmael to free himself from the Thanatos of the Pequod and to survive the descent into the sea. In "Voyages" Crane calls upon the spirit of Queequeg to guide him and his lover through the "sea" of love, enabling him to reemerge triumphant, assured of the power of art to preserve passion from the ravages of time. Melville is Crane's spiritual guide to the body of love, as Whitman will be his guide to the spirit of America. Together they show Crane a faith which will enable him to conquer the despair of the earlier poems; they reassure him that he is not alone in the quest for a love that can transcend death.

The first of the "Voyages" poems was written separately. Although it serves as an introduction to the suite, it does not have the lyrical strength or verbal splendor of the others. Still, it is a strong poem, capturing Crane's poignant regard for childhood as a state of lost innocence. The "bright striped urchins" live in a world of play, which, nonetheless, has ominous overtones of the destructive adult world: they "flay each other with sand" and "have contrived a conquest." But their play is limited by time; they will quickly age and die. The lightning and thunder of the second stanza warn of an impending storm which will bring chaos and death into their world; yet these also accompany the voice of the gods, given in the poet's warning of the last stanza. In his timelessness he foresees their future and would warn them of it, but it is as if God were to warn Adam and Eve of their fall. The fall into experience is both necessary for becoming human and inevitable. The poet's warning echoes a parental concern for the "brilliant kids" that they "must not cross" the line dividing shallow water from deep, childhood from adulthood, innocence from experience. As the children play, they unknowingly touch the symbols of man's timebound nature: the "shells and sticks" that they fondle are "bleached / By time and the elements." They are remnants of previous life, a stern reminder of death. The warning of the last line—"The bottom of the sea is cruel"—has several reverberations: it is death itself which is cruel, but also the exploration of self and the pursuit of passion. The children's innocence resides in their ignorance. As they fondle themselves (their "shells and sticks") they cannot know that their latent sexuality will bring them to a knowledge of passion, "caresses" that are also embraces of death.

If Crane had not continued beyond this point, his poem would seem to be a warning against experience, a yearning for permanent childhood, albeit with some sense that this is an impossible desire. But the second poem of the sequence directly responds to the first, its "—And yet" signaling the poet's acceptance of the temporal nature of love. Time, as a figure of death in the first poem, is transformed in the second by the poet's awareness of eternity. The "rimless floods" and "unfettered leewardings" indicate that to the vision of love time is endless. Time no longer leads in any direction but is cyclical; the sea's "undinal vast belly moonward bends, / Laughing the wrapt inflections of our love." The "inflections" of love, so apparently meaningful to the lovers, are without meaning to the eternal sea, forever ebbing and flowing. The victory over time, absent in the first poem, comes about, paradoxically, when the lovers recognize that they are "in time." What the sea has taken away, it will return; the "prodigal" lover will be restored by the same sea that has carried him off. The sea is no longer an object of fear, no longer an angry god of thunder, but a vast maternal force gathering up her orphaned children (as in the conclusion to *Moby-Dick*). The poet no longer attempts to stop time on its linear way to death, but attempts to immerse himself in its circular flow. At that point the tension of striving, the urge to conquer, is destroyed, and all things come together as aspects of a single whole: "sleep, death, desire, / Close round one instant in one floating flower." The sexual suggestions of "floating flower" contribute to the idea that time is conquered through love. What survives is beyond desire, a timeless love that can know no mortal end. The prayer of the final stanza is addressed to the "Seasons," the gods of the cycle of the Eternal Return. It asks that love be maintained until

> Is answered in the vortex of our grave
> The seal's wide spindrift gaze toward paradise.

In the ecstasy of love the lovers can ask only that it be preserved, that death be but a passage to another shore. The descent into the sea is thus into the "vortex" (an image taken from Poe and Melville), from which one is reborn.

A glimpse of that paradise is provided by the third poem of the sequence. This is the most explicitly sexual of the poems, the center of the sequence and the moment of union. The lovers are together in a world of perfect love. Even the elements seem in harmony: "the sky / Resigns a breast that every wave enthrones." The gentle tones of the first stanza ("tendered," "ribboned," "laved") give way to the rapidly increasing tempo of the second, as the lovers move from gentle caresses to active lovemaking:

> And so, admitted through black swollen gates
> That must arrest all distance otherwise,—
> Past whirling pillars and lithe pediments,
> Light wrestling there incessantly with light,
> Star kissing star through wave on wave unto
> Your body rocking!

This passage is one of Crane's greatest achievements. On the one hand, it is an explicit depiction of a recognizable sexual act: the "black swollen gates" represent the anus of the lover,[24] which finally admits (in a wonderful courtly conceit) the poet, as the lover's body rocks back and forth in the rolling motion of the sea. At the same time its skillful use of repeated sounds ("*P*ast whir*l*ing *p*i*ll*ars and *l*ithe *p*ediments") and words ("light," "star," and "wave") creates an atmosphere of heightened sensibility and desire. The repeated words provide a sensation of urgency, and a symmetry which is appropriate to the subject: man to man as star to star or wave to wave.

The "death" (Elizabethan pun) which occurs in the middle of line 14 (the half line quoted above) is purged of its mortality; there is "no carnage." Passion spent leads not to death but to change. The metamorphosis is double: each of the lovers is reborn as a new being, now part of an enlarged self, and love itself is transformed, as passion is both realized and completed. The "silken skilled transmemberment of song" is the artistic equivalent of the perfect act of love. Far from being *dis*membered (or castrated), the lovers are *trans*membered, as one body enters another. The journey across the "bottom of the sea" is accomplished by a "silken" rope "flung from dawn to dawn": a physical bridge of love. It is the penis itself which, by entering the body of the beloved and carrying to him the poet's love, performs the central act of connection. The poet concludes with his celebrated plea: "Permit me voyage, love, into your hands . . ." But clearly that voyage has already taken place. The following poems are an attempt to accomplish the "song," to construct the work of art that will preserve the moment of sexual union long after its original passion is gone.

The fourth of the "Voyages" addresses the now distant lover. Time and space seem to prevail, yet the poet feels certain that his love can be communicated, a love that although "incarnate" is also immortal. Crane chooses a geological metaphor to which he returns in "The River": the "clay" is the earthbound or mortal, yet it is "aflow immortally" as it seeps down into the river and thence to the sea. It becomes immortal through the poet's "singing," just as in "Voyages" III the ultimate metamorphosis is that "of song." The poet foresees the end of love, recognizing that although the experience can be repeated ("this hour / And region that is ours to wreathe again"), it is unlikely to bear the same intensity as first love. Recognizing this, he nonetheless offers a token of his love, the sign of his own sexuality:

> In this expectant, still exclaim receive
> The secret oar and petals of all love.

In the fifth poem, the lover has returned, but his return only announces a new departure. The symbols of union found in "Voyages" III are transformed into symbols of separation and loss: "lonely," "hard sky limits," "too brittle or too clear to touch!" "shred ends," "one frozen trackless smile." Moonlight is a "wedge" and the sky a "godless cleft." The world is transformed by the end of love, the poet's recognition that his love will be defeated by time and space. Moonlight, once a principle of union and a guiding light of love, is "changed" into a "tyranny." The poet sees only despair where once there had been hope. He cannot understand the lover's response, the lover's desire to return to his voyaging. For the poet it is merely a "piracy." He looks at his lover and realizes that he no longer possesses him, that spiritually he has already departed:

> Your eyes already in the slant of drifting foam;
> Your breath sealed by the ghosts I do not know
> Draw in your head and sleep the long way home.

Love, despite its moments of ecstasy, cannot survive unless it is given a form outside time. The "words" of the lovers are useless, "overtaken" by time.

The transformed world is now one of darkness; the poet is

"blinded," his vision lost in despair. With the loss of the lover, he imagines himself a drowned sailor in a hostile and cold sea. Time now seems endless repetition: "Steadily as a shell secretes / Its beating leagues of monotone." It seems as if the warnings of the first poem had been justified, that he has gone "beyond" the line and entered a world of permanent darkness and death. Even at this point of despair, however, he retains his faith (like Crane's Columbus). He is still the "seer" awaiting the new light of vision. He finds that vision in the figure of the "lounged goddess" (who seems to conflate Venus and Aurora): she offers "eyes / That smile unsearchable repose." Like his vision of Helen, or its source in Pater's description of the Mona Lisa, she remains an eternal source of comfort to man. Her peace is the "repose" which comes after passion and after loss: she is the "white echo of the oar!" As we have noted, the "oar" represents lust or, more specifically, the penis; the goddess, identified with "Belle Isle," represents a perfected lust, lust transformed into desire for the beautiful. That "covenant" (unlike the one given to the Puritans, perhaps) is "still fervid"; the poet gains assurance from the promise that those who serve beauty will find peace.

The final stanza, one of the finest Crane ever wrote, celebrates his faith in a love which transcends the physical to achieve pure spirituality. As in the Platonic paradigm, his love for a beautiful young man leads the poet to an apprehension of pure Beauty. One cannot perceive Beauty directly, but may find it expressed in the perfect form of a young man; the form of that young man then leads to a truer, more eternal form. The final figure, "the imaged Word," expresses what we may call Crane's kinetic poise, his constant search for a balance between the claims of the body and the claims of the soul. Its source is in the mystery of the Incarnation, as expressed by St. John, that most Greek of Christians. The spiritual truth is conveyed through the physical form of the beautiful young man, Christ. For Crane this mystery is at the heart of poetry. In his letters he consistently identified the divine with the physically beautiful, and sought from his lovers a spiritual truth usually found in God. He recognized, in "Voyages," the impossibility of preserving love at such a pitch of intensity. The suite records the passage of a love affair from cautious beginnings, to joyful celebration, to worried anticipations, to despair and loss, and finally to rebirth through the knowledge that in the poet's divine gift of "transmemberment" he has the means of creating a new world of light, of eternally renewing hope. Art alone is "the unbetrayable reply / Whose accent no farewell can know."

The "Voyages" celebrate love, but also that which is achieved through love. Their structure is of interest to readers of *The Bridge* as well. For although *The Bridge* does not narrate a particular love affair, it too moves toward the attainment of a state of suspended balance. Its central metaphor, the relationship between Columbus and Pocahontas, continues Crane's search for a reunion of opposites. And its final section, "Atlantis," celebrates the passage from the city to the underwater kingdom of love, where time is finally conquered in "the circular, indubitable frieze" (an image recalling Keats' "Ode on a Grecian Urn"). That passage to eternity is open to the traveler, "who, through smoking pyres of love and death, / Searches the timeless laugh of mythic spears." By a full exploration of love, a relentless submission to experience, a journey beyond the fear of death, the voyager could regain the lost kingdom. But before Crane could construct his journey to "Atlantis" (although not, interestingly, before he could depict its conclusion) he needed the help of Whitman, to confirm for him that his love bound him to the world, rather than excluding him from it.

Crane and Whitman

Despite the central place which Hart Crane gave to Walt Whitman in *The Bridge*, the relationship between the two poets has remained largely obscured and misunderstood. "Almost all" of Crane's literary friends, John Unterecker reports, "objected to the vaguely Whitmanesque tone" [25] of *The Bridge*. Yvor Winters' review in *Poetry* particularly offended Crane. Winters termed Crane's attitude in "Cape Hatteras" "desperately sentimental." [26] For Winters the problem was not really Crane's use of Whitman so much as Whitman's inherent unsuitability as a poetic model, what Winters called "the impossibility of getting anywhere with the Whitman inspiration"; but he saw the consequence of this influence in Crane's "wreckage." [27]

Allen Tate, while saying that he had not yet read the Winters review, echoed its terms, if not its conclusion. He wrote to Crane, ". . . in some larger and vaguer sense your vision of American life comes from Whitman, or from the same sources in American consciousness as his. I am unsympathetic to this tradition, and it seems to me that you should be too."[28] Tate identified the Whitman tradition as a "high-powered industrialism . . . which . . . is a menace to the spiritual life of this country." In his review of *The Bridge*, Tate repeated much the same arguments. He referred to Crane's "sentimental muddle of Walt Whitman and the pseudo-primitivism of Sherwood Anderson and Dr. W. C. Williams,"[29] and placed Crane at the end of a romantic tradition which Tate abjured.

Crane, while accepting that there was a "personal note" in his poetic response to Whitman, denied that Whitman was "the guilty and hysterical spokesman" for "materialism, industrialism, etc." He suggested that Whitman's critics, including Tate, "never seem to have read his *Democratic Vistas*."[30] Crane was clearly disappointed that his closest friends did not understand the central structure of his most important work, but he remained convinced that his use of Whitman was justified and necessary. It is important, if we wish to come to terms with the nature and extent of Crane's accomplishment in *The Bridge*, to examine Crane's response to the poet he chose to play Virgil to his Dante.

The period during which Crane wrote, the 1920s, was a time of considerable controversy over the cultural role of Whitman and the significance of his poetry. In general, Whitman was identified with the "Midwestern School"—Sandburg, Masters, Lindsay—which was being rejected by the more cosmopolitan poets, who were in touch with European developments such as Dada. Whitman's "meaning" had come to be identified by many with the long, diffuse line, the conversational tone, the catalog, and a rather naive celebration of something vaguely called "life." It is easy to see why those intellectuals who sympathized with the harder lines of Cubism or Futurism might turn against the flabbiness of what they identified (not altogether accurately) as the Whitman tradition. And those who, like Winters or Tate, identified themselves largely with formalism and irony in a philosophical context also wanted to separate themselves from the "sentimentality" of Whitman.

Crane, of course, had ties to all these warring groups. His own origins were in the Middle West, and his early reading seems to have been influenced by the poets of that region. In an early review (of *Winesburg, Ohio*, appropriately enough), Crane had praised Masters' *Spoon River Anthology* as "a mighty seedling of dynamite, cold and intense."[31] And, although his regard for Anderson was somewhat attenuated with time, he never completely lost his admiration for his fellow Ohioan, the author of *Mid-American Chants*, one of the most successful "imitations" of Whitman, and a book that clearly stands between Whitman and an apparently unrelated and "modern" poem such as Crane's "The Dance." At the same time, during the twenties, Crane increasingly moved away from his origins, briefly passing through a Dada period,[32] then finding his mature style in the longer poems such as "For the Marriage of Faustus and Helen," "Voyages," and *The Bridge*.

Crane endeavored to find a way to combine the hard lines, self-conscious modernity of technique, and richness of rhetoric of the "European" school with an admiration for the native land, the typically American, and the exuberant expression of a peculiarly continental heritage which was associated with the "Americanists." In this effort he stood almost alone—sometimes, to a lesser extent, joined by Cummings—and he was never to be classed, of course, with the philosophical poets, although often with the seventeenth-century metaphysicals. Crane's later poems reflect this attempt at integration. His language is almost never in the "Whitman tradition"; he uses instead the forms of the "Eliot tradition" to express the ideas of Whitman. His poetry might most accurately be called Romantic Modernism, for he resolved the clash of American Romanticism with European Modernism by turning Modernism into a tool with which to rediscover his own poetic heritage.

The first indication of the young Crane's interest in Whitman may be found in an early poem, "Episode of Hands," which was written in 1920:

> The unexpected interest made him flush.
> Suddenly he seemed to forget the pain,—
> Consented,—and held out
> One finger from the others.

> The gash was bleeding, and a shaft of sun
> That glittered in and out among the wheels,
> Fell lightly, warmly, down into the wound.

> And as the fingers of the factory owner's son,
> That knew a grip for books and tennis
> As well as one for iron and leather,—
> As his taut, spare fingers wound the gauze

Around the thick bed of the wound,
His own hands seemed to him
Like wings of butterflies
Flickering in sunlight over summer fields.

The knots and notches,—many in the wide
Deep hand that lay in his,—seemed beautiful.
They were like the marks of wild ponies' play,—
Bunches of new green breaking a hard turf.

And factory sounds and factory thoughts
Were banished from him by that larger, quieter hand
That lay in his with the sun upon it.
And as the bandage knot was tightened
The two men smiled into each other's eyes.

The most important source for this poem was *Winesburg, Ohio* (which Crane had reviewed the year before), particularly the tale of Wing Biddlebaum. There can be no doubt as to the interest this book must have held for Crane, who felt himself a misunderstood and lonely figure in a bleak Puritan landscape of repression, intolerance, and isolation. Like George Willard, Crane yearned for escape to the city and fulfillment of his dreams for a literary career. And, like Wing, Crane may well have felt the pain of social ostracism that followed upon others' suspicion that he was different, that his desire for human contact was merely a sign of homosexuality. Unlike Anderson's treatment of the story of Wing, however, Crane's version is hopeful and redemptive. There is no final retreat of an isolated and frightened individual but, instead, the joyful confirmation of human unity through an erotic bond.

It was Whitman, clearly, who enabled Crane to create this variation upon Anderson's theme. For, although Anderson too owed a great deal to Whitman, he had lost the optimism of the earlier poet's vision. And, perhaps because he himself feared the consequences of any affirmation of affection between men, he depicted such affection in terms of frustration and defeat. Crane returned to Anderson's own source and restored the powerful affirmation of Whitman's original vision. For this poem belongs in the tradition of Whitman's "Calamus" poems, as a strong statement of social and political unity founded on sexual bonds.

Crane, undoubtedly drawing from his own experiences in his father's factory, depicts the meeting between the "factory owner's son" and a worker, who holds out his gashed finger to be bandaged by the other man. The scene is portrayed in light, vibrant images that suggest the luminosity characteristic of Anderson, and what Tony Tanner has called the "mysticism of detail,"[33] both attributes reminiscent of certain of Whitman's poems, e.g., "Sparkles from the Wheel." The pain of the cut appears to be overcome by a new sensation, as the man recognizes the interest of the other, just as the bleeding finger is absorbed into the light and warmth of the "shaft of sun." Both the sun and the affection serve as figures of healing, working toward integration and reconciliation. Crane seems to be echoing Whitman's wartime role as the Wound-Dresser, a role which for Whitman was spiritual as well as physical.

In the third stanza the social implications of the poem are introduced, through the hand of the factory owner's son "that knew a grip for books and tennis / As well as one for iron and leather." His fingers are "taut, spare," while the worker's hand is "wide [and] deep." In a strikingly beautiful image Crane compares the owner's son's hands to the rapid, brightly colored flight of butterflies:

> His own hands seemed to him
> Like wings of butterflies
> Flickering in sunlight over summer fields.

It is even possible that Crane here associated, consciously or not, his butterfly figure with the symbol so often associated with Whitman, featured in the famous photograph and often used on the bindings of *Leaves of Grass*. What is certain, in any case, is that the movement of the hands imaginatively creates a scene that is idyllic and pastoral. Through the simile quoted above, the physical scene is transported from the factory to the world of pastoral: suddenly we are in Arcadia.

If the hands of the owner's son are butterflies, those of the worker have other associations. "The knots and notches" of his hand seem "like the marks of wild ponies' play." Again the images are idyllic, associated with freedom and childhood. But they are wilder, more physical, even more masculine, if one likes. The final line of the fourth stanza confirms the association of the meeting of these two men with ideas of spiritual and physical regeneration. Now the marks on his hand are "bunches of new green breaking a hard turf." The associations with Whitman here are unmistakable. The grass breaking through the "hard turf" becomes a sign of Whitman's function, as interpreted by Crane, of restoring new life to a barren earth. Crane's use of "bunches" here in an unusual sense seems likely to have been influenced by Whitman, particularly by the poem once called "Bunch Poem" and now entitled "Spontaneous Me." Although this poem is grouped with the "Children of Adam" section, like many of the poems there it actually seems to belong at least as much to the "Calamus" grouping. It celebrates "the loving day, the mounting sun, the friend I am happy with, / The arm of my friend hanging idly over my shoulder," and then moves from this general scene of friendship to a specific section in praise of the phallus and masturbation. Finally it implicitly compares masturbation and art by portraying the poet after masturbation, with "relief, repose, content," and his poem, offered to the world: "And this bunch pluck'd at random from myself, / It has done its work—I toss it carelessly to fall where it may."

Crane's poem is less explicitly sexual, of course, although there is eroticism in the bleeding finger and the gauze wound around it. But Crane's interest is primarily spiritual, as his last stanza demonstrates. The butterfly hands, the neurotic hands which owe their origin to poor Wing, are now calmed. The factory vanishes completely in the peace of comradeship, as the two hands come together in the sun. It is friendship, Whitman's adhesiveness or love of comrades, which can prevail over work, social class, and pain. In the last two lines, the "knot" of the bandage becomes the knot of friendship (like Ishmael's "Monkey-Rope"), and the blood that was shed becomes the first step toward a Lawrentian *Blutbruderschaft* (without any of the associations with violence that concept may have): "And as the bandage knot was tightened / The two men smiled into each other's eyes." The simple happiness of two men together is the principal theme of "Calamus," where Whitman frequently opposes it to fame or worldly success, as in "When I Heard at the Close of Day" or "No Labor-Saving Machine." Crane, at least in moments of personal happiness and optimism, shared Whitman's belief. In "Episode of Hands" he gave early expression to his commitment to the Whitman of "Calamus" and to the political and social consequences of the sexual vision presented there. "Episode of Hands" presents Crane's view that personal love is the way to break down the barriers of class and destroy the factory system. The idea is, perhaps, "primitivistic," as Tate charges, but it also shows a full aware-

ness of the revolutionary implications of Whitman's poetry at a
very early stage in Crane's own poetic development. He would retain these ideas largely intact throughout his career, giving them
full expression in "Cape Hatteras."

Several years after "Episode of Hands" but still some time
before "Cape Hatteras," Crane returned to a Whitman subject
for one of the most splendid poems of his *White Buildings*, "Repose of Rivers." It is clear that this was a poem of major significance for Crane, one on which he worked with even more than his
usual scrupulous care. Lines from the poem reverberate as far as
"The River" and "The Dance," and parts of an early version of
it appear to have been salvaged and used in "Voyages" VI. "Repose of Rivers" is important as a major autobiographical statement
as well as an early elaboration of his aesthetics of kinetic poise.
The poem is cast as an exercise in memory, an attempt to recall
a past experience, clearly painful. And yet, there is an equally
clear insistence on the need for memory, the need to recollect the
past in order to possess it. Above all, the poem dramatizes the
difficulties of coming to terms with sexuality and the final sur-
mounting of those difficulties:

> The willows carried a slow sound,
> A sarabande the wind mowed on the mead.
> I could never remember
> That seething, steady leveling of the marshes
> Till age had brought me to the sea.
>
> Flags, weeds. And remembrance of steep alcoves
> Where cypresses shared the noon's
> Tyranny; they drew me into hades almost.
> And mammoth turtles climbing sulphur dreams
> Yielded, while sun-silt rippled them
> Asunder . . .
>
> How much I would have bartered! the black gorge
> And all the singular nestings in the hills
> Where beavers learn stitch and tooth.
> The pond I entered once and quickly fled—
> I remember now its singing willow rim.
>
> And finally, in that memory all things nurse;
> After the city that I finally passed
> With scalding unguents spread and smoking darts

The monsoon cut across the delta
At gulf gates . . . There, beyond the dykes

I heard wind flaking sapphire, like this summer,
And willows could not hold more steady sound.

The first two lines evoke the childhood experience of the poet, which had been lost and only recently regained. This experience is associated with a slow, graceful movement, a "sarabande"
that seems almost mournful. The images of mowing and the willows suggest death, yet a peaceful death, accepted within the
larger scheme of things. But these memories were lost "till age
had brought me to the sea." The marshes connote a hidden world,
a place of dark sexuality, "seething" in Crane's word. There is a
melancholy about them, heightened perhaps by associations with
Sidney Lanier's "The Marshes of Glynn," one of several poems
which inform this one. In Lanier's poem the poet creates an "impression" of the gloomy twilit world of the marsh, seeking to find
in the passage to the sea a freedom from his preoccupation with
moral and ethical questions. The marshes in Lanier's works evoke
a world of hidden love, of "deep" passages, and of confused human
existence. They are an image for the unconscious, but one without the frightening sexual connotations found in the Crane poem.

Crane derived the half-land, half-sea world of the marshes
not only from Lanier but, more important, from Whitman. The
marshes are akin to that special landscape which Whitman celebrated in "Calamus," particularly in the opening lines of the first
poem of that section: "In paths untrodden, / In the growth by
margins of pond-waters." Whitman's marshland was a spiritual
as well as physical place, its half light more a result of social necessity than picturesque chiaroscuro. For the life of the homosexual
is life in the "margins," in "untrodden" paths; by his sexuality
he is placed on the border of society and, in Whitman's view,
must embrace that "marginal" identity and refuse to accede to the
ways of the world:

Escaped from the life that exhibits itself
From all the standards hitherto publish'd, from the plea-
    sures, profits, conformities,
Which too long I was offering to feed my soul

Whitman's first "Calamus" poem is a statement of his liberation
from conventional standards and his acceptance of his poetic desti-

ny "to sing no songs to-day but those of manly attachment." Crane turned to the figure of the "Calamus" poet implicitly in his first stanza, then explicitly in the second and fourth stanzas.

The startling beginning of the second stanza, with its two words, "Flags, weeds," recalls Whitman's celebration of his own body as worthy of worship: "Root of wash'd sweet-flag! timorous pond-snipe! nest of guarded duplicate eggs! it shall be you! / Mix'd tussled hay of head, beard, brawn, it shall be you!" The "flag" is, in other words, Whitman's "calamus." But Crane's narrator, at the time of the experience, cannot see it as anything but a weed. It is a disorder, something undesirable to be pulled out of any tended garden. And so he judges and condemns himself, associating his memories ("remembrance of steep alcoves") with death ("cypresses") and damnation ("they drew me into hades almost"). Even the sunlight, usually associated with brightness and joy (as in "Episode of Hands"), is here merely "the noon's / Tyranny." As it is cast on the "mammoth turtles" it seems to cut and penetrate them: "rippled them / Asunder . . ." The horror of this memory is eloquently suggested by the placement of the last word of the stanza, and the terrible pause following it. Here the poet has reached the depth of his memory, the realization of his total self-hatred and fear of death. Whitman's model has not yet helped him but, rather, stands as an ironic contrast of freedom and self-declaration against corruption and self-destruction.

The third stanza is transitional, continuing the images of enclosure ("black gorge," "singular nestings"), which culminate in "the pond I entered once and quickly fled." If the first sexual experience was fleeting and unsatisfactory, its recollection provides a key to the past, which is now reclaimed: "I remember now its singing willow rim." The failure of memory in the first stanza is overcome, by a sort of Freudian return to the scene of the crime.

The entry into the pond is associated with other images of penetration and the passage of the river into the sea (recalling the last line of the first stanza, "Till age had brought me to the sea"). This association is particularly manifest in "the city that I finally passed," which from the reference to "the delta" would seem to be New Orleans. When this section of the poem was expanded and rewritten for "The River," the allusion to New Orleans was made clearer: "past the City storied of three thrones." The river's flow past New Orleans is part of its "will" to rejoin the sea, as the title "Repose of Rivers" implies. (In fact, in some senses, the

"I" of the poem may be said to be the river, which can only come of age once it has reached the sea, having passed the dangers of ponds and other diversions.) As the sexual imagery of "scalding unguents" and "smoking darts" makes clear, the passage of the river to the sea is a consummation, in which the phallic power of the river reaches its ultimate expression in its absorption by the embracing sea. The repose which the poem proposes is *post coitum*.

The reference to New Orleans is significant, however, not merely for that city's geographical position, in the Mississippi delta, but also for its important role in the poetry and the popular image of Whitman. Crane's use of New Orleans here and in "The River" is based largely on his relationship to Whitman, specifically his acknowledgment of Whitman as a father, not only a poetic model but also a model of the homosexual seeking to find adequate expression for his emotional life in largely heterosexual forms. Crane's "city that I finally passed" recalls Whitman's poem about New Orleans, "Once I Pass'd through a Populous City." Here too the subject is memory and forgetfulness: Whitman opposes the memory of a personal experience to the forgetting of impressions of "shows, architecture, customs, traditions." As the poem now stands in most editions of Whitman, it reads, "I remember only a woman I casually met there who detain'd me for love of me." The manuscript of the poem, however, read, "I remember only the man who wandered with me, there, for love of me," and later, "I remember, I say, only that youth" or "only one rude and ignorant man." Normally one would not expect Crane to know the original manuscript version of a Whitman poem, but in this case considerable attention was given to the discovery of the manuscript changes by Emory Holloway. Holloway published the original version of the poem in an article in *The Dial* in 1920 and also included it in his edition of Whitman notebooks and manuscripts the following year.[34] Crane had, almost certainly, seen the original version or, at the very least, had heard about the changes in the text. For these changes seemed to indicate clearly the possibility that all the apparently heterosexual references in *Leaves of Grass* were actually disguised homosexual passages. Even Holloway, who was hardly sympathetic, and who later went to absurd lengths to "prove" Whitman's heterosexuality, concluded that "the poem was altered . . . in order to conceal the fact or the nature of that manly attachment," and suggested that the theory of a "secret romance" with a woman was "unproved . . . if not erroneous."[35]

In other words, according to theories prevalent in the 1920s concerning Whitman's sexuality, it seemed likely that Whitman's New Orleans "romance" was with a man, and that this was the occasion for his discovery of his homosexuality. While modern scholarship would probably reject the idea of a simple and sudden origin of homosexuality in Whitman, this is most likely the view which prevailed at the time Crane was writing "Repose of Rivers." Thus his reference to New Orleans is a way of conveying, in discreet terms, his own homosexuality. The poem suggests clearly that once he has "passed" New Orleans, that is, has come to terms with his sexuality, he can return to the memories of unhappy early experiences and find a calm of acceptance. Having passed through the ordeal of fire ("scalding unguents" and "smoking darts"), he can attain a peace which yet is a state of flux, beyond desire, and pass into the fulfillment of "this summer" and its "steady sound." Characteristically, Crane uses a sexual metaphor to describe the ideal aesthetic state, a state of suspended animation. While his poems describe the search for a state of calm, it is not a calm without motion but rather a calm after motion. As in this poem, he frequently represented that transition by opposing the images of river and sea, taking the river as a symbol of unfulfilled desire from Whitman's "From Pent-Up Aching Rivers." Although Crane is often thought of as an "orgasmic" poet, his most characteristic state is an achieved (or desired) peace; while it is Whitman who sings "the mystic deliria, the madness amorous, the utter abandonment."

The opposition between the river and the sea which underlies "Repose of Rivers" is more clearly visible in a related "unpublished" poem, "Belle Isle."[36] Here, as in "Voyages," it is not so much the sea which is imagined as the ideal world but that which the sea contains and encloses—the island. This concept of the island as a place of perfect peace, an idyll of bliss in the midst of a sea of chaos, was almost certainly influenced by Melville's *Moby-Dick*.[37] It might be interpreted as a primitivistic desire for a return to a simpler, childlike existence. Or one could speculate on the significance of Crane's family home on the Isle of Pines for his repeated use of the image of the island, as well as his own frequent desire to return there. In "Belle Isle," however, there is no "noble savage" theme and no childhood innocence. Instead the island is a figure of the state of mind after passion, a figure of achieved sexuality: "the grace / Shed from the wave's refluent gold." It is a spiritual calm which can be achieved after the passage through experience, a "still point of grace."

In "Belle Isle" as in "Repose of Rivers," there is a movement back in time, as the poet attempts to "search back" and recapture the past. He identifies himself with Narcissus seeing only his own reflection in the pool, as Echo has vanished: "now there is / Only this lake's reluctant face." Recalling his past experience, the poet returns to its anguish and its promise:

> And remembering that stream of pain
> I press my eyes against the prow,
> Waiting . . .

The "stream of pain" refers both to the river which will "sow" an island at its base and to the seminal fluid itself. There is the remembered pain of first sexual penetration and the longing for renewed penetration. Here again Crane insists upon his precarious balance: if the river seeks expression in the sea, the sea can also become a figure of death and loss of consciousness. The lake is a "too placid tide," for it has brought separation and the death of love.

The problem which the poem confronts is that of retaining the heightened consciousness of passion, and it is presented in explicitly sexual terms. The state of desire is by itself incomplete and yearns for fulfillment; that very fulfillment must, however, be the death of desire. Love seems to die once it is returned. The moments of greatest sexual ecstasy arrive and then abate. Although the lovers of the poem have given "an absolute avowal," it is "termed" by time, "by hours that carry and divide." The searing moment of passion, the moment of penetration, "that sharp joy," cannot be sustained. The poet asks, in a poignant question central to this poem as well as to "Voyages" and *The Bridge*, "How could we keep that emanation / Constant and whole within the brain!"

But just as the act of anal intercourse depicted here passes through pain to Freud's "oceanic" state, just as pain becomes its own cure through a burning out of passion, just as the act of penetration brings "that instant white death of all pain," so the poet must pass beyond the world of striving passion into the world of memory and art. Crane's position here combines a Whitmanic belief in the sexual origin of feelings of transcendence and spiritual unity and of art ("the origin of all poems"), with a Symbolist idea of art as the calm recollection of a previous spiritual state, and thus the recreation of that state. The world of time and loss can be defeated by access to a timeless world, a world of "grace" and "gold." The opening and closing of the island world—"a place / The water lifts to gather and unfold"—recreates the movement of sexual intercourse, but also suggests the revelation of a private, interior world which has its origins in the Symbolist tradition.

The final stanza of "Belle Isle" is almost identical to the final stanza of the sixth poem of the "Voyages" suite. The "hushed willows anchored in its glow" betray its relationship to "Repose of Rivers" and illustrate Crane's kinetic poise; the willows are not silenced but hushed, not still but anchored. One significant change in wording occurs, in the first line: in "Belle Isle" it is "the after-word," in "Voyages" it is "the imaged Word." The change in "Voyages" clarifies the poem's aesthetic statement, and links the role of the artist to that of God, making the Word flesh. But "after-word" contains an interesting pun which is helpful in understanding Crane's attitude toward time. It is also much closer to the sexual origins of the poem. In neither "Voyages" nor "Belle Isle" is Whitman's influence explicit; that influence can be seen only in "Repose of Rivers." Once the three are read together as related poems, however, Whitman's role in Crane's developing aesthetic is clear. Whitman helped Crane understand the sexual origin of art and gave him the confidence to write poems as a tribute to his own loves and so preserve them from time and loss. The greatest record of this influence is, of course, "Voyages," Crane's sequence of love poems, which was eventually offered in tribute to Emil Opffer but was begun long before Crane had met Opffer.

The homosexual poet seeks poetic "fathers" who in some sense offer a validation of his sexual nature. Whatever he may learn poetically from the great tradition, he cannot fail to notice that this tradition is, at least on the surface, almost exclusively heterosexual. The choice of a model like Whitman is, therefore, an important element of self-identification, an act of declaring one's sexual identity and of placing oneself in a tradition. Whitman's sexuality was not, of course, the only influence on Crane; but it was a major influence, and the first aspect of Whitman to mark Crane deeply. It must be remembered that for a homosexual poet like Crane there was no model to equal Whitman. No other modern poet had written so openly of his sexuality and his love. There were, of course, a few other models available for a young homosexual poet. There was Wilde, to whom Crane wrote his first published poem; but although Crane could sympathize with the persecuted Wilde, he could find little in his poetry to emulate. Many of the Decadents, both English and French, were taken as models by other homosexual poets of this period, such as Crane's friend Wilbur Underwood. But, although Crane passed through a brief Decadent period, it was not to be of lasting influence. And in any case the self-dramatization of suffering and the self-pity that often characterized these poets were not congenial to Crane's expansive and assertive nature. It was also important for Crane to find American models, since he was never at home with European languages or culture, and because he believed in Emerson's (and Whitman's) call for a national poetry. Unfortunately none of Crane's friends at the time, nor critics later, was able to understand the nature of Crane's act of allegiance to Whitman. None of them would have understood the concept of homosexual identity as Crane was struggling with it, although Tate, in retrospect, appears to have come to some understanding. When he was interviewed by Unterecker, Tate attributed Whitman's influence on Crane to "the homosexual thing . . . the notion of 'comrades,' you see, and that sort of business."[38] Although, in a changed climate of opinion, Tate recognized the nature of Crane's indebtedness to Whitman, he failed to understand it.

As we have already suggested with regard to "Episode of Hands," Crane was also aware of Whitman's social criticism, an awareness that appears to have been rare at the time (and not all that common even now). Crane responded enthusiastically to the "social" Whitman, which was, after all, rooted in the sexual, as his comment in *Democratic Vistas* indicates: "It is to the development, identification, and general prevalence of that fervid comradeship, (the adhesive love, at least rivalling the amative love hitherto possessing imaginative literature, if not going beyond it,) that I look for the counterbalance and offset of our materialistic and vulgar American democracy, and for the spiritualization thereof."[39] This text is almost a gloss on Crane's earlier poem (i.e., "Episode of Hands"), but it may also serve as an introduction to Crane's later idea of Whitman. The one friend of Crane's who shared his view of Whitman and taught him to appreciate Whitman increasingly as a social critic and mystic was Waldo Frank. Frank's *Our America*, which Crane read and encouraged his friends to read, declared, "*Democratic Vistas* is quite as clearly our greatest

book of social criticism as *Leaves of Grass* is our greatest poem."[40]
Frank's book was a call for a new awakening, and he turned to
Whitman for an example of the kind of spiritual vision he sought:

> This then is our task. Whitman foresaw it and warned us.
> We must go through a period of static suffering, of inner
> cultivation. We must break our impotent habit of constant
> issuance into petty deed. We must begin to generate within
> ourselves the energy which is love of life. For that energy,
> to whatever form the mind consign it, is religious. Its art
> is creation. And in a dying world, creation is revolution.[41]

It was precisely in these terms that Crane addressed Whitman in
The Bridge, seeking a way out of "this new realm of fact" which had
led man into the folly of "the dream of act." Like Frank, Crane
saw Whitman as a creative and regenerative force, who could lead
him through what Frank called "inner cultivation" and help him
emerge from his descent into the self.

Crane's Proem bears some relationship to Whitman's "Crossing Brooklyn Ferry" in its geographical setting, its inclusive attitude toward the multifaceted life of "mast-hemm'd Manhattan,"
and its use of the gull as a model of flight and a unifying figure.
Crane seems to have had in mind Whitman's depiction of the
birds' flight, as they "wheel in large circles," in his construction
of the first image of *The Bridge*, the "dip and pivot" of the sea-
gull. Whitman's world of unity through flux thus contributed to
Crane's concept of the "curveship." But the first explicit appearance of Whitman in *The Bridge* occurs in "Indiana," where Crane
borrows an episode from "The Sleepers." In Crane's dramatic monologue, spoken by a pioneer mother to her son, the woman recalls
a symbolic meeting with one of the manifestations of Pocahontas,
here reduced to "a homeless squaw." The meeting between the
two women—both wanderers, the Indian heading west as her
land is stolen by the whites, the white woman heading back
east after a failed attempt to find gold—is a moment of instant
recognition, communion, and love. The squaw's eyes "sharp with
pain" shun the men, but light "with love shine" when she sees
the other woman. The source of the episode is section 6 of "The
Sleepers," where Whitman recounts the meeting of his mother "on
the old homestead" with "a red squaw." Here too the meeting is
one of deep and unspoken affection: "The more she look'd upon
her she loved her." In both poems the encounter of the two women

is an emblem both of selfless love and of the reconciliation of warring races through personal love. It is the masculine principle
which has sown hatred through conquest and enslavement (in the
first editions of *Leaves of Grass*, the episode precedes a passage on
black slavery), and it is, symbolically, the feminine principle
which can restore harmony. Just as in his earlier poem Crane has
Faustus "marry" Helen and thus reconcile opposites, so in *The
Bridge* the Columbus principle must wed the Pocahontas principle.[42] Crane invokes Whitman's dream poem to the night in order
to call up the darkness—the intuitive, the primitive, the feminine—as a counter to the questing of the son, the unsatisfied male
who remains a "pent-up" river seeking the sea.

By far the section of *The Bridge* most important for an understanding of Crane's relationship to Whitman is his "ode to Whitman,"[43] "Cape Hatteras." Crane's epigraph is taken from section
8 of "Passage to India." Although he cites only one line (1.220),
the entire stanza should be read to provide the full context of
Crane's allusion:

> Reckoning ahead O soul, when thou, the time achiev'd,
> The seas all cross'd, weather'd the capes, the voyage done,
> Surrounded, copest, frontest God, yieldest, the aim attain'd,
> As fill'd with friendship, love complete, the Elder Brother
>   found,
> The Younger melts in fondness in his arms.
>
> (ll. 219–223)

As this passage makes clear, Crane's epigraph evokes the transition
which Whitman had called for, from physical exploration to spiritual discovery, the transition which is itself the principal theme
of *The Bridge*. Like Whitman, Crane uses Columbus as "the chief
histrion," but, again like Whitman, he makes use of more than
the actual journeys. The subject of *The Bridge* is, of course, Columbus as the type of the spiritual quester, whose journey ends when
he reaches not India but Atlantis, the Platonic lost paradise. The
model for completion given in Whitman's stanza is the physical
love between two brothers, which, as an emblem of adhesiveness,
stands as the long-sought goal at journey's end. Crane's use of this
passage as his epigraph suggests that, in *The Bridge* as in "Voyages," the conclusion is to be a triumphant celebration of love,
now rendered timeless and complete. Insofar as God exists in
Whitman's poem, he is not a distant Father but a loving "Elder

Brother." He is the creation of man's efforts, built out of man's acts of faith, as the architectural metaphors "copest" and "frontest" show.

Crane's indebtedness to "Passage to India" is not restricted to the stanza from which he drew his epigraph. As we have seen, the entire structure of *The Bridge* derives from Whitman's idea of the completion, through spiritual exploration, of the journey begun by Columbus. No wonder Crane placed Whitman at the center of his poem; and no wonder that this section was so difficult for him to write, because so crucial. It was in fact the last section to be completed, while the rest of the poem was already being set in type in Paris—just as the keystone must be laid last at the apex of the arch. *The Bridge* shares with "Passage to India" the idea of an organic continuity between present and past (ll. 13–15) and of America's role as the spiritual descendant of Columbus, with a divine mission to accomplish:

> (Ah Genoese thy dream! thy dream!
> Centuries after thou art laid in thy grave
> The shore thou foundest verifies thy dream.)

Crane also shared Whitman's view of the poet as "the true son of God," a position derived from Emerson's belief in the calling of the poet, and Whitman's faith that the poet in this role could reconcile Nature and Man. He believed with Whitman that the journey undertaken by the poet went beyond reason, rediscovering a prelogical mind, the so-called primitive or poetic: "the voyage of his mind's return, / To reason's early paradise / Back, back to wisdom's birth, to innocent intuitions." He turned Whitman's "rondure of the world" into his "curveship," the principle of the curve or the eternal return. Above all he adopted Whitman's "worship new," including engineers and architects who built "not for trade or transportation only, / But in God's name, and for thy sake O soul."

The first stanza of "Cape Hatteras" begins with a typographic representation of geological shift, which indicates organic balance. A sinking in one place is countered by a rise in another; what appears to be death or destruction is merely an inner adjustment, a physical equivalent of the transmigration of the soul. In this state of apparent chaos the poet returns home, abandoning the death-seeking journeys of the mind so agonizingly portrayed in "Cutty Sark." The return home and the announcement of his reading of

Whitman are linked: the self-seeking quest of Ahab gives way to the love of Ishmael and Queequeg, while the Ishmael-like poet survives the drowning of "Cutty Sark" to be reborn through his acknowledgment of the spiritual guidance of the crude, American Walt Whitman. Crane's insistence on his Americanness was of great importance; an acceptance of European literary models seemed to him a fatal weakening toward effetism or an indulgence in the antihuman games of Surrealism. Only in the American soil, in "native clay," could he find a source of strength for poetic survival, just as Whitman had insisted upon the American poet's own subject in "the United States themselves . . . essentially the greatest poem." [44]

The address to Whitman as "Walt" is undoubtedly one of the instances of "sentimentality" that critics have attacked. But the use of the first name here seems entirely appropriate. If Crane were addressing Eliot he would hardly say "Tom," of course. And his address to Poe in "The Tunnel" is not to "Eddie." But "Walt" is the name of a persona as much as a poet. (We recall that "Song of Myself" mentions "Walt Whitman, an American, one of the roughs," but that *Leaves of Grass* was copyrighted by "Walter Whitman.") It is the Walt Whitman of the poems who is being addressed as comrade and brother, the Walt who is the speaker of "Calamus." One can hardly create a new world of brotherly love without employing the only modern English equivalent of *tutoyage*; later in the poem Crane would also adopt the archaic second-person familiar for a related purpose.

Having announced his allegiance to Whitman, Crane now proceeds to illustrate the apparent failure of Whitman's dream. This was a subject which frequently troubled him. After reading Spengler he had concluded that Whitman's "confidence" in America's spiritual future was "lonely and ineffectual." [45] But once back on the Isle of Pines he regained his confidence, characteristically citing Whitman, from "Passage to India": "I feel an absolute music in the air again, and some tremendous rondure floating somewhere." [46] In "Cape Hatteras" the earth to which Whitman recalled his readers is "sweetness below," a hidden vein beneath the machine-age world, and his starry sky is "sluiced by motion." Despite man's worst efforts and the apparent prevalence of war, space is still a "salver of infinity . . . subjugated never." There is no naive optimism in Crane's treatment, but a severely tempered optimism, which recognizes that Whitman's faith is as yet unrealized but which remains undaunted, in the conviction that Crane, by assuming the mantle of the older poet, can resume and complete his mission.

Crane expresses his doubts in the opening lines, by quoting, to ironic effect, Whitman's "Recorders Ages Hence" from "Calamus." While the title as quoted by Crane might be taken to refer in general to Whitman's place in history, in fact the poem itself has particular significance for Crane. It is here that Whitman asks to be remembered not as a poet but as a lover: "Publish my name and hang up my picture as that of the tenderest lover." The failure of Whitman's faith is thus even more poignant than might at first be evident, for Whitman had not succeeded in being remembered as a fond lover. Whitman had counted upon future generations to complete his mission, to recognize that beneath his "passive exterior" as a "rough" he was actually tender, loving, and gentle. Crane's response demonstrates that he has understood Whitman's legacy and has assumed it himself. Greatest pride is not to be reserved for man's accomplishments, for his "songs," but for "the measureless ocean of love within him." It is the acknowledgment of Whitman as lover which underlies his role in "Cape Hatteras." The destructive nature of Crane's world is seen as resulting from the failure of that love, the failure of Whitman's society to respond to his call.

So, too, when Crane evokes "Starting from Paumanok" and "Out of the Cradle Endlessly Rocking" (in ll. 4–5 of the fourth stanza), he is calling upon Whitman the lover. The two poems are in fact closely related, both using the song of the bird as a model for the source of poetic art in the acceptance of death. "Starting from Paumanok," which serves as an introduction to *Leaves of Grass*, boldly announces, "I will write the evangel-poem of comrades and of love." The song of the bird is "a charge transmitted and gift occult for those being born"—a charge which Crane accepted. The bird suggests to Whitman that all poetry is ultimately an act of love, which is expressed not merely to the beloved but also to all future readers, and that the transformation of love into art renders it eternal, enabling the love to survive long after the death or departure of the beloved. This view, expressed clearly by Whitman in these two poems, is central to an understanding of Crane's "Voyages" ("the unbetrayable reply / Whose accent no farewell can know") as well as *The Bridge*. Thus the answer to Crane's question:

Walt, tell me, Walt Whitman, if infinity
Be still the same as when you walked the beach
Near Paumanok

is that the message of the bird in "Out of the Cradle" ("Death, death, death, death, death") cannot be altered. Infinity remains the same for all men in all ages, and is "the key" to art.

A poem like "Out of the Cradle" is also a crucial indicator of Whitman's ability to transcend personal loss, to retain his faith in love despite the loss of a particular lover. This faith was essential to Crane, whose poems are almost obsessively concerned with the search for love and the anguished fear of its loss. In "Cape Hatteras" Whitman is recognized by his eyes (the poem is, in fact, structured largely around imagery of the eyes and vision), which are the eyes of a seer. They are "sea eyes" (the pun is intentional), which are transformed as they pass underwater, but not closed. Whitman's eyes are everywhere—in Wall Street, in Connecticut farms, in the sea. Man is lost in a "labyrinth," the way out of which can be indicated only by Whitman, whose position above or below the level of the earth enables him to see the pattern and find the passage away from the monster, the "cooler hells" of "Cutty Sark," where one meets only the Drowned Sailor.

Whitman's Ariadne-like role is further emphasized here by contrast with other literary echoes present in this section. The major one, of course, is of Melville's "Bartleby the Scrivener," who inhabits the "prison crypt / Of canyoned traffic." Bartleby represents a dead end, his death apparently symbolic of Melville's own passage into silence. In a world so totally hostile, Bartleby can assert his selfhood only negatively, by denying. Thus death becomes his victory. Crane admired Melville enormously, of course, but here he clearly sees the dangers of submission to the pressures of life without brotherhood or love. Melville passes from the affirmation of Queequeg and Ishmael to the terrible denials of "Bartleby" and *The Confidence Man*; Whitman remains "undenying."

Another echo is of T. S. Eliot, particularly his portrayal of Phlebas the Phoenician. The sea eyes of "Cape Hatteras" recall Ariel's song from *The Tempest*, quoted by Eliot in *The Waste Land*: "Those are pearls that were his eyes. Look!" (l. 48). Unlike Eliot's "drowned Phoenician Sailor," Crane's sailor-narrator who drowns in "Cutty Sark" is reborn through the vision of Whitman. Crane is suggesting here that the cultural despair (and what we may now see to be personal despair) of *The Waste Land* can be resolved only through the example of Whitman. He presents the dilemma as a choice between poetic models, and announces clearly his rejection of the pessimism of Eliot, as well as the despair of Melville's later works.

Another example of a poetic dilemma resolved for Crane by Whitman may be observed in the brilliant stanza 10 of "Cape Hatteras." Here the alternate model is Cummings, to whom Crane renders homage by imitating his style. Crane's stanza is virtually a concrete poem, visually depicting by the use of broken lines, eccentric hyphenation, and wild alliteration and internal rhyming, the crash of a plane drunk on space. The conclusion to this section—"By Hatteras bunched the beached heap of high bravery"—refers not only to the destruction of man through his misuse of technology and his abandonment of his spiritual role (his "Sanskrit charge"), but also to the ultimate sterility and destructiveness of verbal experimentation such as that of Cummings. Cummings, as Crane explained in "General Aims and Theories," was an impressionist, albeit a brilliant one. His work lacked a spiritual basis which would permit him to do more than depict the desperate nature of man's condition. He offered no new "illumination." Thus the major transition of "Cape Hatteras," from stanza 10 to 11, is from physical to spiritual exploration, marked by the move from Cummings to Whitman.

Man has misused his new power over space, and so is destroyed, as nineteenth-century America was rent apart by the strife of the Civil War. But the crash of the airplane need not be final. Whitman offers the "rebound seed." The reference here is double. At the simplest level Crane is alluding to Whitman's central symbol, the grass, suggesting the ability of the earth to accept death into its cycle of life, to bring new life out of apparent destruction. But at another level the "rebound seed" is the sperm, as Whitman sees himself in "Song of Myself" "jetting the stuff of far more arrogant republics." As the apparent death of the phallus gives way to its procreative force, so the death of man's phallic power, represented by the "Falcon-Ace," must yield to the new life of man's fraternal love. The model here is Whitman during the Civil War, as he offers not only physical healing but also love and gentleness that may replace the hatred and aggression of war. Christ-like, Whitman raises the dead through his self-sacrificial love:

                    O, upward from the dead
        Thou bringest tally, and a pact, new bound
        Of living brotherhood!

The isolated phallic pilot gives way to the brotherhood of lovers, in which the phallus is no longer an aggressive instrument of death, but the seat of pleasure. In the last lines there is almost certainly an echo as well of Pound's "pact" with Whitman: "We have one sap and one root— / Let there be commerce between us." Appropriately enough, when Pound finally comes to terms with his old antagonist, he too must choose a phallic metaphor; the pact is finally one of love.

        The following stanza continues the apostrophe to Whitman, as well as the contrast between Whitman and other poets. In this case the others are Poe and Coleridge—two "mystical" poets who are rejected not, as Eliot is, for their pessimism, but for the limitations of their vision. The ravens of line 2 and the condor of line 3 evoke Poe, and Crane's feeling that Poe, although recognizing the spiritual despair of man and calling for a Platonic flight of the imagination, is unable to sustain a flight beyond the wordly. So, too, the albatross of line 4, in its associations with Coleridge, suggests the English poet's inability to resolve the problem of death. The communion wine of line 5 offers no transcendence, since both Poe and Coleridge are unable to go "beyond"; for both of them death remains the final obstacle to man's yearned-for escape from the limitations of self. The death-birds of Poe and Coleridge are contrasted with the image of Whitman, "as a strong bird on pinions free, / Joyous, the amplest spaces heavenward cleaving." His eaglelike flight takes him beyond the death obsessions of "the poets of other lands" and proposes itself as an alternative to the wrecked debris of the warplane. Whitman alone can take the poet through death: "thy wand / Has beat a song, O Walt,—there and beyond!" For the first time in the poem Whitman is associated with the figure of Hermes (through the wand), whom Whitman called "a beautiful and perfect young man"[47] and who serves here as a psychopomp, the guide who can lead man to an acceptance of death and abandonment of striving. (The wand is at the same time, of course, a metonym for the orchestra conductor, as Whitman "orchestrates" the music of the earth and "directs" the performance of future poets, including Crane. It is also the phallus.) The "vigil" which Crane recalls is like the one imagined or recounted by Whitman in "Vigil Strange I Kept on the Field One Night," with its "vigil for boy of responding kisses, (never again on earth responding)." In this "Drum-Taps" poem Whitman displays his role as what Crane calls "mourner," transforming his love for the young men into a loving care for them at the moment of their death and a death-watch passed beside their bodies, until he buries them the next morning and his love aids them on the journey from one world to the next. Whitman's view of this matter was consciously Greek, and Crane responded to the death-love of the earlier poet with full acceptance. The battle against death had ironically brought only more death; now death was to be seen as passage to another existence, guided by the beautiful boy, the angel of death.

Suddenly, in stanza 13, there is a transition from the elegiac tone of the preceding stanza, and the "glacial sierras" are replaced by the flowers of spring. The burgeoning of this stanza suggests the spiritual renewal effected in Crane himself by the example of Whitman. Whitman not only had acted as spiritual guide to America, but also had been an agent of personal rebirth for the poet. Thus the spring of this stanza is "that spring / When first I read thy lines." This first use in the poem of the first-person singular is startling, yet entirely appropriate. We move from generalized experience to particularized; Whitman means experience, not in theory, but in the life of the poet. Crane's style becomes celebratory, as he rejoices in the new life. He celebrates the continent as well, following Whitman's habit of encompassing space by using American place names, chosen for their aural relationships as well as their geographical spread: Potomac lilies, Pontiac rose, and Klondike edelweiss.

Whitman is not merely the means to this renewed life; he is also an expression of the sanctity of life itself. Thus he is addressed as *"Panis Angelicus!"* Crane's use of this phrase, repeated twice in the last two stanzas, has often been criticized by readers who have imagined that Crane misunderstood the meaning of the Latin and thought he was referring to Whitman as Pan. Certainly the Pan reference is there; no poet with Crane's sense of wordplay and indebtedness to Joyce could fail to imply it. But the primary meaning is indeed the religious one: Whitman is the heavenly bread, the earthly and secular communion which is to replace the ecclesiastical. As in Emerson, there is no need for transubstantiation, since the bread is already divine. While Crane was not a Catholic, he almost surely knew the "Panis Angelicus" as a piece of music, in the famous setting by Franck (Crane's taste in music was late Romantic—Scriabin, d'Indy—and early Modern—Bloch, Schoenberg), whose lush ecstasy would surely appeal to the poet of "Atlantis" as he sought a way to express his enraptured regard for Whitman. Again it is to Whitman's eyes—"Eyes tranquil with the blaze / Of love's own diametric gaze, of love's amaze" —that Crane responds.

Yet Crane does not overestimate Whitman, whose poetic limitations he knew very well. Whitman is "not first, nor last,—but near"; it is his very ordinariness which makes him Crane's greatest model. As Whitman himself insisted at the end of "Song of Myself," he was not to be found in the places of the great, but underfoot and everywhere.

> I bequeath myself to the dirt to grow from the grass I love,
> If you want me again look for me under your boot-soles.

Whitman is hailed as he who "flung the span on even wing / Of that great Bridge, our Myth, whereof I sing!" It is he who first sang of the love of men, who offered a way for men to cross the boundary between life and death without fear. He is "our Meistersinger," the spirit of music hovering over us. This reference to Wagner recalls Edwin Arlington Robinson, whose ode to Walt Whitman begins, "The master-songs are ended, and the man / That sang them is a name." In fact the whole opera, with its treatment of poetic "influence" in Sachs and Walther, and its theme of the conflict between conservative "high" art and a popular art which violates convention and restores art to its proper place, is of interest as a gloss on the poetic relationships of Whitman, Robinson, and Crane. Robinson, like Crane, had faith in the ultimate triumph of Whitman, despite the apparent loss of his vision:

> But there are some that hear him, and they know
> That he shall sing to-morrow for all men,
> And that all time shall listen.

Crane here accepts the destiny which had been offered to Robinson—the fulfillment of the promise of the tradition begun by Whitman—but which Crane, by his reference here, implicitly suggests that Robinson did not realize. Crane, by acknowledging the Meistersinger at the same time that he reminds his reader that Whitman was "not the greatest, thou," simultaneously establishes himself as the only worthy successor to Whitman, surpassing both Robinson and Pound, and as the poet who by continuing may complete and fulfill Whitman's poetic mission.

The symbol of Whitman's legacy is the grass itself, "something green, / Beyond all sesames of science." Science, which has apparently offered new opportunities to man, fails because its magical powers do not bring man to any understanding of death. Science continues to tempt man with the illusion of his own power to conquer death individually. For Crane, victory over death can only come, however, through an acceptance of Whitman's spiritualization, an understanding of the pattern of life and death within nature. As Whitman had put his hope for a new poet in *Democratic Vistas*:

> What the Roman Lucretius sought most nobly, yet all too blindly, negatively to do for his age and its successors, must be done positively by some great coming literatus, especially poet, who, while remaining fully poet, will absorb whatever science indicates, with spiritualism, and out of them, and out of his own genius, will compose the great poem of death. Then will man indeed confront Nature, and confront time and space, both with science, and *con amore*, and take his right place, prepared for life, master of fortune and misfortune.[48]

Crane hoped to be that poet, and signalled that fact by his acceptance of Whitman as his precursor, thereby announcing that he, Crane, would by his art justify Whitman's faith in the future.

And so, paradoxically, in the midst of an age of apparent chaos, where "vast engines" assume "seraphic grace," Crane sets about to integrate the world of technology into his poetry, to create a modern *De rerum natura*. He will reclaim the vision of the Open Road, Whitman's adhesiveness, which will prevail "through struggles and wars," and which "cannot be countermanded." "The shuddering longing ache of contact" is to be resolved, as the "camerado" accepts Whitman's offer of companionship, taking his hand in direct response to Whitman's

> Camerado, I give you my hand!
> I give you my love more precious than money,
> I give you myself before preaching or law;
> Will you give me yourself? will you come travel with me?
> Shall we stick by each other as long as we live?
> ("Song of the Open Road," ll. 220–224)

Thus Whitman's "heritage," which is "signalled to our hands," is literally a call to join hands in fellowship and love. Crane's repeated use of the image of the hand when thinking of Whitman is fully justified; for Whitman repeatedly uses the hand to symbolize the act of friendship, the physical joining-forces of two men who shall remain comrades and lovers, as Crane had first suggested in "Episode of Hands."

Now Crane can triumphantly repeat the words of the "Calamus" poem, "recorders ages hence," without any doubt or question. Instead the words are followed by Crane's yes. Accepting the "aureole . . . of pasture-shine" on Whitman's head, the sign and natural nimbus of his divinity, Crane calls upon the poet of "Crossing Brooklyn Ferry," with his affirmation of unity in diversity, of "the glories strung like beads on my smallest sights and hearings." Crane holds out his hand to Whitman and thereby forms a bridge of flesh, a span of faith to his poetic past and eternal future. Crane's last sonnet (each of the fifteen stanzas of "Cape Hatteras" is, with slight modifications, a sonnet) is completed by six rhymed couplets, the lines of which are broken, thus representing visually Crane's act of completion. As the last line progresses horizontally across the page,

> Not soon, nor suddenly,—no, never to let go
> My hand
> in yours,
> Walt Whitman—
> so—

it recalls its "obligation" to the past, its need to rhyme. This brilliant exercise in form confirms Crane's sense of himself and his relationship to Whitman. The last lines clearly recall and rewrite the conclusion to "Starting from Paumanok":

> O Camerado close! O you and me at last, and us two only.
> O a word to clear one's own path ahead endlessly!
> O something ecstatic and undemonstrable! O music wild!
> O now I triumph—and you shall also;
> O hand in hand—O wholesome pleasure—O one more desirer and lover!
> O to haste firm holding—to haste, haste on with me.

Crane becomes Whitman's "camerado," taking his hand, accepting his word, sharing his triumph. Although Crane's line looks like something written by Cummings, its proclamation is Crane's renunciation of anything less than visionary poetry such as he found in Whitman, having as its essence the love of comrades and the ability of love, through art, to transcend death.

Any reading of Whitman must take into account his need to be completed by the future.[49] His readers were his lovers, his comrades. Only as they returned his love could it be justified. He never doubted that his love would be reciprocated, but he also knew that this would take place only with the passage of time. In "Poets to Come" he was to the future what Emerson had been to him, calling for "a new brood, native, athletic, continental" who could "justify" him. For he recognized that his own reputation depended upon the future, that his own greatness would ultimately be measured by the response of others. And he also recognized that, frank as he was, he could do no more than speak a few "indicative words." Any work of art is incomplete without a reader (or perceiver). But the prophetic art of Whitman would be particularly empty. He wanted lovers—finally he wanted to be loved by all the world. And Crane, almost alone among the poets of the early twentieth century, gave him love.

But Crane always tempered his praise with a recognition of Whitman's limitations. In particular, he distinguished between the significance of Whitman's vision and the inadequacies of Whitman's style. He wrote in his essay, "Modern Poetry":

> The most typical and valid expression of the American *psychosis* seems to me still to be found in Whitman. His faults as a technician and his clumsy and indiscriminate enthusiasm are somewhat beside the point. He, better than any other, was able to coördinate those forces in America which seem most intractable, fusing them into a universal vision which takes on additional significance as time goes on. He was a revolutionist beyond the strict meaning of Coleridge's definition of genius, but his bequest is still to be realized in all its implications.[50]

Crane's comment allows him to make Whitman into a poet much more consistent with his own aesthetics, by downplaying the technical aspect, with which Crane sympathized least and which seemed to lead to Sandburg or Lindsay, and by validating the revolutionary vision, to which Crane could then give new form. The bequest is "still to be realized," and it is Crane who shall realize it.

Crane's relationship to Whitman might fall within Harold Bloom's category of *tessera*.[51] Crane both completes and, in so doing, "misreads" Whitman. That is to say, he makes Whitman into Crane. Or at least makes Whitman into the patron of his art. Crane's completion of Whitman is a tribute to the older poet's genius, and a statement of his own inadequacy. As in any such relationship, imitation and homage are a double-edged compliment: Crane praises Whitman, yet suggests his own superiority, for only Crane can make Whitman whole, by becoming his perfect reader and lover. Once the relationship is established, it is Crane alone who journeys to Atlantis.

Far from writing in a "vaguely Whitmanesque" tone, Crane used *The Bridge* to respond in very clear and carefully defined ways to Whitman's example. Whitman had always been for Crane a source of confidence in his own homosexuality and in the expression of his love in his poetry. In *The Bridge* he returned again to Whitman to reaffirm his indebtedness and to suggest the crucial importance of Whitman to his own victory over death. The critics' failure to understand the "personal tone" in Crane's response to Whitman is largely due to their own inability[52] to read the texts accurately and their insensitivity to Crane's needs as a homosexual poet. For the homosexual poet, the past must repeatedly be invented anew, the tradition created afresh. Whitman called for a poet who would be American—as Crane so deeply was—and who would be the poet of the new adhesive order—as Crane wished, but did not quite dare, to be.

4. Some Contemporary Poets

CRANE HAD SIGNIFICANTLY enlarged the possibilities of homosexual poetry, by extending it beyond "mere" subject matter. In Crane, the poet's sexuality is rarely the subject of the poem, as it is in "Calamus," but it nonetheless helps determine the nature of the poem's images and even its structural patterns. "Atlantis," the culminating section of *The Bridge*, is introduced by an epigraph from *The Symposium*, offering us a major clue to reading the poem as a whole. Crane had, however, little direct influence on the poets who followed him. When homosexuality came to be a major element in poetry again, among the Beat poets of the 1950s, the emphasis was on social protest. The avowal of homosexuality became part of a larger rebellion against bourgeois values.

The last twenty-five years have seen an enormous change in public attitudes toward homosexuality. While Whitman's dream of an adhesive America has not been realized, the kinds of disguise once felt necessary by all but the very bravest have begun to disappear. Being homosexual is no longer likely to make one lose one's job; as a result gay poets have no longer felt the same impetus to establish a connection between their sexuality and their political views. While this may have resulted in a loss of political fervor, it has also meant an extension of the forms of gay poetry. It would be impossible to define gay poetry now in the relatively simple terms of one hundred years ago. At that time a gay poet had only two choices: he could "come out" in the manner of Whitman and risk mockery and scorn, or he could cast his verses in the approved forms of Greek and Persian convention.

Gay poets since World War II have not abandoned the sense of tradition. One can find poets working in almost every conceivable form, using every conceivable model. Edward Field writes simple (some would say simplistic) verses of affection, expressing a belief in the revolutionary power of love. Robert Duncan works

in a highly complex style, considerably evolved since his beginnings as an imitator of Eliot but still concerned with language
and mystic awareness. Thom Gunn often writes traditional formal
verse that may express existential dilemmas or describe the scene
in an S & M bar. None of them feels that his homosexuality determines any particular form or even, in many cases, any particular content.

All the poets whom I consider in this section are aware of
themselves as homosexuals and use that awareness as part of the
subject matter of their poems. It is clearly still important for the
gay poet to feel himself linked to a tradition and to acknowledge
those who have gone ahead. In some poets, such as James Merrill,
one can see an important change brought about by a growing willingness to acknowledge his homosexuality openly. Merrill's work
has always been meditative and self-exploring; but it is only recently that he has expressed his homosexuality in direct terms.
Significantly, he turned to Crane, consciously or unconsciously,
at that point. For Thom Gunn, too, the acknowledgment of homosexuality has brought about changes in the poems. In his case,
one can argue that the poetic form was altered to suit a new sense
of himself. Even poets who seem very far from the traditions we
have discussed have made use of a gay tradition in very explicit
ways: Frank O'Hara's "Homosexuality" imitates "Song of Myself"
in a very amusing way, both invoking the spirit of Whitman and
distancing himself from it, as in this parodic couplet: "The song
of an old cow is not more full of judgment / than the vapors
which escape one's soul when one is sick." [1]

Allen Ginsberg

In the 1950s it often seemed that the only openly gay poet was
Allen Ginsberg. The enormous publicity that Ginsberg received
made him an important figure, whose avowal of homosexuality
was part of his larger attempt to undermine American society and
its pretensions to respectability. Although many of the Beat writers were homosexual or bisexual (such as Burroughs or Kerouac),
it was Ginsberg who made his sexuality an integral part of his
public image and his poetry. "Howl" was the first poem to bring
Ginsberg public attention, and its treatment of homosexuality is
characteristic of Ginsberg's position during this time. "Howl" is

a lament for "the best minds of my generation," the "angelheaded hipsters" destroyed by the cruelties of American society. The homosexual functions in the world of "Howl" as a figure of angelic innocence, his love a protest against the insensitivity and madness which surround him. Ginsberg writes for those

> who let themselves be fucked in the ass by saintly motorcyclists, and screamed with joy,
> who blew and were blown by those human seraphim, the sailors, caresses of Atlantic and Caribbean love,
> who balled in the morning in the evenings in rosegardens and the grass of public parks and cemeteries scattering their semen freely to whomever come who may,
> who hiccupped endlessly trying to giggle but wound up with a sob behind a partition in a Turkish Bath when the blond & naked angel came to pierce them with a sword,
> who lost their loveboys to the three old shrews of fate the one eyed shrew of the heterosexual dollar the one eyed shrew that winks out of the womb and the one eyed shrew that does nothing but sit on her ass and snip the intellectual golden threads of the craftsman's loom[2]

It is easy to see why this poem had such an extraordinary effect on its first readers. Its celebration of the specifics of homosexual life was calculated to shock, particularly its radical redefinition of the holy, and partly its deliberate use of "forbidden" words. Had Ginsberg's American readers followed French literature, they would have realized the extent to which Ginsberg's ideas were influenced by those of Jean Genet.[3] But Americans had not read much (if any) Genet in 1956, and so Ginsberg was successful in his attempt to *épater les bourgeois*.

Ginsberg's relationship to Whitman is clear in "Howl." Ginsberg learned from Whitman the use of the long line, the repetition of the subordinate clause ("who let," "who blew," "who balled," etc.), and the celebration of phallic energy. The third line quoted above shows Ginsberg's assumption of Whitman's democratic sexuality—the celebration of anonymous sexuality and the sharing of the poet's seminal energy. At the same time one can see a great deal of the private mythology of Ginsberg—the search for the sexual encounter as perfect religious experience. While this might seem to originate in Whitman's depiction of the sources of mystic vision as sexual, it should be remembered that

Whitman's sexuality is portrayed as both active and passive, and that Whitman devotes as much attention to the image of two lovers simply happy to be together as to actual moments of sexual penetration. In Ginsberg the desire for religious vision is transformed into a desire to be fucked, whereas in Whitman the experience of sexual pleasure leads to a greater understanding of the world. Although Ginsberg calls on Whitman, he transforms an ultimately peaceful vision of human unity into an affirmation of the homosexual's alienation from the "straight" world and a desire to become an object of love rather than a participant in it. Here, as in the later poems, Ginsberg links his passive sexuality to his poetics, as he rejects the "craftsman's loom" for the orgasmic scream.

Ginsberg's most poignant tribute to Whitman is his "Supermarket in California," which looks to Whitman as "dear father" and "lonely old courage-teacher."[4] Whitman is called upon for his "enumerations," his celebrations of variety, which Ginsberg locates, rather amusingly, in a California supermarket. Whitman evokes for Ginsberg the dream of a return to lost innocence, a surprisingly Freudian dream of "every frozen delicacy." The California supermarket is the American world of beautiful young men, which Ginsberg imagines himself sampling. It should be noted that for Ginsberg, however, the dream is marred by guilt (or fear) —"followed in my imagination by the store detective"—and that it does not assuage Ginsberg's sense of himself as an isolated outsider. Whitman is the American poet with whom Ginsberg feels a certain identity, yet that identity is vitiated by Ginsberg's failure to share Whitman's affirmation of American life. Whitman, even when he saw himself most clearly as a homosexual, identified himself with America; Ginsberg repeatedly denies that identification, affirming his isolation and loneliness. "Howl" effectively expressed the rage of frustration felt by Ginsberg's generation, as he worked toward continuing and extending the Whitmanic tradition of aural poetry.

Ginsberg's whole work has been in some sense radical, as an attempt to revolutionize the sensitivity of an insensate public, and as a conception of poetry as political action. But he has become frozen in gesture, and sometimes seems to be tilting against windmills. His volume *Planet News 1961–1967*[5] was clearly situated in the political atmosphere of the fifties, against the blandness of which Ginsberg opposes a reborn sexuality:

> Che Guevara has a big cock
>   Castro's balls are pink
> The ghost of John F. Dulles hangs
>   over America like dirty linen[6]

The statement is there, an indictment of timid, repressed America, but it remains flat and didactic. There is no magic, no transformation, not even any humor. The visionary poet seems to have lost his vision, and even Ginsberg himself seems to sense this loss.

His homosexuality poses certain problems, as "This Form of Life Needs Sex"[7] makes clear. His desire to "continue the race" will make him "have to accept women." His love of men is a love of beauty, but he sees it as ultimately sterile:

> But no more answer to life
>   than the muscular statue
>
> I felt up its marbles
> envying Beauty's immortality in the
>   museum of Yore—
> You can fuck a statue but you can't
>   have children

For Ginsberg homosexuality appears to be linked to its traditional aesthetic implications. It is still a cult of Beauty, which he finds difficult to bring into harmony with his more radical political vision. Furthermore, his desire for continuity through procreation makes him wonder about the need to embrace some form of heterosexuality. Ginsberg's poem suggests that the price of the immortality of art is sterility. It is unable to accept the aesthetic consolation of continuity through one's creativity. The dilemma is frequently expressed (nowhere better than by Yeats), but it may have particular urgency for a homosexual who feels that there is an obligation to participate in the continuation of the species.

One of Ginsberg's most important poems from this collection is "Kral Majales,"[8] which deals with his experiences as May King. Although Ginsberg is aware of the mythic significance of his role —and in fact sees himself as playing the May King throughout life, constantly erecting the phallus—the poem ends in a state of defeat which seems to symbolize Ginsberg's spiritual condition in a world which has not accepted his divine mission:

> And *tho* I am the King of May, the Marxists have beat me
>   upon the street, kept me up all night in Police Station,

followed me thru Springtime Prague, detained me in secret and deported me from our kingdom by airplane

As Ginsberg has become more and more aware of the failure of
his self-appointed mission as Redeemer, he has turned to a kind
of mystic awareness that amounts to an abdication of all poetic
responsibility. One simply cannot, however, make a life-long pose
out of visionary rage unless one is able to transform it into art.
Ginsberg's successful selling of himself as representative of the
avant-garde has managed to conceal the fact that he has little new
to say and no new way to say it, and that his joylessness is far
from the world of the more traditional gay poets of the same time.
    His following volume, *The Fall of America: poems of these states
1965–1971*,[9] confirms Ginsberg's failure. The volume is dedicated to Walt Whitman; yet in conjunction with Ginsberg's attempt
here to develop "found poetry," a kind of artless collage, Whitman's words are taken and used without reflecting back on Whitman's poetry or forward toward the creation of a new poetry equivalent for our time to Whitman's in his. The poems of this volume
are apparently meant to express a new mood of acceptance and contentment, as Ginsberg wanders through America in Whitman's
footsteps. There is to be a change:

> Done, finished with body cock desire, anger
> shouting at bus drivers, Presidents & Police.[10]

The anger of "Howl" is to be replaced with a new receptivity to
the universe. But there is a very fine line between the vaunted
receptivity and a total passivity which amounts to complicity in
the universe. Ginsberg's "Graffiti 12th Cubicle Men's Room Syra-
cuse Airport"[11] is simply a copy, one assumes, of the content of
the walls of this particular men's room; the poet has only to find
poetry and then present it, in an utterly debased version of Emerson's "I am a transparent eyeball" theory. Found poetry succeeds
when it uses a random discovery as a way of revealing something
not otherwise apparent. It can remind us of the poetic in the ordinary. But Ginsberg seems to find the entire world a found poem,
which reduces the element of joy in discovery and makes the poet
an echo of an ominipresent truth.
    The new mood of passivity is not only philosophical and po-
etic, it is also sexual. Ginsberg's poem "Please Master"[12] is a successfully erotic evocation of the desire to be fucked, a desire which
one supposes is equivalent to the poet's desire to be fucked by the

universe, to be overcome by its sensations. But here again Ginsberg betrays the heritage of Whitman, always a poet of multiple
possibilities, who clearly depicted in "Song of Myself" the turning
over in bed as sexual roles were exchanged and fucker became
fucked. The fact that "Please Master" is indeed erotic is likely
to obscure the fact that it is a dangerous vision of the world. To
be a field of sensation is indeed to revive one's own erotic po-
tentialities, and Ginsberg's poem is a necessary political-sexual
statement of the need to admit openly one's desire for anal intercourse. It is no good, of course, pretending that a homosexual revolution can take place without fucking. Were the poem to appear
alone, one would admire its sensuality, its pornographic excel-
lence, and its revolutionary implications; seen, however, in the
context of Ginsberg's other poetic statements, it becomes a general
resignation. Ginsberg's master is unnamed, undescribed, totally
anonymous; he is the coming to life of a statue, a fantasy embodied, which can lead only to destruction of oneself as lover and
poet.[13]

Robert Duncan

Despite the far greater popularity of Allen Ginsberg, Robert Duncan is perhaps the most interesting and most accomplished of the
recent gay poets, because of the wealth of his reading, which has
become the richness of his language and allusion, and because he,
more than any other poet of his time, has spoken of himself as
poet and homosexual and of the meaning of his homosexuality
for his work. When he collected his early poems in 1966, he wrote
a preface which is both an autobiographical statement and an essay on poetics, in which he outlines the major influences, literary
and personal, on his early work. He gives what must be one of
the finest statements of the position of the homosexual and poet
with regard to American society:

> In 1938 when I was nineteen, I had fallen in love and left
> college in my sophomore year, following my lover East. That
> first experience of a sexual relationship took over my life.
> I was moved by violent conflicts and yearnings, a need to be
> reassured in love that all but obscured my expression of lov-
> ing. The opposites played in me: male and female, love and

hate, tenderness and jealous anger, hope and fear. Here too there had been the awakening of a rhythm, the imprint of a cadence at once physical and physiological, that could contain and project the components of an emerging homosexuality, in an ardor that would prepare for the development of Eros and, eventually, for that domesticated or domesticating Love that governs the creation of a household and a lasting companionship. Perhaps the sexual irregularity underlay and led to the poetic; neither as homosexual nor as poet could one take over readily the accepted paradigms and conventions of the Protestant ethic.[14]

The homosexual poet is, insofar as he recognizes his homosexuality, obliged to view society from the outside and to question the accepted ideas of his own culture. Needless to say, a heterosexual may well come to the same point of view; the difference lies in the imperative with which the homosexual is confronted.

The consequence is a freeing of the homosexual, the gift of a radical perspective which often is expressed in an awareness of his own body. Because the homosexual is defined by his sexuality, it is much harder for him to sublimate that sexuality into generalized sentiment and forget the body of love. He is able to see his own body as end rather than as means. Because sex between men cannot be procreative, gay men are freed from the traditional economic imperative (breeding to preserve the family and provide cheap labor) and the traditional religious imperative (breeding to glorify God—the conservation of sperm), and able to see their sexuality as play which can be good in itself.

Duncan's poetry, from his earliest work to the present, is deeply erotic. He is in love with words: their surfaces, their sounds, their shapes. His poetry continually strives to escape the bounds of convention and transport the reader into a new awareness centered in the body rather than the mind. To enter into a Duncan poem is to experience language in a fresh manner. L. S. Dembo has spoken of Duncan's "Dionysian vision of poetic language as a transconceptual rhythm or force."[15] This is the cadence or rhythm of which Duncan speaks in his preface and which he sees as rooted in his homosexuality. The homosexual is, for Duncan, a Dionysian in an Apollonian world.

Duncan's poetics reflect a reaction against the rationalist world of logic and order. His poetry serves the mystical end of altering the consciousness of the reader, of transporting him into the magical realm of poetry, which combines a state of religious exaltation with one of sexual excitement. His use of language is similar in many ways to that of Poe, with whom he shares a sense of magical, esoteric poetry (even though Duncan may have come to Poe's vision through the familiar circuitous route, via the French *symbolistes*, then Eliot and Crane). He shares with Crane the abiding metaphor of the body of the world, which may be found in much mystical literature but which has been discovered anew by these poets of twentieth-century America.

Crane, as Dembo has also observed, is one of the most important influences on Duncan's work, even though Duncan does not seem to have written about his poetic relationship to Crane. For Duncan as homosexual poet, Crane has a special significance. One can observe in Duncan's work a number of references to poets who were homosexuals; these references serve partly as code, indicating to his readers the meanings to be found behind some of the poems, and partly as elements of the foundation of a tradition. One of the greatest problems facing the homosexual poet in America is the absence of a clearly defined homosexual tradition. Heterosexual criticism almost always overlooks or distorts the element of homosexuality and leaves the homosexual to establish his tradition through a kind of underground, in which young gays learn through whispers about Shakespeare's sonnets, Marlowe, Whitman, Crane, Auden, and so on. For Duncan the influence of Crane is not limited to the recognition in him of a fellow homosexual; that recognition may, in turn, give rise to the exploration of poetic possibilities.

Duncan shares with Crane the metaphor of the bridge, and of poetry as a bridge toward the eternal. He uses the image in "A Letter to Jack Johnson" from *The Years as Catches*: "our bridge toward the waves."[16] Poetry remains an attempt to cross time and space and catch a glimpse of what lies beyond. Vision and memory are combined, since time future and time past are identical. Duncan provides a very moving recollection of lost love—a poem similar in tenderness to Crane's splendid "My Grandmother's Love Letters"—in his "Structure of Rime XI":

> There are memories everywhere then. Remembered, we go
>   out, as in the
> first poem, upon the sea at night—to the drifting.
> Of my first lover there is a boat drifting . . .[17]

The world is occasion and embodiment. The things of the world "recall" (Crane's phrase) memories from the past and begin a journey to recapture that past, variously imaged as lost Eden, Atlantis (in both Crane and Duncan), or meadow—"Often I am permitted to return to a meadow." Just as memories are remnants of previous experience—fragments—so too the physical world is seen as remnant of a larger spiritual world. The aim of the poet is to recapture the lost world and the lost love. But neither the cosmos nor love are attainable; the experience of fleeting love leads to a recognition of mutability. Art remains the road to love and cosmos.

Art for Duncan is never static; the world is not contemplated in moments of quiet reflection, but grasped, seized in moments of visionary insight which can be compared to moments of love. Duncan's poetry is composed of glimpses, caught images, seconds of truth which disappear as soon as they occur. His words explode, and in the shower of their broken pieces may be found an instant of recognition. His poetry is orgasmic, a poetry of concentration and eruption. Although the universe cannot be grasped, it can be known (the carnal pun is intentional). Loving is an attempt at knowing, which leads, never to understanding, but to realization. Duncan constantly reminds us that "love is the body of the soul, desire."[18]

Crane was for Duncan a way to the discovery of Whitman as well. Whitman remains the most persuasive model for any gay poet writing in America, for no other poet has so convincingly and unabashedly written of his love, both physical and spiritual, for other men. What is surely important for Duncan is Whitman's awareness of the body, his celebration of the self through the body of the self, and his sense of the physical act of love as occasion for a mystical perception of unity. Duncan's poem, "The Torso" (*Passages* 18), shows his indebtedness to Crane and Whitman, and deserves quotation at some length:

> and at the treasure of his mouth
>   pour forth my soul
>   his soul   commingling
> I thought a Being more than vast, His body leading
>   into Paradise,   his eyes
>   quickening a fire in me,   a trembling
>   hieroglyph

·   ·   ·   ·   ·   ·   ·   ·   ·   ·   ·   ·   ·   ·   ·

> At the root of the groin
> *the pubic hair*, for the torso is the stem in which the man
>   flowers forth and leads to the stamen of flesh in which
>   his seed rises
> a wave of need and desire over   taking me
>   cried out   my name
> (This was long ago. It was another life)
>   and said,
>   What do you want of me?
> I do not know, I said. I have fallen in love. He
>   has brought me into heights and depths my heart
>   would fear without him. His look
>   pierces my side   .   fire eyes   .
>
> .   .   .   .
>
>   wherever you are
> my hand in your hand   seeking   the locks, the key
> I am there. Gathering me, you gather
>   your Self.
> For my Other is not a Woman but a man
>   *the King upon whose bosom let me lie*[19]

The first stanza illustrates Duncan's mystical-sexual vocabulary. The occasion of the poem is, of course, an act of fellatio, with the poet describing his feelings as he achieves climax in the mouth of his lover. Duncan, like Crane and Whitman, sees the orgasm as religious ritual, in which the worshiper-poet finds expression through his sperm-soul (which, as we see, becomes his poem). Through the body of love into Paradise—but at the moment of orgasm we are left with a hieroglyph, a coded word, a mystery language. If all loving is an attempt to regain Paradise, then all art is an act of love, written in a secret language accessible only to the initiate.

The poem is in a sense confessional, as so many of Duncan's poems are, and gives expression to the poet's homosexuality. It also turns to seek the figure of the lost lover, who has been assimilated into the Poet, Walt Whitman, and into God. Duncan has taken verbal echoes of "Song of Myself" and Hart Crane's *The Bridge* and interwoven them, providing for himself a place in the tradition. Crane takes the hand of Whitman as spiritual guide in "Cape Hatteras" and thus fulfills Whitman's promise

to his reader-lovers; Duncan now takes both their hands. But because of the echoes of Crane's "The Tunnel," with its last lines:

> Kiss of our agony Thou gatherest,
>   O Hand of Fire
>   gatherest—

the experience is given spiritual significance as well. The agony
of suffering leads to redemption; the final meeting with the God-
lover is assured. Love for the homosexual Duncan leads to self-
knowledge because it always leads to a reflection back on self: "For
my Other is not a Woman but a man."

The encounter with self is the subject of one of Duncan's
early poems from *The Year as Catches*, "An Encounter," a poem
which also reveals his indebtedness to Eliot, so marked in these
first poems. The encountered stranger has a Prufrockian timidity,
which gives great scope and depth to this depiction of the hesitan-
cy with which one man may respond to another's cruising.

>   . . . And he asks
> —Are you insane? Your eyes are strange. I
> cannot meet them—He pauses and his gaze
> is restless, having no intent nor answer,
>   so that we look back
> each into his own eyes, uneasy,
> seeing no end to the questioning perspective.
>
> His abstractions avoid the ultimate decision
> —how can the room itself be faced or the derision
> of those others in the room, would-be Gods with voices
> and eyes at tension, wooing the distance between them.
>
>   .   .   .   .
>
> Any stranger is dangerous, holding perhaps
> the locks of self, who may release a flood.[20]

If the poem is perhaps too dependent upon its Eliotic tone (even
to rhyming "decision" and "derision"), it shows Duncan's desire
to confront the self, in a world which prefers evasions. The search
for random sex is a sign of the spiritual wasteland in which these
strangers live, and yet they fear to find a passionate encounter,
which might break down the structures they have erected against
themselves.

There is a Freudian influence in a number of Duncan's poems, such as this one, due to Duncan's commitment to the idea of polymorphous perversity (the childhood ideal) and Freud's concept of underlying bisexuality.[21] The locks of self may, of course, be a metaphor for the repressive techniques which are developed to keep the dangerous tendencies of the id in check. In this view, the homosexual who refuses to sublimate himself serves as a constant social gadfly, an ever-present social id that will not be repressed. It is not surprising, then, that Duncan should speak so positively of the homosexual, as in his lines, "This place rumor'd to have been Sodom is blessed in the Lord's eyes."[22]

Duncan's celebration of polymorphous pleasure (if I may alter a very annoying misnomer) is probably nowhere clearer than in his delightful and playful "Dance early spring weather magic." The poem begins,

Hug the girls, boys. Hug the boys, boys.
Hug the girls, girls, Hug the boys, girls.
Round, and around and around.[23]

It is a round, in which boys and girls are constantly interchanged in every possible variation of words and relationships. But it is also a metaphorical round, in which the world is seen as a circle and sexual definitions are as fleeting and impermanent as points on a rapidly revolving wheel. Girl and boy—How different are they? the poem asks, as it seeks an end to definitions and a rediscovery of pleasure, a time when girls and boys will hug and kiss indiscriminately, when all will dance and magic will prevail. Duncan's is a world of white magic and revelry, in which the dance is a central image for ever-changing and joyful relationships.

Duncan's belief in the dance may derive from his reading of Nietzsche, who has had a strong philosophical influence on his career, and whose distinction between Apollonian and Dionysian in *The Birth of Tragedy* underlies Duncan's Dionysian vision. In several poems Duncan turns to the figure of Apollo, traditionally associated with the sun and with reason, and reminds us that Apollo once loved Hyacinth:

AI   AI

The hyacinthus springs, love's flowering
in the year's renewal, white and blue-red
as the violet-blooded beloved youth.

How, when he fell, your heart was torn
And you tasted the depth of our mortal regret.

AI   AI

The mocking blood, the mocking flesh, beckons
and flowers in the wan pale light. See!
the beloved mouth, to be kisst, is closed.
The eyes are closed. The beloved body lies,
to be seized to your body, broken.

.   .   .   .

heedless and eager to prove your love,
you have cut love down. Inscribe then your grief
upon love's bloom.

.   .   .   .

AI   AI

Deathless Apollo, Thou too hast loved, and Thou
immortally must bear
mortality's bourne.[24]

It is Apollo's destruction of his beloved Hyacinth which may bring
him to an understanding of love and death. Love makes human
the inhuman; and because all love is transitory, it bears within
it the knowledge of death. To love is to accept suffering, to accept
the irrational. Apollo's love for Hyacinth is seen by Duncan as
redemptive, promising an awakening from the world of rational
order through the power of love.

Apollo is the power of the head, and its rejection by Duncan is total. The poet's power is the power of illogic, of the absurd, of the suspension of syntax, of unreason, and, above all,
of the body. His series of poems, "The Structure of Rime," might
well be called his Zarathustra poems, for they are modeled on
Nietzsche's *Thus Spake Zarathustra* and follow in that tradition
of prophetic books. The voice of the poems is the voice of the
prophet who announces the coming of the New Man and celebrates
the awareness of the mystery which is a necessary preparation for
that coming. The eighth poem uses the figure of the magician as
a force for good (unlike Nietzsche, in part 4 of *Zarathustra*) to
announce what is in fact a central statement of Duncan's poetics:
"This the magician taught: Let the Flesh be given lips that It

may talk."[25] The language of Duncan's poetry is the language of the flesh, not of the head; it is the magical language spoken only in moments of heightened consciousness, when the spirit is allowed to escape through the music of the body.

These moments are moments of vision, in which the poet goes beyond his ordinary existence and glimpses something of the eternal. Duncan's metaphor for these moments is frequently sexual, and perhaps nowhere better expressed than in his second "Night Scene," where his orgasmic vision is made explicit:

> youth spurts, at the lip the flower
>   lifts lifewards, at the
> four o'clock in the morning, stumbling
>   into whose room, at whose
>
> mouth out of slumber sweetening,
>   so that I know I am not I
> but a spirit of the hour descending into body
>   whose tongue touches
>   myrrh of the morgenrot
>
> as in a cowslip's bell that in a moment comes Ariel
>   to joy all around
> but we see one lover take his lover into his mouth,
>   leaping, Swift flame of
> abiding sweetness is in this flesh.
>
>   Fatigue spreading back, a grand chorale
> of who I am, who he is, who we are,
>   in which a thin spire of longing
> perishes, this single up-fountain of a
>   single note around which
>
>   the throat shapes![26]

Dawn, the new life, the flower, all are images which represent the penis, celebrated in its moment of triumph. The way back to the spiritual is through the body: thus Duncan is again firmly in the tradition of body mysticism established by Whitman and continued by Crane. No poet, however, has equaled Duncan in his ability to compare the powerful evocation of the erotic with a highly literate sensibility and an awareness of the possibilities for both using and transforming the western literary tradition.

Duncan remains preeminently the poet of the soul known through the body.

Although Duncan has spoken forthrightly for the significance to his art of his homosexuality, he has also maintained that his homosexuality is a sign of his participation in the human community, rather than of his exclusion from it. In his thoughtful essay, "The Homosexual in Society," Duncan warns against the creation of a second, outcast society to replace the one the homosexual feels excluded from. Duncan makes a poignant plea for a homosexual who is "willing to take in his own persecution a battle-front toward human freedom." Speaking of Hart Crane's poetry, and arguing against the cult of Crane, he writes,

> Crane's suffering, his rebellion, and his love are sources of poetry for him not because they are what make him different from, superior to, mankind, but because he saw in them his link with mankind; he saw in them his sharing in universal human experience.[27]

Thom Gunn

Robert Duncan has expressed his relationship to Thom Gunn in his "Poems from the Margins of Thom Gunn's *Moly*."[28] Gunn seems nonetheless far removed stylistically from the poetry of Duncan. Duncan is a magician of words, who revels in their hallucinatory and incantatory powers, while Gunn is a craftsman and sculptor. His poems are spare and lean, while Duncan's are sprawling and agitated. Gunn's is the art of control and order, even when he is writing about the world as experienced under the effects of LSD.[29] Every line is finely honed, the tone cool and reasoned. Gunn uses his powers of discrimination to create a poetic world which has two principal subjects: the nature of order in a disordered universe and the nature of love in an essentially loveless world.

It is significant to note that Gunn's poems do not deal with the act of love. They are not poems of the body in the way that Duncan's are, nor do they offer any apocalyptic future in which we shall all be united in sexual bliss. Their mood is one of prevailing sadness, which derives from an overwhelming sense of impossibility. Much of the imagery that is most clearly homosexual is devoted to the description of male homosexual fantasy figures, notably the motorcyclist and, by extension, all "rough trade," but also in one notable poem ("From the Wave") the surfer. Gunn clearly feels guilt and unhappiness about his homosexuality, and these feelings pervade his poetry. He cannot reconcile the needs of the body with the claims of the mind.

"On the Move"[30] is the first of a number of Gunn's poems to deal with the figure of the motorcyclist, seen here in heroic terms: "In gleaming jackets trophied with the dust." Gunn's attitude toward this figure is determined by his identification of the motorcyclist with a Nietzschean will. "The Boys," as he terms them, have chosen their style and thereby their route. Their continual movement and energy become the expression of an existential attempt to overcome the senseless universe. They are not afflicted with the intellectual's disease, doubt, which they "strap in," thus managing to become what they pretend to be. They dominate the scene and prevail over nature: "Much that is natural, to the will must yield." They are *created* persons, who make their own lives:

> Men manufacture both machine and soul,
> And use what they imperfectly control
> To dare a future from the taken routes.

In the last two stanzas the poet turns from description to commentary. He sees in the motorcyclists "a part solution," because they do not accept the human conditions of discord in a world in which man is "half-animal."

> One joins the movement in a valueless world
> Choosing it, till, both hurler and the hurled,
> One moves as well, always toward, toward.
>
> A minute holds them, who have come to go:
> The self-defined, astride the created will
> They burst away; the towns they travel through
> Are home for neither bird nor holiness,
> For birds and saints complete their purposes.
> At worst, one is in motion; and at best,
> Reaching no absolute, in which to rest,
> One is always nearer by not keeping still.

The perpetual motion of the cyclists becomes an assertion of their humanity, in absurdist terms. In the "valueless world" it is movement itself which assumes value.

A similar version is presented in the other motorcycle and "tough" poems of *The Sense of Movement*. "The Unsettled Motorcyclist's Vision of His Death"[31] continues the theme of the cyclist as representative of the human will in conflict with nature. "I am being what I please," he maintains; or, "My human will cannot submit / To nature, though brought out of it." The element of choice is again crucial: "I urge my chosen instrument / Against the mere embodiment." All men are viewed as hurtling toward their deaths in a world they cannot comprehend; the nobility of the cyclist lies in his attempt to control and master the universe. Such an attempt is inevitably futile, as the cyclist realizes in his vision, but Gunn clearly sees virtue, or at least beauty, in the attempt to deny that futility.

"Lines for a Book"[32] extends Gunn's vision beyond the personal eroticism of his motorcycle poems into a philosophical and historical statement which will value "the toughs through history." Gunn's poem is a defense of action against contemplation, presented in terms of a series of contrasts. It represents the homosexual cult of virility and may well speak for the most dangerous aspect of homosexuality: the creation of a Spartan ideal which excludes all "feminine" behavior. We are here far from the bisexuality and polymorphous vision of Robert Duncan. Gunn is quite clear on a number of points that one can most charitably call morally dubious:

> . . . It's better . . .
> To be a soldier than to be a cripple;
> To take an early weaning from the nipple
> Than think your mother is the only girl;
> To be insensitive, to steel the will,
> Than sit irresolute all day at stool
> Inside the heart . . .

Although Gunn's motives may be clear to a certain extent and deserving of some sympathy, the need for the homosexual to react against the effete and decadent seems to be considerably overstated here. One must suspect that it derives not entirely from a reaction against gentility, but more from a personal need to refuse softness and assert hardness. Gunn's rejection of Stephen Spender and "pale curators" (the poem is a parodic version of Spender's "I Think Continually of Those") seems a bit simplistic, although one can sense his despair at the widely held idea that the homosexual must be a frustrated, gelded man-woman. To that extent

Gunn's call for "disturbing images" could be a call for the revival of the erotic, but the links between the erotic and the violent make his vision suspect. He is responding to the Decadent image of the androgynous self with a new image of the self-contained male.

"Market at Turk" [33] indicates by its title—an allusion to a hustler neighborhood of San Francisco—Gunn's erotic associations. The hustler depicted is ennobled by his description, which places him in the context of ancient warriors: "prepared / for some unique combat in / boots, jeans, and a curious cap." The boots, straps and Marine belt of the hustler's costume are "reminders of the will." His lack of knowledge or awareness does not tarnish his nobility, for he "gestates action," in an image of the force that sets the world in motion. A very similar figure—working-class hero—recurs in Gunn's second volume, in the poem "Black Jackets." [34] Here he is "the red-haired boy who drove a van / In weekday overalls, but, like his friends, / Wore cycle boots and jacket here." He is both erotic—"He stretched out like a cat"— and noble—"with fierce devotion."

Gunn seems to have realized the hopelessness of this ideal and the dead-end lives of those whom he captured in his poems. Perhaps nowhere does he create so effectively his mixed mood of admiration and despair as in the first of his Hogarthian "Modes of Pleasure" [35] poems. The ferocity of his other heroes remains, but it is now somewhat sadly misplaced in the figure of "The Fallen Rake." His very success as rake has been due to his unwillingness to domesticate Eros, to return to Duncan's phrase. He is a master of lovemaking, but not of love, knowing "the sensual skills as skills alone." But Gunn sees him as tragic hero, for he is

> . . . condemned
> To the sharpest passion of them all.
> Rigid he sits: brave, terrible,
> The will awaits its gradual end.

Gunn's admiration of the will, of rigidity, and of pose is both personal and poetic. His poems seem to possess the hardness he admires and to reflect the fierce isolation of the poet. They too are "brave [and] terrible."

In a very controlled poem, "The Beaters," [36] Gunn makes explicit what was only implicit in the motorcyclist poems: his concern with sadomasochism. The beaters are given a nobility of purpose and manner; they too exercise the will, in what Gunn sees as an assertion of self. They choose their own definitions, set limitations; and the forms they use to indicate their sexual tastes—the swastika or the chains—are "emblems to recall identity; / Through violent parables their special care / Is strictly to explore that finitude." The fourth stanza marks a change in the tone of the poem, as Gunn turns from the beaters as they meet and determine their preferences to a view of them after sex, as they are released from their bonds. Gunn sees one loosing the other, lifting him up "with an ultimate gentleness" and realizing

> It was no end, merely extremity.
> They know they shall resume pursuit, elsewhere,
> Of what they would not hold to if they could.

Their cruelty becomes a form of self-exploration and of yearning for death. In the last stanza Gunn leaves his reader with the purely physical, now transformed into a gentleness that replaces words:

> The lips that meet the wound can finally
> Justify nothing—neither pain nor care;
> Tender upon the shoulders ripe with blood.

Gunn's lyrical treatment of the sadomasochist seems to be a way of saying, "this too is love," as he looks for tenderness in the most unexpected places. Perhaps he means to remind his readers of the element of cruelty that forms a part of all lovemaking, and to demand of homosexuals that they not relegate their sadistic or masochistic brothers to the inferno of scorn where once all homosexuals lived.

Gunn is, of course, aware that the homosexual "tough" is a poseur, but that is precisely why he is admired. Gunn's poetry is marked by a concern with style, conceived as definition of self. This idea, so important in contemporary literature, undoubtedly owes a great deal to turn-of-the-century aesthetics, and particularly to Oscar Wilde; but in Gunn's case it may come as well from his interest in Renaissance poetics and mannerism. It is perhaps this which enables him to express the importance of style in art through the figure of a modern rock singer: his poem "Elvis Presley." [37]

The "Elvis" poem is significant because it forms a link between the motorcycle poems and Gunn's concept of style, or, in other words, because it demonstrates the connection between

Gunn's aesthetics and his "erotics." Presley, like the cyclists, is turned into a warrior. He is seen "wielding a guitar" in a "posture for combat." Presley is Gunn's self-defined man, in large part because the scope of his work is narrowly defined—"the limitations where he found success." He is a figure of the man who creates himself, through the medium of style;

> He turns revolt into a style, prolongs
> The impulse to a habit of the time.

To "turn revolt into a style" is, of course, to make art out of life; and Gunn's admiration is given to those who live their lives as a continual work of art, an idea derived in large part from the aesthetic theory of Wilde. The pose is valued over the inconsistencies of reality, because it represents a gathering together of the self, a hardening of life into style. The "truth," or reality, is of little significance: "Whether he poses or is real, no cat / Bothers to say."

The transformation of dull reality into transcendent art is the subject of what is perhaps Gunn's most famous single poem, "Blackie, the Electric Rembrandt." [38] Both Blackie, the tattoo artist, and the tattooed boy are clearly part of Gunn's preferred milieu of the tough and noneffete. Their relationship, in which the boy's body becomes the ground and element of Blackie's art, is subtly eroticized:

> . . . the point
> that touches (quick, dark movement!)
>
> a virginal arm beneath
> his rolled sleeve: he holds his breath.

There is nothing accidental about their relationship; there is "concentration" on both their faces, and Blackie's hand is "steady and accurate." Blackie is the conscious and careful artist, whose art is nonetheless an act of love which can transform the beloved into a work of art (as the poet transforms his erotic impulses into art). The boy who is tattooed, turned into a work of art, is thereby redeemed, as he transcends his own existence: "Now he is starlike."

The anonymous erotic relationship recurs frequently in Gunn's poetry, as it does in the poetry of a number of homosexual artists. Such a relationship may be seen as devoid of feeling or human concern. Or the artist may interpret such a relationship as a way of defending a promiscuity based on the centrality of the ego. The rediscovery of the erotic self, in the absence of an objectified other, may lead toward the poem of masturbation, in which only subjective pleasure is felt. Gunn has two poems in particular which deserve examination in this regard, "Touch," from the volume of the same name,[39] and "The Feel of Hands," from *My Sad Captains*. Both show the indebtedness of Gunn to Whitman.

"Touch" is a delicate lyric about the poet's relationship to an unidentified lover, whose name and gender are not given in the poem. In many homosexual poems, particularly before the last ten years or so, the anonymity of the lover was a strategy of concealment, permitting the homosexual poet to publish love poems in "respectable" places without fear of censorship or scorn, yet still conveying to knowledgeable readers the "truth." In some cases this even led to the argument that the gender of the beloved did not matter, was somehow irrelevant to the "real" poem. In Gunn's poem, however, namelessness and genderlessness are essential to the poem and its view of human relationship. The poet-narrator views his deathlike state with a certain ironic detachment:

> . . . my skin slightly
> numb with the restraint
> of habits, the patina of
> self, the black frost
> of outsideness, so that even
> unclothed it is
> a resilient chilly
> hardness, a superficially
> malleable, dead
> rubbery texture.

At such a point the "you" of the poem can be seen only in vaguest outline as "a mound of bedclothes." But the touch of the two leads to a transformation, as warmth begins to "break down that chill." The "you" of the poem responds without knowledge to an equally anonymous lover, but in this vague touch there is nonetheless hope; a process of "continuous creation" is begun, and in their isolation, their "dark enclosing cocoon," a radical metamorphosis is underway. For that cocoon is also the "dark / wide realm where we / walk with everyone." The individual's discovery of his isolation is a discovery of his common humanity. His butterfly soul will be freed through love. The publication of *Touch* in 1967 marks an important change in Gunn's attitudes. He presents a much more sensitive view of life, in which the abiding recognition is of human isolation and death, and in which love, rather than style, becomes an attempt to defeat death. Gunn puts his point most clearly in the last poem in this volume, "Back to Life," [40] which seems to me a statement of the poet's own return "to life," a declaration of the change that we have witnessed in his poetry, and in particular an acceptance of love and the erotic, life-giving forces. The last stanza employs the running of sap as a metaphor for sexual arousal, and concludes:

> A small full trembling through it now
> As if each leaf were, so, better prepared
> For falling sooner or later separate.

The realization of the post-coital state of isolation and separation can lead to an understanding and acceptance of death, just as Whitman suggests.

The earlier poems reveal much less acceptance and little love. There is even a kind of defiance about them, as in the statement from the second "Modes of Pleasure" poem, [41] "This is a momentary affection." Nonetheless, this poem shows Gunn's need to argue against himself, the first signs of a disintegration of the armor so carefully built up, particularly in the *Sense of Movement* poems. The poses of "Modes of Pleasure" are by now familiar: lust is "dark in his doubtful uniform." The "you" is "apart, contained," and the "I" and the "you" have a "callous glance." The questions of the fifth stanza embody the poet's argument with himself, as he asks "Why should that matter? Why pretend / Love must accompany erection?" The poet feels a need to justify sex without love, and yet seems to have difficulty doing so. It is not until the following volume (*Touch*) that he can write openly about love. "The Feel of Hands," [42] published in the same volume with "Modes of Pleasure," successfully captures the rhythms of love, as exploration turns from light touch to fury, "hunting without scruple." The last stanza depicts the poet alone, "in the dark" (literal and spiritual): "I do not know whose hands they are." The conclusion echoes, in theme and language, section 11 of "Song of Myself":

> The young men float on their backs, their white bellies bulge
> to the sun, they do not ask who seizes fast to them,

They do not know who puffs and declines with pendant and
    bending arch
They do not think whom they souse with spray.

It is perhaps significant to note, however, that Whitman's poem,
unlike Gunn's, ends with ejaculation, just as a comparison of
Whitman's "Is this then a touch?" (sections 28 and 29) with
Gunn's "Touch" reveals the comparative absence of the physical
in Gunn and the extraordinarily erotic imagery of Whitman.
    One way to measure the change that has taken place in Gunn's
poetry is to compare two poems concerned with the same concept
—the dualism of body and soul. The earlier poem, "The Allegory
of the Wolf Boy," [43] clearly accepts the division, while the later
poem or cycle of poems, "Tom-Dobbin," celebrates the moments
of its overcoming. The first stanza of the "Wolf Boy" deals with
the wolf as boy, animality successfully hidden beneath the surfaces
of civilization:

> . . . At tennis and at tea
> Upon the gentle lawn, he is not ours,
> But plays us in a sad duplicity.

Gunn suggests that civilization is repressive and leads to the concealment of our "real" animal natures under a façade of behavior.
The poem may be read as an allegory of the homosexual, who must
hide his animal, "bestial" nature in order to succeed in the world
of tennis and tea. Gunn's early work is a constant defense of the
primitive against the effete, a reaction against a specific public
image of the homosexual. His famous poem "Carnal Knowledge"
discusses the techniques of evasion through its famous play on
knowing: "you know I know you know I know you know" and
admits "even in bed I pose." [44] But his earlier work seems to
suggest countering one pose with another, as the effeminate and
civilized are replaced by the aggressively "masculine" and primitive. "The Wolf Boy" is about breaking out, escape from the bonds
of convention, from the world of reason and understanding, into
"the dark and dust" and the world of "insect lust." The "infertile
light" of the moon which consecrates the world of the werewolf
restores the original self and frees the wolf from his boy-body.
Now he is "only to instinct and the moon . . . bound."
    Gunn returned to this theme in "Tom-Dobbin," which he

subtitles his "centaur poems."[45] Here the formalism of Gunn's earlier work is somewhat relaxed, and he experiments with various shapes of a poem. The first of the five poems in this cycle uses irregular lines and page settings in a way that resembles Duncan's work. It establishes, not the distinctions between body and soul, animal and man, but rather the "imperceptible transition." As the first poem of the cycle makes clear, these poems are concerned with the interrelatedness of apparent opposites (the hair of the man is a "beginning" down—with a pun on that—and the "chestnut brown" of the stallion is also "a beginning upward"), as well as the "instant / passage between the two." The second of the poems more clearly identifies the mode by which the two elements are to be reconciled. Here the rhyming couplets are used for comic effect in this deliberately bawdy poem:

> Hot in his mind, Tom watches Dobbin fuck,
> Watches, and smiles with pleasure, oh what luck.

Tom's pleasure is intellectual, while Dobbin's is physical, but orgasm joins the two: "In coming Tom and Dobbin join to one." The physical and intellectual are joined "only a moment," but it is a moment which transcends all others:

> A shock of whiteness, shooting like a star,
> In which all colours of the spectrum are.

The third and fourth poems of the cycle are depictions of forms of unity, rooted in the natural world, whose perception depends upon the kind of cosmic consciousness announced in the second poem. Here Gunn has again come much closer to Whitman, whose spirit seems to hover over these poems as inspiration and guide. In the third, "he plunges into orgy," the sexual and physical becoming a metaphor for his relationship with the world, as he moves toward a Whitmanic acceptance of the world and joy in its diversity. That acceptance is based upon a radical refusal of the distinction between self and other and a perception of the elements of the created world as "extensions of self." The world as orgy is the world as total body, ultimate and universal polymorphous pleasure, in which one is restored to the child's innocent inability to distinguish between subject and object. Birth is another sign of the inner relationships of things, and the mammal with her child is seen in the fourth poem as "one breaking outline that includes the two." To see the two animals as one is to link past to future, give to take, and mother to son. It is only in the fifth and final poem of the cycle that the meaning of these perceptions becomes clear. The poet imagines himself as a swimmer, moving slowly through a state of semiconsciousness. The surrounding water becomes environment and atmosphere, as lover and loved are united. Their growing loss of individuality and acquisition of universality are marked by their loss of identity in a vague underwater world:

> Gradually closing in, until we enter
> The haze together—which is me, which him?
> Selves floating in the one flesh we are of.

The affirmation manifest in this group of poems is central to understanding the "new" Thom Gunn, who has acquired a faith in the restorative powers of love and sees a possibility for the reconciliation of all opposites in the moment of orgasmic or mystic perception.

Clearly he has not rejected his entire poetic career up to this time, but he has modified his position significantly. One sign of this change is "From the Wave," [46] which is as much an erotic poem to a distant beloved object as the motorcycle poems, but which nonetheless displays an important new sense of harmony with nature. The surfers described in this poem are again emblems of control, suspension, and order: "they poise their weight / With a learn'd skill." But they are not really masters of nature, since they must establish "balance" and must "wait until / The right waves gather." They are dependent upon the very nature they control, and express a harmony which is discovered within the individual rather than one imposed from without by stylistic artifice. Significantly, they are last seen in a playful and waiting mood, in which one senses an almost Romantic concern for the carefree play of boys together. Thom Gunn seems to have come to terms with the world and with himself.

The idea of a continuity between self and world is central to many of Gunn's finest poems from his latest volume, *Jack Straw's Castle*.[47] As he puts it in "Thomas Bewick,"

> he reverts
> to an earlier self, not yet
> separate from what he sees.[48]

Gunn is now striving for a deliberately naive point of view, hence his echo of "There Was a Child Went Forth" as well as his acknowledgment of the influence of Gertrude Stein's *Three Lives*. "The Geysers," [49] his most significant poem to date, shows not only the influence of Whitman but also that of Robert Duncan. Here we are no longer concerned with modes of dress, but rather of undress: "We get up naked as we intend to stay." The final section of the poem depicts "The Bath House," in which knowledge is replaced by feeling, and the search for the ideal lover becomes a submission to the sensations of pleasure. Genders and identities are deliberately mixed, as the narrator reaches a climax that is both the destruction of Pentheus and a moment of orgasmic consciousness, an instant of selflessness. There is a growth toward community and the development of a newer, more androgynous self as, Whitman-like, Gunn writes, "I am part of all."

Edward Field

If Thom Gunn's poems display a slow but certain movement toward a consciousness of the body and a celebration of pleasure, Edward Field's poems take bodily pleasure as their starting point. Field's first volume of poems, *Stand Up, Friend, With Me*, [50] attracted considerable attention and quickly established him as an important poet of the sixties. As Richard Howard pointed out in a perceptive article that will provide the basis for all further criticism of Field's work, [51] the title poem (omitted from the collection) identifies the penis as the friend in question, and establishes the foundation of Field's poetry in an autoerotic and masturbatory vision that is joyfully orgasmic. Field is a pleasure to read because of his pervasive sense of humor, his delight in the things of the world, and his refusal to take himself or others too seriously. His poems are often playful spoofs that come close to being Camp —his second volume, *Variety Photoplays*, [52] must be considered an element of Camp culture—but usually avoid crossing that line by their sense of the holiness of being.

In general Field seems free of overwhelming poetic influences; he is very much his own man, creating his own categories. Nonetheless, if one poet were to be seen as a source of inspiration, it would be, again, Walt Whitman. (It is likely that no homosexual poet can write without a sense of indebtedness to the "Good

Gay Poet.") Whitman's influence may be seen in particular in the natural, simple world that Field admires and which he locates, in *Stand Up, Friend, With Me*, in Greece. The quiet lyric celebrations of male love in Cavafy have contributed as well to Field's "Greek" world. There exists, of course, a rich tradition of homosexual poetry concerned with Greek themes, perhaps inevitably, as it is only in Greece that the homosexual may find a culture in which he might have had a place and whose literature speaks directly to his own sexual experience. Most of the homosexual literature concerned with Greece is, however, unfortunately suffused with the thickest of Romantic sentimentality and expressed in the oldest of clichés. The banal affections of schoolmasters for their pubescent charges seem often to have given rise to an attempt to turn that frustrated and hardly acknowledged eroticism into some kind of Greek ideal. Field, however, is far from that world, even if his choice of Greece as model for the ideal world is determined by his homosexuality. For what remains unsaid in his Greek poems is what is still known as Greek love, and it forms the core of this natural erotic order.

His poem "Donkeys" [53] shows how the Greek landscape can be transformed by Field into a vision of utopian existence that seems out of Freud by way of N. O. Brown. The poem is written in Field's characteristically understated style. There is considerable charm to his almost conversational manner and the laconic way in which he is able to present a scene of considerable pathos. The crying donkeys are of interest to Field because they "never grew up / But stayed children." Like children they know the ideal world and would be capable of creating it, except that they "do not own their bodies." He admires their crying, for it is a sign that they do not passively accept their plight, any more than he wishes men to accept the slavery of adulthood. Let us all become children again, says Field, who "would sit in a field of flowers / Kissing each other." What the donkeys know is what "everyone knows who stays as sweet as children"; they have rejected the work ethic and cannot understand what Field presents ironically as "my wisdom." By the end of the poem Field has masterfully transformed the donkeys into perceptive and joyful children and their masters into asses. In Field's world, animals and children are blessed with a kind of simplicity that permits them to enjoy pleasures that adults cannot. His next poem in this volume, "Goats," [54] concludes in a similar fashion:

> So let us be as joyful as he was
> Eating our goat stew,
> Making the movement of dancing and the noise of singing,
> Taking each others' bodies in our arms
> And then filing simply off to bed.

Pan, the goat-god, is of course somewhere behind this poem, but, as is typical with Field's poems, he does not make too overwhelming an appearance. We do not have to know about Pan in order to sense the world of primitive pleasure. Life is meant to be pleasurable, Field maintains, even (or especially) in light of death—that we all, too, shall wind up as goat stew.

It is strange that none of the poems in this volume deals explicitly with male homosexual love,[55] although Field has included one dealing with two female homosexuals, "Ruth and Naomi."[56] The poem is again simple and playful, with allusions to Field's knowledge of suffering (as in the first two lines: "If one is a Jew who has a history / —Meaning simply to remember and be sad—"). Ruth becomes a Jew through her acquaintance with suffering and her love of Naomi. The poem moves quickly, however, from such allusions, which recur throughout Field's work, to a celebration of the victory of love. The rabbis in the end "loved her, since she was lovable," and

> All of Israel blessed this union
> (Which they had been secretly admiring anyway)
> As Ruth and Naomi, lip to vaginal lip,
> Proclaimed their love throughout the land.

Field's poetry is marked by its romantic sense of joyful discovery, of the glory of the created world, and of an egotism which comes from a reawakening of the self. As Field's "Song" ("as the musician")[57] declares, the poet's art is his penis, an extension of himself by which he can touch and make love to the world. The poet, following directly in the tradition of Whitman, makes love to thousands of readers through the medium of his poem: each poem is an act of love. And, as Field explains in "Prologue,"[58] a poem directly in response to Whitman's "Starting from Paumanok," to love the world is to love oneself, since self and world are coterminous.

Like Whitman, Field calls for us all to undress, confident that in our nakedness (devoid of conventions, of repression, of civilization) we should intuitively know our way. In his poem "Spring"[59] he writes of the reawakening that comes with each spring, opening up before us "three-hundred-and-sixty degrees of possibility." Faced with an infinity of choices civilized man may find himself lost, but

> If I were naked I think my body
> Would know where to go of its own accord.

Without clothing the penis could rise freely and men could follow its lead. The tone of this poem, like that of a number of others, reminds us that Field is sometimes a kind of urban Robert Frost, both in language and in theme (adding, of course, Field's phallic joy).

For all of Field's joy there is also in his poetry a strong sense of the homosexual as other, of his love as strange and impossible, which a number of poems from this first volume illustrate. "Sonny Hugg and the Porcupine"[60] is one of Field's more amusing treatises on loving, using one of his favorite personae, Sonny Hugg. The porcupine is a symbol of impossible love because with his bristles "he couldn't be kissed." His impossible love gives Sonny "impossible dreams." He even thinks of removing the bristles, but realizes that without them the porcupine would no longer be the object of his affection. The first three stanzas function as metaphor for the plight of the homosexual as "impossible" love object; but then in the fourth stanza Field gives the game up, settling not for an impossible lover, but for "those creations / Not quite as darling but with bodies good for hugging."

Field clearly has moments of despair about his homosexuality, expressed particularly in "Poem for the Left Hand,"[61] where he deals with homosexuality as an invisible deformity. When the poet's left hand is removed, he becomes "one of the obviously crippled," but he also realizes that he has "been one of them for as long as I can remember." The poet comes to terms with his "deformity"—his homosexuality—through his realization that it is better to make the deformity clear than to conceal it. The recognition and public acknowledgment of homosexuality are seen as part of a process of liberation. In the second stanza the poet defends his own existence and announces his decision no longer to apologize:

> . . . Something is wrong with people

Who say it's me that's wrong, my nature needs changing.
Our nature is god's various will
And each oddity precious for the evolving animal kingdom.

A similar self-acceptance is presented in Field's poem "It,"
from *Variety Photoplays*.[62] The "it" in question is, of course, the
penis, and Field's poem is an account of his discovery of his penis
as a boy and his acceptance of it years later. Field dramatizes the
mechanisms of guilt and shame: "What do you do with stuff when
it spurts out?" and "nowhere to hide." His desire for masturbation—"the terrible act I couldn't help doing"—is overwhelmed
by the desire to conceal his secret and his fear of dreadful consequences:

You must control yourself, I ordered desperately,
or your life will be ruined like it says in the handbook.

But he cannot control his masturbation or conceal his penis, any
more than he can control his sexuality or conceal his homosexuality. The attempt to "destroy it," to eliminate the penis, becomes
an attempt to destroy himself. The poem concludes with the poet's
realization, presented in the simplest terms, of the need to accept
himself. Once liberated he finds it hard to imagine how he could
have so fully refused himself:

Only now, after years of struggle,
I face the simple facts of nature
And think how useless to have suffered.

It is interesting to contrast this poem on masturbation with Gunn's
"Courage: A Tale" (from *Jack Straw's Castle*); Gunn's tone is light
and witty, Field's didactic.

Field praises those who do not attempt to destroy themselves,
who assert their sexuality in the face of a priggish and disapproving
world. This is the subject of his "Graffiti."[63] Field grants his
"blessings" to the "bright-eyed kids" who are still in the polymorphous paradise of childhood, and who reflect their glorious
state of sexuality through their "defacing" of the subway signs,
which Field accurately sees as improving them. The kids do not
accept the bland, sterile world of American advertising, nor the
imposed asexuality of the bodies depicted on the billboards. They
restore sexuality to an asexual world, by seeing the truth beneath
the surface. Boobies, cunt, prick, and balls—these are the forbid-

den words as well as the forbidden images, and the graffiti-drawing kids have not yet accepted the sexual taboos of respectable adulthood, the "winter that will freeze them forever." He is aware that most of them will grow up, forget their dreams, and become disapproving respectable citizens. For the moment, however, they are children, and on their passage into the world they leave behind a work of art: "a wall scrawled all over with flowers / That shoot great drops of gism through the sky."

Field's faith in the redeeming power of love, even in this most fallen world, is presented in "Giant Pacific Octopus." [64] The octopus is the poet's lover, a metaphor again for the apparently unlovable. But his many arms are also figures of a world in which touch is restored, feeling is everywhere, and one's whole body is a field of pleasure. To make love to an octopus is like making love to four men; thus the poem is a vision of a radically restored sexual and sensual utopia. The lover's vision transforms the octopus:

> and I kiss him and make him into a boy
> as all giant pacific octopuses are really
> when you take them into your arms

But he does not turn love into possession, nor try to live in an undefined future. Aware of the possible transitoriness of their relationship, he merely rejoices in its moments:

> for as long as he will stay, one night or a lifetime,
> for as long as god will let you have him.

Although Field's poetry is highly sentimental and seems not to have grown beyond the world of the 1960s, his best work is redeemed by his sense of comedy. He revels in the absurdities of our lives, just as he enjoys humorous manipulations of language. One of his funniest poems is surely the "Ode to Fidel Castro," [65] which begins with the classic invocation to the Muse, seen here as "Boy God, Muse of Poets." Castro is depicted in his various roles: as Latin sex object (his picture next to Rudolph Valentino's), as idealistic social reformer, as statesman and politician, and as Camp hero. Field proposes sex as an answer to politics:

> Perhaps the only thing to do is to look upon each other
> As two men look when they meet solitary in the deep woods
> Come black man let us jerk off together
> Like boys do to get to know each other.

He recognizes Castro's imperfections (not the least of which are the Cuban government's ruthlessly antihomosexual policies), but he sees the Cuban leader through the poet's eyes—"It's your spirit we love and the glamour of your style"—and dreams of the day when the poet's kiss will replace Krushchev's:

> A kiss of the poet that will make you truly good
> The way you meant to be.

Fidel Castro, like all of Field's Camp heroes, is a little bit of ourselves, gaining by his freedom from convention the possibility for self-expression and narcissism, as Richard Howard puts it. We love our heroes because they offer the tiniest hope of escape from our dull world of repression and boredom.

Richard Howard

Richard Howard came to poetic maturity with his discovery of the form that he has made his own, a variation on the Browningesque dramatic monologue. His last three volumes have successfully made use of this form, which he is continuing to modify and develop. It has permitted Howard to exercise his extraordinary mimetic talent, and to bring poetry to the boundaries of drama. The monologue, in its various incarnations, offers a presentation of self (or, if one prefers, a dramatization of self) which appears to be revelation of truth. For Howard, as for Wilde (to whom he owes so much), the truth is only the most complicated of masks; all selves are created, which is to say fictive. He makes use of his poetic fictions as part of the presentation of himself. The words of Browning, cited in the Dedication of *Untitled Subjects*, serve as an introduction to Howard's monologues: "I'll tell my state as though 'twere none of mine."

One of the monologues of that volume, "1889," [66] is written by an exiled English homosexual to Robert Ross, the friend of Oscar Wilde. It evokes the sad milieu of wealthy English homosexuals at the end of the nineteenth century, lonely, homeless, and pretentious, finding solace only in the purchased affections of young boys. The speaker bears a certain resemblance to Lord Alfred Douglas, Wilde's embittered and volatile lover, but he is not to be identified with anyone in particular; he stands for a class of men. (Likewise, the dating of the poem is not to be taken too seriously. Havelock Ellis, whose research for *Sexual Inversion* is mentioned, did not actually begin work on that book until about 1892.)[67] Howard wittily evokes all the mannerisms we recognize as part of the fin-de-siècle world of Camp that set the tone of homosexual discourse until recently; his speaker, with a little of Fr. Rolfe in him, comments:

> I confess,
> myself, to a Chinese sort of love for red—
>   the very names, vermillion, scarlet,
> warm me, and to dress in floating crimson silk
>   I half understand
> being a Cardinal, a woman wholly . . .

But Howard also makes us see the queen's grand manners as defenses against the recognition of self. His constant search for love with Pippo and his friends is an urgent denial of his own loneliness and isolation. As the speaker declares, "We are all and everlastingly / alone." He is unable to become a participant in love, settling for the purchased charms of boys. His defiant maleness prevents him from returning the affection he craves. Howard makes use of the tradition of late nineteenth-century homosexual artists —there has rarely been a time when so many of the greatest talents have been homosexual—but although his monologues in part continue that tradition, they also depict its inner stresses and the forces that will lead to its destruction.

It is quite natural, therefore, that Howard's next book should have been *Two-Part Inventions*.[68] In the majority of these poems there are two speakers, a confrontation of two voices. These voices point up the central conflict in Howard's art: the need to allow for the erotic core of art, while keeping it in balance with the necessary artifice and control. Three of the six poems explicitly deal with homosexuality, but all recognize the sexual sources of art. One of the most delightful is Howard's imagined encounter[69] between Wilde and Whitman (a meeting that actually took place).[70] The two define the possibilities of homosexual art in the nineteenth century: Whitman's homely verse of self-declaration and Wilde's elaborate metaphors for the masks of self-concealment. Their coming together in the poem represents Howard's confrontation with his own possibilities and his own past. The question is, how to reconcile Wilde and Whitman—on the one hand the voice which declares, "I want only Form," on the other the voice which declares,

"I keep nothing together." For Howard, the encounter between Wilde and Whitman must lead Wilde to reconsider his position as aesthete. Whitman, for all his commonness, must reveal the truth of the sources of art, the reason why *Leaves of Grass*, with all its flaws, is ten times greater than Wilde's poems:

> Without the boys—if it had not been for the boys
> I never would have had the *Leaves*,
> the consummated
> book, the last confirming word.

Howard's pun on "consummated," accentuated by the line break, is crucial. Whitman's art is "consummated," a fulfilled sexuality; by acts of love he consummates his book, in a way the deceits of Wilde do not permit (the poem is set in 1882). Howard clearly instructs us that Wilde will learn from the experience, although the only poem to reflect his learning will come "from a deeper place than these," by which Howard means us to think of the "Ballad of Reading Gaol," or perhaps even *De Profundis*. Thus Howard offers the reader an interpretation of the two writers through his "invention." He asserts the central significance for Whitman of the "Calamus" poems and of the "boys," while suggesting that in Whitman's old age he grew cautious. In Wilde's case, he asserts Wilde's failure to understand the importance of his own sexual nature, his need to come to terms with his homosexuality and to supply to his art a vivid truthfulness that was strikingly absent from the early poems. But one must not read Howard as if he were merely proposing criticism in verse; his accomplishment is to have provided voices for his subjects, and so to have dramatized the inner, intellectual conflict. Each of his "inventions" is both a historical tableau and a scene from Howard's own inner life.

"The Lesson of the Master" [71] is an amusing scene drawn from the homosexual circle around Edith Wharton and Henry James. It depicts Wharton the day of "Gerald Mackenzie's" funeral, as she drives to Versailles with his ashes, accompanied by "Gerald Roseman." Roseman reveals to Wharton the homosexuality of her friend, a fact she has managed to suppress from her consciousness for a long time, as the historical Edith Wharton seems to have done with her friends. Howard questions the effect such repression may have had on the lives of all concerned: Gerald "must have had a Great Barrier Reef / of the soul, and behind it he kept / his heart." Howard is concerned with the radical split such men have

established in their lives between affection and desire; Wharton,
who has known his affection, and Roseman, who has known his
desire, come together in a brief moment, which represents the
center that might have been—love. The entire delicious scene
has been arranged by Henry James, who, Howard imagines, delights in picturing the effect of this confrontation on his two
friends. But they have the final turn of the screw: they reserve
silence for Mr. James. It is a marvelous *tour de force* by Howard.

In "Contra Naturam" [72] (the title is Latin for the "sin" of
homosexuality) a similar confrontation occurs, this time between
Rodin and an unnamed fellow-traveler. The traveler asserts his
indebtedness to Rodin: "You have been, from the first, the inspiration / of us all." But the traveler's frankness about his homosexuality embarrasses Rodin, who denies any kinship:

> Why must you add me to your lineage?
> Surely my line of descent is clear, from
> Praxiteles to Michelangelo
> and then Rodin. I have no part in yours . . .

Despite this disclaimer, the traveler insists, claiming to recognize
a "fellow-traveller" (that is Howard's joke, of course) in Rodin.
He insists upon the close relationship between the ecstatic vision
of art and that of sexuality. When he sees a young boy in a bath,

> . . . it is neither Jacques nor Jean
> I look at, once they are naked before me,
>   but Endymion
> who stands, momentarily illuminated
>   in a clearing . . .

His insistence forces Rodin to recall the (historically based) episode
when a furiously jealous Diaghilev found Nijinsky and Rodin lying together and denounced Rodin as a "pédéraste." The incident
is the sort of delightful gossip that Howard often makes use of,
but it is also an occasion for Rodin to reveal himself, as he thinks
back longingly on that moment of congruence, "the identity of the
evanescent / with the enduring." Art is imagined as the attempt
to prolong Nijinsky's wittily portrayed erection: sculpture freezes
movement and preserves it from time. Just so the pederast undertakes a lifelong quest to preserve the fleeting moment of perfect
beauty, between childhood and adulthood. But Rodin rejects what
he himself recognizes; a tired man, moving toward death, he can

only express his own fears: "Ecstasy is always a danger." His fellow-traveler accuses him, however, of "the supreme transgression of failing / to appreciate" himself. Rodin, while creating a body of art visibly inspired by an ecstatic appreciation of male beauty, finally betrays the sources of his art, out of fear. The inner conflict portrayed here is not merely between heterosexuality and homosexuality, but between classic and romantic. Throughout his work, Howard affirms the failure of an art that is not romantic, that denies its own sensual energy, while at the same time recognizing the claims of classic control, without which the inspiration would remain only a moment of sexual encounter and never be transformed into a permanent work of art. While the traveler is "right," in that his avowal of his tastes is more honest, it is hard to accept that his vision of Endymion in a steam bath is a greater accomplishment than Rodin's vision of Endymion in Nijinsky and his transformation of that vision into a work of art.

For Howard more than almost any other modern artist, it is important to define a line of descent. A major figure in the contemporary scene both as poet and as critic, Howard has nonetheless insisted upon the poet's relationship to the past. The clearest evidence of this desire to understand the present through the past may be his volume, *Preferences*,[73] for which he asked fifty-one contemporary poets to choose their "preference," an older poem of special meaning to them. The modern texts help us read the past, as the older texts help us read the present. This is precisely the sort of dynamic relationship which Howard believes exists between two works of art. The concept owes something to the critical theory of intertextuality advanced by the *Tel Quel* critics (and no one knows more about modern French criticism than Howard), but it owes more to Howard's belief in a deep sense of sympathy, what he calls, in the title of his latest volume, *Fellow Feelings*.[74]

For Howard, the Muse is *les autres*, those artists who have gone before and who in their work have created a form of permanent inspiration. The job of an artist *now* is to define his relationship to an artist *then*, and to create a living bond between them. Like Pater's Denys, cowled and leaning over medieval illuminators, the past is present, in "visible sympathy" with the artist in the process of creation, and no art is new, but merely renewed. *Fellow Feelings* are records of the moments when one realizes sympathy—when one knows what one feels for one's fellow artist, and he has really become one's own. The confrontation here is not be-

tween two historical figures, but between Howard and another artist; and the moment of recognition is the moment of realizing
what is shared.

"Decades," [75] a cycle of five poems for Hart Crane placed
first in the collection, is concerned with fatherhood and treats bril-
liantly the poet's relationship with his poetic fathers.

Section 4, "Sands Street Bar & Grille," for instance, evokes
Crane's barroom "Cutty Sark," with its own treatment of Crane's
literary paternity. Crane's poem is steeped in Melville and strives
to give form to Crane's own feelings for the earlier artist, as poet
of the sea, explorer of the unconscious, "diver," and would-be
lover. In the same way Howard takes off from "Cutty Sark," leads
us both backward and forward through *The Bridge*, from the Proem
"under thy shadow," through Crane's acknowledgement of Whitman in "Cape Hatteras," to the River and Harbor of the city
viewed from the other side of the Tunnel, and deftly carries us
back to Crane's celebrated elegy "At Melville's Tomb" as well as
his beautiful "Praise for an Urn." Howard asks,

> . . . What did you learn,
> steeped in the great green teacher of the gradual,
> when all you knew was sudden, a genius in need
> of a little more talent, a poet not by grace
> but the violence of good works?

Knowledge is sudden, learning gradual. What Crane learned in his
descent was presumably what he believed Melville's Pip learned,
or Poe's Pym: the need to discover oneself in the darkness, to come
face to face with the unthinkable and the unseeable. The way down
is the way back, a journey that leads always to death, eternally
feared and eternally yearned for.

The last section of *Decades* represents Howard's coming to
terms with his albatross, Crane. We all finally accept our fathers
or invent them. As Howard puts it,

> I press your poems as if they were Wild Flowers
> for a sidelong grammar of paternity.
> We join the Fathers after all, Hart, rejoin
> not to repel or repeal or destroy, but to fuse,
> as Walt declared it: wisdom of the shores,
> easy to conceive of, hard to come by, to choose
> our fathers and to make our history.

A poet like Crane represents a difficult paternity for Howard. Crane's occasional vulgarity, his lewdness, his ceaseless adolescence must grate on this more polished surface. And yet Howard cannot and will not extricate himself from the burdens of High Romanticism evoked in this poem: Poe, Melville, Coleridge, the high priests of madness and excess. His work, controlled as it is, must come to terms with its demons as much as, or more than, its more exuberant brothers. And, too, Howard must acknowledge Crane's place in the tradition of homosexual poetry, just as Crane had to acknowledge his masters, Melville and Whitman. Acknowledging one's father is a way of acknowledging oneself, and the work of art is a record of such discoveries of self, in others:

> Why write unless you praise the sacred places, encounters
> when something is given over, something taken as well?

The point made by Howard and attributed to Whitman is essential: the poet's relationship to his fathers is not one of violence and hatred, *pace* Freud. For Howard, Crane's poems are pressed like flowers, for they are love-tokens. Whether the poets are contemporaries like Whitman and Wilde, or the older poet is dead when the younger is four (Crane and Howard), their meeting is one of love and fraternity. Howard's metaphor for vision is sexual and religious; it is a descent of the Spirit, a sacred rape. Howard emphasizes rightly the element of choice implicit in the poet's relationship to the past. He invents, or finds, his fathers, just as he chooses his lovers; and the history of those he chooses is the history of his construction of self. To finally know our fathers is to finally know ourselves.

James Merrill

People sometimes speak of what they call a "gay sensibility." They usually mean a particular elegance, a sensitivity to the surfaces of things, a taste for order, and an ironic distance between the self and the world. The roots of this attitude are in the 1890s, with the writers of the Aesthetic tradition. While, as Susan Sontag pointed out in her essay on Camp,[76] such attitudes are not necessarily homosexual, they are particularly attractive to homosexuals and have formed the basis of what may be called the gay subculture, particularly in the eastern United States, until very recently.

James Merrill is the most brilliant contemporary artist identified with this sensibility. While the space available here in no way allows for a full examination of Merrill's impressive body of work, it is worth looking at least briefly at the ways in which Merrill's work has reflected the change in social attitudes toward homosexuality. Merrill's early work always assumed and implied his homosexuality but did not state it. It was taken for granted that those who knew would know. The sense of shared readership was created by a body of taste rather than by any presumed sexual preference. Merrill, that is, wrote for those who cared about opera, porcelain, Oriental art—subjects which have, among American men at least, tended to have a homosexual audience.

It should not be thought that Merrill's taste for the objects of haut-bourgeois culture implies a thoughtless acceptance of America's industrial society. On the contrary, Merrill has consistently been a witty satirist, as in these lines from "Days of 1935" [77] (the title of the poem recalls any number of poems by Cavafy entitled "Days of . . ." celebrating a lover):

> Tel & Tel executives
> Heads of Cellophane or Tin,
> With their animated wives
> Are due on the 6:10.

It is precisely, in fact, Merrill's commitment to the values of art that enables him to reject the mindless vulgarities of a plutocratic society. The entire poem is a wonderful example of Merrill as Camp writer, recalling as it does a childhood dream, inspired by the Lindbergh case, of being kidnapped and held for ransom. The kidnappers, Floyd and Jean, represent for the child-narrator an exciting new world far from the calm regularities of suburban life. The three inhabit a never-never land of the erotic; he observes their "prone tango," and later Floyd comes to sleep with him while he feels the gangster's "nipple's tender fault." The dream comes to an abrupt end, as the child imagines their arrest and trial, realizing with horror his own betrayal: "You I adored I now accuse . . ." But awakening brings back a world emptier by far, whose mundane life can know nothing of the world of art, the dream world that in Merrill is always part fairy tale, part erotic fantasy, and all guilty desire. The poem is a celebration of the forbidden; and as the tradition of Camp (and psychoanalysis) insists, its desirability is directly related to its interdiction. "Days of 1935" seems to

offer homosexuality as a way of combating the father, the assertion of a permanent childhood world of pleasure against an adult
world of duty.

The relationship to the past, particularly to the family, is an
important, almost obsessive, subject in Merrill's work. Merrill is
constantly working out the difficult balance between the personal
self and what we might call the historical self. "The Friend of the
Fourth Decade," from *The Fire Screen*,[78] is an interesting record
of one meditation upon the self. The poem has the ironic under-
cuttings of the Camp style, but it also begins to look toward a
stripping down of these defenses. The "friend" of the poem, in a
very funny moment, declares:

> I'm tired of understanding
> The light in people's eyes, the smells, the food.
>
> (By the way, those veal birds were delicious.
> They're out of Fannie Farmer? I thought so.)

We are warned not to take his taste for simplicity too seriously
(in any case he tells us, "I *despise* Thoreau!"). Still, the confrontation with the friend is something of a confrontation with self;
the poet is struck by his friend's determination to rid himself of
language ("I mean to learn, in the language of where I am going, /
Barely enough to ask for food and love") as well as the past (represented by the postcards he soaks in water to remove their stamps,
thereby leaving only the image "rinsed of the word"). The poet
attempts to do the same with his mother's postcards, but "her
message remained legible." "Certain things," he writes, "die only
with oneself." Although the friend achieves an identity of "individual and type," the poet remains fixed in his world of indelible
memories, unable to relinquish the civilization that he knows both
nourishes and maims him. The last section of the poem is a dream,
in which the poet sees his friend divested of "his whole civilization" and finally confronted with his naked self:

> See his eyes darken in bewilderment—
>
> No, in joy—and his lips part
> To greet the perfect stranger.

The ambiguities of that last line are central to Merrill's own reaction to the problems he has posed: the conventional "perfect strang-

er" is also a *perfected* stranger and, of course, the Stranger, Death.
What would we be without the "swaddlings" which surround us?
Merrill asks. While tempted by his alter ego to seek the answer,
he also fears that we, like the mummy released from its grave-
clothing, will not survive our exposure to the elements.

Characteristically, Merrill's view of this is double. The fire
screen, which gives its name to this collection, was made by his
mother, and depicts *her* mother's house (there is no escaping history!); it is designed to protect the family from the fire. But in a
footnote to the poem Merrill refers to this interpretation, given
by the poem itself, as "the obvious," and suggests instead that
the fire screen be read as the "screen *of* fire," alluding to Wagner's
Ring. By leaving the poem unchanged and adding the note, Merrill leaves the question neatly balanced. One cannot imagine that
this apparent indecision is less than intentional; it would be odd
for a poet to name a collection of poems after an image that he
had somehow misinterpreted. As Merrill wryly comments in his
note, "Our white heat leads us on no less than words do. Both
have been devices in their day." [79]

The same volume contains a delightful love poem, "To My
Greek," [80] which suggests that the implications of "The Friend
of the Fourth Decade" are taken somewhat more seriously by the
poet than that poem would indicate. In the joy of this love, the
poet lives in a triumphant present: "Let past and future / Perish
upon our lips, ocean inherit / Those paper millions." Language
is no longer seen as puzzle, but as vibrant surface and sensual tex-
ture. In a wonderful section, inspired by Wallace Stevens (the
greatest single poetic influence on Merrill's work), he exclaims:

> Let there be no word
> For justice, grief, convention; *you* be convention—
> Goods, bads, kaló-kakó, cockatoo-raucous
>
> Coastline of white printless coves
>
> Already strewn with offbeat echolalia.
> Forbidden Salt Kiss Wardrobe Foot Cloud Peach
> —Name it, my chin drips sugar.

The relationship with the "Greek" brings Merrill to divest himself
and discover a primitive pleasure in things, a sheer sensual delight.
The lovers, prevented by language from transforming the physical

relationship into an intellectual one, preserve the intensity of their desire. Their communication transcends language; as Merrill puts it,

> Come put the verb-wheel down
> And kiss my mouth despite the foot in it.

This is still Camp, of course; but something very different is taking place in Merrill. For the object of irony is the poet himself, and there is nothing arch about his admiration for this Greek. The poem records Merrill's acceptance of love as a powerful force, one which is heightened by its associations with ancient Greece (and perhaps by the distance from America), and which is not merely dream but reality. The final lines of the poem echo Crane's "Voyages" I, in order to respond to that warning with a new poem of acceptance:

> Let schoolboys brave her shallows. Sheer
>
> Lilting azure float them well above
> Those depths the surfacer
> Lives, when he does, alone to sound and sound.

These lines are recognizably Merrill's, in their extraordinary verbal play and command of meaning and sound. But they also announce an attitude that one does not usually associate with the early Merril. While no one will ever mistake Merrill for a primitivist, one can recognize the poet's discovery, through an encounter with a beloved Greek, of the possibility of a joy that rises above language.

Not that such love can be realized between unequals only. A later poem, from *Braving the Elements*, the first book to announce the "new" Merrill, records a very American experience—two lovers go on an expedition into the country. "In Nine Sleep Valley," [81] like "To My Greek," relies in part upon echoes from Hart Crane. In this case the echoes are of *The Bridge*, both "The River" and "The Dance," sections in which Crane evokes and celebrates the American landscape, and "Atlantis," Crane's triumphant "paradise regained," as well as "Voyages" II. [82] In section 7, for example, Merrill speaks to his lover:

> I want to show you how the clumsiest love
> Transfigures if you let it, if you dare.
>
> There was a day when beauty, death, and love
> Were coiled together in one crowning glory.

> Shears in hand, we parted the dark waves . . .
> Look at me, dear one. There.

The third and fourth lines quoted here echo the following lines from "Voyages,"

> Hasten, while they are true,—sleep, death, desire,
> Close round one instant in one floating flower.

Crane is invoked here because his love poem gives strength to Merrill for the creation of his own. Crane's poem is a magnificent testimony to the power of love, even when clumsy, to "transfigure" the lovers; while Crane's life seems to illustrate the difficulty that so many of those he loved had in "daring" to let love work that transformation. Merrill's poem reminds us that it is sometimes more difficult to be loved than to love. The poem is his love-offering, his flawed "flower." As his last line declares, "accepting them's the art."

The eighth section of the poem is an interesting meditation upon separation. It draws upon the same Platonic theory which we have seen to be an important source for many of the poets considered here, the view that the homosexual man is a twin, half of an original male whole. Merrill treats the subject with his usual elegance and wit; for him that original whole is represented by the geode formed by nature and "then cloven in two / By the taciturn rock shop man, twins now forever." But minerals, he suspects, unlike men, do not yearn for completion:

> Enough for them was a feast
> Of flaws, the molten start and glacial sleep,
> The parting kiss.

In the end, we see, Merrill's American setting for his poem was no accident. If America is a "botched country," it has nonetheless had a dream of perfection (as suggested by the mention of the murders of Robert Kennedy and Martin Luther King in section 2). The American Beauty rose of the poem is both the land and the individual beloved, but Merrill's lesson is that nature can finally be loved only in its specifics, not in general. The difficulty for America has always been in accepting nature on its own terms, and Merrill sees in that dilemma an instance of the universal search for love. His men, unlike James Dickey's, return to the wilderness, not to rape and be raped, but to cry out with Faust, "Ah stay! Thou art so fair!" In his own way, and probably quite without intending it, Merrill returns to Whitman's view that only in the rediscovery of the warp of American life, only in adhesive love, can the American democratic dream be realized.

Alfred Corn

Alfred Corn is the most talented of the poets of his generation (he is now in his thirties) writing in America. His first volume of poems, *All Roads at Once*,[83] was considered by Harold Bloom the most distinguished first book of poems since Crane's *White Buildings*. The recent appearance of his second volume, *A Call in the Midst of the Crowd*,[84] confirms the promise of the first, particularly in the masterful title poem—a long piece in four parts on New York City, firmly established in the tradition that begins with "Crossing Brooklyn Ferry" and *The Bridge*. Although the poem bears obvious comparison to *Paterson*, it is a far more accomplished and satisfying work.

One of the most interesting poems in the first collection is "To Bunny, Remembering Those Days."[85] Two twelve-line stanzas compose an intense meditation upon time and love. The first stanza recalls a past love, its "first new days" in Union Square. Those days are part of a new world, a world created by the birth of love, as Corn's astonishing opening makes clear: "In the beginning there were the open air / lunches." The word is indeed made flesh. Corn wittily plays with his scene: as the lovers lunch, they are "sandwiched together on a bench," and they "digest" their days together. But their sacred meal also takes place under a sign, the emblem of the square, "a weathered relief of immortal workers." The political significance of that symbol is then undercut, as Corn imaginatively transforms the scene of the workers to "some ideal / symposium in Socratic Greece." The idealization of these Art Deco male bodies becomes a bridge to another past, and other familiar spirits are invoked. The *déjeuner sur l'herbe* is now under the protection of *The Symposium*, with it promise of ascending love. The final lines complete the scene, evoking "courting pigeons" who provide a neat counterpart to the courting Socratic lovers. In a wonderful conceit the pigeons are seen "hissing like little pewter teapots," both completing the lunchtime associations of the first stanza and looking toward the developments of the second. Finally, the significance of the "square" is subtly altered by the final line's "hexagonals," suggesting a pattern that is increasingly complex.

In the second stanza the poet speaks from a point of view in the present, the "now" of line 2, and looks both backward and forward. The trade union implied by Union Square has now become a distinctly personal one—"our odd, problematic union." And the square remains a hexagon, with "neat matchings" and "funny / non-congruences." The deliberate ellipsis at the precise middle of the second stanza marks a turn from the poet's meditation upon a relationship to an image of it, which seems to rise out of the mists of memory—"seen as through a vapor of steam." The process of memory depicted here, skillfully prepared for by the teapots of line 10, seems directly influenced by Proust's celebrated madeleine. Specific images of the past are preserved intact and may be called up by the mind. They seem part of the "green frieze," the oxidized monument of "immortal workers," a perfect figure for the poem's situation both within and outside time. The frieze with its echoes of Keats' Grecian Urn is a symbol of eternal love as quest; its greenness carries both ecclesiastical associations of hope and physical suggestions of the ways in which time can transform even what appears to be most permanent. The poem's final image is deliberately unresolved, as befits such a dream-poem:

> two figures leaning together,
> leaning toward some form of the future.

While no "form" is determined for that future, it is significant that the figures lean together. Although this poem is in some sense informed by its Keatsian model, it does not offer a figure of perpetual nonconsummation. Instead it returns implicitly to the suggestions of the first stanza. These lovers are to be seen not as seeker and sought, but as comrades (in both the Marxist and Whitmanic senses). Union Square can preside over their union, since it provides a model of love as sharing, a figure of men together, an adhesive union of equals in a Socratic world that draws as much upon hopes for the future as memories of the past.

Another poem, "The Bridge, Palm Sunday, 1973,"[86] inscribes Corn directly in the tradition of Whitman and Crane, and thus looks forward to *A Call in the Midst of the Crowd*. Corn's title would seem to suggest a random notation of time and place, in the manner of a casual "New York School" poem.[87] His epigraph, however, makes it clear that there is nothing random about the

place; the specificity of reference serves only as an ironic counter-
point to the triumph over time and place. The epigraph is line 20
of "Crossing Brooklyn Ferry," which it is useful to cite in its full
context:

> It avails not, time nor place—distance avails not,
> I am with you, you men and women of a generation, or ever
>   so many generations hence,
> Just as you feel when you look on the river and sky, so I felt

Whitman's words promise a continuity which vanquishes time,
and enable Corn to call upon the elder poet as guide and mentor.
At the same time, since Corn is crossing not the ferry but the
bridge, he must also call upon Crane. As in Whitman's poems, the
"you" of Corn's poem is deliberately left unclear. At some points
he seems to be calling upon a friend or lover, as in stanza 4. But,
given the epigraph, the "brother" and "old buddy" of the first
stanza would seem to refer to Whitman himself. It is he who joins
the younger poet in his pilgrimage to Crane's apartment overlook-
ing the bridge; the three—Corn, Crane, and Whitman—are
joined by bonds that both affirm and deny history.

The relationship between the artist of the past and the artist
of the present is a crucial one; it is wittily construed by Corn's
opening lines:

> The bridge was a huge sentence diagram,
> You and I the compound subject, moving
> Toward the verb.

All subjects (that is, subjective consciousness) may be said to be
compound, as all are composed not merely of the present self but of
those selves that have gone before (one thinks of Richard Howard's
"fellow feelings" and James Merrill's "secular guardian angels" [88]
as parallels). It is through these compoundings that one can discover "the verb," that is, find the strength that will create an artistic record of experience. Corn's poem mixes an act of brotherhood
("I put my arm on your shoulder") with a recognition of the universality of death. Even the conventional symbols of Christian faith
in Resurrection—the hatching Easter eggs—are but reminders of
death, for they are merely "feathered skeletons." Thus the bridge
becomes an emblem of the journey of life, from birth to death (and
back?). Corn's poem is in effect a reading of the two poems which

give birth to his, recalling Crane's need to build upon Whitman and so escape the dangers of the bedlamite, who recurs here as a reminder of Crane's Proem. The "sentence" of the first line is revealed to be a pun, suggesting both a verbal structure and a judgment. The unity perceived by Whitman in his passage across the river comes from a recognition of the evanescence of life— "glories strung like beads"—and the universality of death.

Corn's attitude toward Crane is complex. *The Bridge* is for Corn "grand enough to inspire disbelief and to suspend it." If Crane's masterwork requires our suspension of disbelief, it also achieves the leap of faith through quite another suspension—the suspension bridge. Corn accepts Crane's trope, recognizing that his visionary genius lies in the conception, and that like all visionaries Crane requires completion by those who follow. Thus Corn places himself in that great American visionary line of descent from Whitman to Crane, and takes his place as the final reader, that is to say, the fulfiller of their destinies. Poetic truth consists in relationships which are, to use Howard's term, "invented"— Corn's is the more Romantic "imagined":

> The truth may lie in imagining a connection
> With him or with you; with anyone able to overlook
> Distance, shrug off time, on the right occasion . . .

Corn's extraordinary power comes from his ability to combine a colloquial and relaxed voice with a celebration that is intense and ecstatic. The tone is derived in part from Auden; but the matter is in the great Romantic tradition, and the union of the two is exceptionally felicitous.

Although he can conceive total vision or total transcendence, Corn cannot assert it. The end is a Platonic perception of ecstatic unity: "an acute perfect convergence." But the last lines are phrased as questions, recording the poet's yearning for vision rather than the vision itself. The conditional "would" implies the distance yet to be traversed, as well as a grain of doubt as to the possibility of achieving that crossing, except as an act which is imagined, which is to say willed. Corn remains a skeptical visionary, in the sense intended by Harold Bloom when he says of Keats, "He felt the imagination's desire for a revelation that would redeem the inadequacies of our condition but he felt also a humorous skepticism toward such desire." [89] As Corn puts it in another poem, "[Corot] perfected the world; but I resist / And will not see symmetry if none is / There." [90] Corn remains acutely aware of the distance between the ideal and the real, a distance rendered more painful by our ability to conceive the ideal and even to obtain a momentary glimpse of it. Still, the final lines of Corn's "Bridge" ask for an affirmation of love, Forster's "connection," as a means, indeed *the* means, of overcoming the isolation of the self:

> Would a new sentence be pronounced, a living connection
> Between island and island, for a second, be made?

Upon what does this conditional rest? Corn's answer is clear: "If I called him a brother—help me with this, Hart—" Corn echoes Crane's appeal to "Walt" in "Cape Hatteras" and thus asserts the power of brotherhood, of fraternal love, to act as a force toward the redemption of experience and the rebirth of a fallen world. If Corn records, in Anthony Hecht's words, "the filth, confusion, and steeliness of urban life," [91] he also records, as did Whitman and Crane before him, the moments of vision (Whitman's "sparkles") which transform it, and identifies those moments with the possibility of shared love.

The most important of the poems in *All Roads at Once* is "Pages from a Voyage," [92] which looks forward to the remarkable accomplishment of the title poem of Corn's second volume. The poem is structured around a reading of Darwin's *Voyage of the Beagle*, and weaves together the poet's reflections as he recuperates from an illness, with his observations of the world around him and fragments of texts drawn from Darwin and from Melville's "Encantadas." It records a spiritual passage, the survival of a winter of discontent through the realization of the joys of discovery, the attempt to catch a fleeting moment of time and hold it. Corn records this desire of the artist to capture experience by knowing or seeing so precisely, that a world indeed seems to come alive within his hands:

> So many minds to become, events that might be
> Beheld, the heart of matter through which a conditional
> World springs colored, solid; seizes there.

Although it is Darwin's *Beagle* which is explicitly evoked, his *Origin of Species* is also a major source for Corn's poem, suggesting as it does the twin questions of origin and survival. For the poet these become questions of his own historicity, his relationship to past and future. As in his "Bridge," the central act of the poem is an affirmation of brotherhood (here, it should be noted, the relationship is one of the artist as naturalist, without any sense of shared sexuality). Following the handclasp of section 8, the poet proclaims his own sense of the past:

Introductions arranged by books;
The true heritage, where descent
Is called tradition . . .

This sense of poetic descent forms the core of "A Call in the Midst of the Crowd," a long "Poem in Four Parts on New York City."[93] Technically it resembles *Paterson* more than any other poem, with its long excerpts from journals, newspapers, guidebooks interwoven with the poet's own account of the passage through a year. Corn seems to have learned from Williams (and Marianne Moore) the possibility of making use of the apparent trivia of the real world in the composition of a new whole. But Corn brings in addition a strong lyric voice and a visionary commitment that finds permanence in the transitory, as in these splendid lines:

My bike,
My charger turns toward home. Towers rise
And swell as I come closer, the pedals
I pedal like a pump that pumps them up—
As such, I am the builder. Though what proof
But in saying it, an act, much like love,
That enjoins substance on what comes and goes?
Streets, stay with me. Desire, match with a moment;
See, that there always be one of this day.

Corn's mastery of tone is evident in such lines, from the ironic juxtaposition of "bike" and "charger" to the delightfully silly alliterations and repetitions of "pedal" and "pump," both of which, by their frivolity, prepare for the emotional declarations of the final lines and save them from falling into sentimentality. Corn here declares himself an urban (and urbane) Romantic; though he will proclaim the supreme power of art and love to conquer time and transcend mere experience, he does so in a disarmingly witty and colloquial manner. The effect is to heighten the power of his commitment, as the mock-questioner is suddenly transformed into Renaissance wit.

Corn's title is drawn from "Song of Myself," section 42, and

from "Calamus" 32. A reading of the "Calamus" poem is central
to an understanding of Corn's accomplishment:

> What think you I take my pen in hand to record?
> The battle-ship, perfect-model'd, majestic, that I saw pass
>   the offing to-day under full sail?
> The splendors of the past day? Or the splendor of the night
>   that envelops me?
> Or the vaunted glory and growth of the great city spread
>   around me?—No;
> But I record of two simple men I saw to-day, on the pier,
>   in the midst of the crowd, parting the parting of dear
>   friends,
> The one to remain hung on the other's neck, and passionately
>   kissed him,
> While the one to depart, tightly prest the one to remain in
>   his arms.[94]

Whitman's poem makes two important statements, both of which
are pertinent to Corn's invocation of the Calamus poet. The first
is Whitman's antiepic stance, his conscious rejection of the "important" subjects of poetry, particularly the epic, and his choice
instead of a lyrical and ahistorical subject, a deliberately "insig-
nificant" moment. The second, closely related to the first, is Whitman's insistence upon his role as a love poet and, more specifically,
as a poet of adhesive love. Bearing the Whitman source in mind
helps one understand the importance of "A Call" as a love poem,
a celebration of a shared moment of love "in the midst of the
crowd." Corn has learned from Whitman the need to record accurately the generally unobserved details of love, those that give
a special luminosity to its kaleidoscopic apparitions. As his "double" puts it in "Birthday Lunch," "stay close / To the facts you
see." It is a matter of seeing clearly, and, in Whitman's terms,
of choosing to make the kiss of the two men more important than
the battleship or the growth of cities. The central problem is, as
Corn puts it, "How capture all this / Without being taken captive
in turn . . . ?"

Part of the solution to this dilemma may be provided by Hopkins, who manages to capture the details of a world lovingly observed while at the same time retaining a sense of that world's
innate luminosity, its *quidditas* or inscape. Corn has organized
his poem of the world on a seasonal order, with each season also

being assigned an element. The influence of Hopkins is felt, appropriately, in the "Fire" section, in a poem which celebrates the turning point of the larger poem, a birth of love which coincides with Fourth of July celebrations. The first half of the poem records the poet's concern with details, his affirmation of the artist's role as the inventor of order (again he writes "imagine":"The first to consider imagining stars / Constellations" makes "some brilliant connections"). The second half is an exuberant celebration of light, the points of fire which illumine the night and offer a "covenant." The verbal exuberance of this section is daring; and Corn succeeds all the more for having risked so much. His lines have few equals, except in Hopkins and in the Crane of "Atlantis":

> Air aspirant with fractioned voices, feverfew
> Of the sensed illusion, higher ground, progressions
> Sounded in the spheres . . .
> There is a fire that surpasses the known burning,
> Its phoenix center a couple that must be there,
> Blast furnace, dynamo, engendering a city,
> Phosphor spines that bend and meet to weld, to fuse
> As a divining rod—sluicings, spillway, braid,
> Chorded basses that set myriad threads afire,
> Newborn limbs and reach of the proven tendon now
> Let go into empowered brilliance, rayed showers,
> The garden regained.

Echoes of Crane and Whitman run throughout the poem. Corn's "Declarations, July 4" is Whitmanesque in its celebration of the diversity of American life, and makes use of a catalog to record that diversity, recognizing, as Whitman did, the relationship between the openness of American experience and the openness of an American language. As Corn wittily puts it:

> Temples and libraries stand cheek by jowl with
> The native clapboard, International Style,
> White Castles, cast-iron, urban high-rise
> Vernacular, Prairie School, pizza parlor,
> And Greek Revival. For language here is
> Federal, eclectic, ad hoc, laissez-faire.

Like the postmodern architects whose views he seems to echo, Corn celebrates the healthy disorder of the American scene, finding vitality in the willingness to develop a language (of poetry or of buildings) that will reflect the nature of life as lived rather than an idealized version of life as it ought to be lived. No one has given a better justification for Whitman's joy in "foreign" words and phrases than his fellow poet. Yet, if there are moments of Whitmanic joy, there are also passages through hell, which testify to Corn's reading of Crane (and Lorca). A section from "Summer Vertigo," for instance, is closely related to Crane's "The Tunnel," the section of *The Bridge* which is derived in its turn from Edgar Allan Poe:

> Willfulness takes you underground:
> A labyrinth filled with victims, dressed
> In several secondhand myths.
> To barrel through darkness at 2 or 3 G's,
> Venom coursing through the third rail
> And poured into the flywheel at a screeching
> Halt: you do the stations and take the cross-
> Town shuttle to Grand Central—nothing.
> Then, head of a man, body of a bull.
> Cold sweat beads the chrome fixtures
> Or a virginal urinal. . . .

Corn's indebtednesses are not mere gestures of erudition; his poem is constructed upon the past, the elements of which coalesce and become tools for the construction of a future. Crane, above all, is celebrated for his "dark laughter," his ability to see the moment transformed, the final identity of tears and laughter. In Corn's words, "we / all make toward engulfment, doomed; and joyful."

Is "A Call in the Midst of the Crowd" a gay poem? Although the Whitman of "Calamus" is invoked as a guardian spirit, Corn's poem does not have the political self-consciousness of the earlier poem sequence. "A Call" is gay insofar as it addresses the poet's own life and celebrates a love in which the reader comes to share. Corn addresses the problem of gay identity in his poetry in the delightful section of "A Call," "Billie's Blues," set in a gay bar, where "one cruises / Mainly to cruise." But the poet's recollection that he met "you" there leads him to speculate on the need for the specific gender and identity of the "you." He wonders

> Whether dispensing with names,
> An apparent gender, showed, oh,
> Cowardice, betrayal; or good sense.

The problem arises from the fact that a poem addressed by a man to another man will not be considered "universal," while a poem from a man to a woman will be. Billie Holiday herself, the Billie of the title, has an "ambiguous first name." However, the poem concludes,

> Nothing vague about the voice, certainly.
> Listen: love mixed with a little hate for
> Him. Sounds universal to me.

However one may conceal a "name," one cannot conceal a "voice," and it is by this that a poet or a singer lives. Corn seems to point toward a definition of gay art which will emphasize, not merely honesty of gender, but honesty of experience. At that point, it is by being honest about the specifics that (ironically) one becomes universal. "Blues" are surely "about" love, and not "about" heterosexuality. Still, the blues singer, as she sings about her man, can find a response in the poet and his love song for his "man"— as the significant placement of "him" in the last line indicates. One fails to be universal, Corn seems to say, not by the gender of one's beloved, but by failing to be true to one's experience, by writing an emotionally dishonest poem. There lies the danger of the hidden pronoun.

Corn announces the development of a gay poetry which can transcend its gayness. He is fully aware of his identity as a gay, an identity to which he testifies in his relationship to Whitman and Crane. They retain a special meaning for him because they have been poets of the city who brought to their views of New York not only their religious sensibility but also their sexuality, and embraced its meaning and fulfillment in the city, Sodom-on-Hudson, as Frank O'Hara called it. Still, Corn seems to suggest, one must explore one's sexuality, so that finally one may forget it.

Conclusion: The Future

GAY LITERATURE has always, since the Greeks, been a literature of indirection. It has operated through a series of more or less coded references. One of the more immediate effects of gay liberation may be the elimination of the need for such a code. Will this mean an impoverishment of the literature? It seems certain that no one will again write a novel like *Dorian Gray*, in which we never know exactly what Dorian's "vices" are. But, as *Maurice* shows, art does not necessarily gain from directness. Poetry is a somewhat different matter from fiction, of course, since poems need not have characters and plots. Will gay poetry simply mean poems addressed by men to men? How will they differ from poems addressed by men to women?

For many, homosexuality is not *per se* an interesting subject, that is, no more nor less interesting than heterosexuality. It has become important because of its social status. In other words, in this view homosexuality is a response to antihomosexual prejudice. If that prejudice were eliminated, homosexuality as we know it (that is, self-conscious homosexuality) would disappear; homosexuality would occur as but one of a large number of forms of sexual expression. At that point the half-hid warp would no longer be half-hid, but an acknowledged part of the fabric of American life.

For others, homosexuality is different in its essence from heterosexuality, since it is based on the union of sames rather than opposites. In this view, the acceptance of homosexuality would lead to considerable changes, ranging from art to philosophy to social organization. It was to this view that the visionary Whitman of *Democratic Vistas* spoke, imaging a different order of love "at least rivaling . . . if not going beyond" the heterosexual order in the fulfillment of the American Dream. The revelation of the warp, in this view, is only the first step toward a reshaping of the fabric.

There can be at present no way to know with certainty who is right. Gay literature, although tracing its history back over two thousand years, is still in its infancy. Conclusions must be tentative. Whether homosexuality becomes one of many sexualities or becomes a force for social change, the men who used their craft as a way to explore its possibilities have established a tradition that seems certain to grow, confident in its readers and lovers.

Notes

Introduction

1. Cleveland, 1962. First published 1960.
2. The present study is confined to men. Although there have been important Lesbian poets whose sexuality was a major element of their self-definition—such as Amy Lowell and May Sarton—they should be studied separately. They do not share the assumptions or traditions of gay male poets, and their identity as Lesbians should be linked to their identity as women. The word "homosexual," of course, means same-sex, not sex between men. Nonetheless, because Lesbians prefer the term "Lesbian," and to avoid awkward repetition of the phrase "male homosexual," in this study "homosexual" applies only to men who are sexually attracted to other men.
3. *Democratic Vistas*, in *Complete Prose Works*, p. 240n.
4. Unpublished letter to Wilbur Underwood, 14 February 1932. The prejudices active in Crane criticism can be seen in this recent and typical statement about the affair with Mrs. Cowley: "This ironic heterosexual relationship, the only such well-documented affair of his life, was but a brief period of relative stability sandwiched between his homosexuality, excessive drinking, brawling, and irrational behavior" (Alfred B. Cahen, "Hart Crane's Ghost Written Suicide Notes," *Hart Crane Newsletter* [Fall 1977]: 12). Homosexuality is considered the equivalent of other forms of irrationality.
5. There is a preliminary attempt to deal with O'Hara in these terms in a review by Stuart Byron, "Frank O'Hara: Poetic 'Queertalk,'" *Real Paper* (Boston, April 24, 1974): 20–21.
6. James E. Miller, Jr., *T. S. Eliot's Personal Waste Land: Exorcism of the Demons* (University Park, 1977).

Walt Whitman

Whitman, the Critics, and Homosexuality
1. Elizabeth Corbett, *Walt*.

2. Holloway, "Walt Whitman's Love Affairs," *The Dial* (November 1920): 473–483.
3. Holloway, *Walt Whitman: An Interpretation in Narrative*.
4. James E. Miller, Jr., *A Critical Guide to 'Leaves of Grass*,' p. 50n.
5. Jacob Stockinger, "Homotextuality: A Proposal," in Louie Crew, ed., *The Gay Academic* (Palm Springs, 1978), pp. 135–151.
6. Newton Arvin, *Whitman*, p. 277.
7. Mark Van Doren, "Walt Whitman, Stranger," in *The Private Reader* (New York, 1942), p. 82.
8. *Critical Guide*, chap. i.
9. Crawley, *The Structure of Leaves of Grass* (Austin, Texas, 1970), p. 112.
10. Walter Lowenfels, ed., *The Tenderest Lover: The Erotic Poetry of Walt Whitman* (New York, 1970).
11. Cf. note 47 below.
12. Edwin Haviland Miller, *Walt Whitman's Poetry: A Psychological Journey*.
13. Ibid., p. 147.
14. The letter is in Horace Traubel, *With Walt Whitman in Camden*, 5: 330–331.
15. "Walt Whitman: Ein Charakterbild," *Jahrbuch für sexuelle Zwischenstufen* 7 (1905): 155–287.
16. "Whitmans Forderungen sind augenscheinlich nur aus seiner homosexueller Naturanlage verständlich und würden schon zum Beweise seiner Homosexualität genügend sein, auch wenn wir nichts von seiner Persönlichkeit und seinem Leben wußten" (193).
17. Minden, 1906.
18. *Der Yankee-Heiland: Ein Beitrag zur modernen Religionsgeschichte* (Dresden, 1906); *Whitman-Mysterien: Eine Abrechnung mit Johannes Schlaf* (Berlin, 1907).
19. *Der Yankee-Heiland*, p. 232. "Als Verkünder der leidenschaftlichen Liebe des Mannes zum Mann gehört Whitman zu den falschen Propheten."
20. "The 'Feminine Soul' in Whitman," *Current Literature* 41 (July 1906): 56.

The Dream-Vision Poems

Unless otherwise noted, the Whitman poems are cited from the Norton Critical Edition of *Leaves of Grass*, ed. Scully Bradley and Harold W. Blodgett, based on The Comprehensive Reader's Edition published by New York University Press.

21. Leslie Fiedler, Introduction to *Whitman*, Laurel ed. (New York, 1959); Edwin Haviland Miller, *Walt Whitman's Poetry: A Psycholog-*

ical Journey, pp. 66–84; James E. Miller, *Critical Guide*, pp. 130–141.

22. All citations from "The Sleepers" are to the 1855 text, and are taken from the convenient reprint edition edited by Malcolm Cowley, *Leaves of Grass*.

23. *Critical Guide*, pp. 133–134.

24. *Walt Whitman's Poetry*, pp. 83–84.

25. See Alice Ford, *Edward Hicks: Painter of the Peaceable Kingdom* (Philadelphia, 1952); and *Edward Hicks: A Peaceable Season* (Princeton, 1973). Hicks was a cousin of the Quaker leader, Elias Hicks, of whom Whitman wrote.

26. Thomas L. Brasher, ed., *Walt Whitman: The Early Poems and the Fiction* (New York, 1963), p. 263.

27. *Walt Whitman's Poetry*, p. 90.

28. Line references are to the 1855 text.

29. See the Eakins painting *The Swimming Hole*, used as the cover for the Penguin edition of Whitman's *Complete Poems*, ed. Francis Murphy. See also any of the celebrated bathing paintings by H. S. Tuke, one of which is reproduced as plate 15 in Brian Reade, ed., *Sexual Heretics: Male Homosexuality in English Literature from 1850 to 1900*. There is an interesting discussion of the implications of the "boys bathing" theme in the poetry of World War I in Paul Fussell, *The Great War and Modern Memory* (New York, 1975), pp. 299–309. It is worth noting that Whitman writes "young men" while later writers use the terms "boys" or "lads." Their eroticism is considerably more pederastic than Whitman's.

30. *Walt Whitman's Poetry*, p. 94.

31. See Frederick Engels, *The Origin of the Family, Private Property, and the State* [1884]; Lewis H. Morgan, *Ancient Society* [1877] and *League of the Ho-dé-no-san-nee or Iroquois* [1851].

32. *Walt Whitman's Poetry*, p. 99.

33. Quoted in Clifton Joseph Furness, *American Literature* 13 (January 1942):424–425.

34. Ibid.

35. Whitman's use of the "e" in "amie" testifies to his faulty French, not to any sexual ambiguity. He later settled on "camerado" as his word for "special friend." It is clear that the English word "friend" seemed to him inadequate, perhaps too depleted of meaning.

"O a word to clear one's path": Adhesiveness

36. *Democratic Vistas*, in *Complete Prose Works*, p. 240n.

37. Edward Hungerford, "Walt Whitman and His Chart of Bumps," *American Literature* 2 (January 1931):350–384.

38. The question of Whitman's attitude toward women and its relationship to his ideal of "manly" friendship is complex, and deserves separate treatment. Clearly Whitman was concerned that his ideal be seen as manly, that is, not effeminate, and so emphasized his role as a "rough." This was basically a response to the unspoken assumption that homosexual love was unmanly. In an age of increasing "feminization" of culture, particularly in the church and the academy, Whitman spoke on behalf of more "masculine" values. These have come to have disastrous cultural effects on twentieth-century figures such as Hemingway. But unlike Hemingway, Whitman was not a misogynist. He took pains to announce, in "Song of Myself," "I am the poet of the woman the same as the man, / And I say it is as great to be woman as to be a man." While Whitman was thus a theoretical advocate of the equality of women, he does not seem usually to have thought of women in connection with adhesiveness. However, "The Sleepers" includes (section 6) a very moving account of what appears to be an episode of female adhesiveness. And in the 1876 Preface he wrote, "I also sent out 'Leaves of Grass' to arouse and set flowing in men's *and women's* hearts [my emphasis], young and old, endless streams of living, pulsating love and friendship . . ." The same passage, however, defines comradeship as "the beautiful and sane affection of man for man, latent in all the young fellows" (*Complete Prose Works*, p. 277n). Like most nineteenth-century men, Whitman appears to have had a blind spot concerning female sexuality, particularly Lesbianism, despite his determination to reject "impassive women" in favor of those "that are warm-blooded and sufficient" ("A Woman Waits for Me").

39. 2 Sam. 1.

40. Douglas, "Two Loves."

41. Horace Traubel, ed., *An American Primer*, p. 15.

42. The attempt to distinguish between homosexuality and homoeroticism, as many critics do, seems to me at best pointless. Both mean essentially the same thing: a sexual attraction between two (or more) members of the same sex. If a distinction is drawn, it comes down to determining whether or not there has been any genital contact (and so one arrives at the ever greater absurdity of homogenitalism). Not only can we never really know this, it also does not matter in the least. One can properly use the term "homoerotic" when one begins to say "heteroerotic" as well.

43. The textual evidence is presented by Fredson Bowers in his edition of *Whitman's Manuscripts: Leaves of Grass (1860)* (Chicago, 1955). The "crisis" theory is presented by Stephen E. Whicher, "Whitman's Awakening to Death: Toward a Biographical Reading of 'Out of the Cradle Endlessly Rocking,'" in *The Presence of Walt*

Whitman: Selected Papers from the English Institute, ed. R. W. B. Lewis, pp. 1–27. In fairness I should point out that, despite wide acceptance, this theory has not been universally believed. Both Edwin Haviland Miller and James E. Miller, Jr., have expressed their doubts. And earlier, Malcolm Cowley wrote of Whitman: "He was not 'unconsciously' or 'half-consciously' homosexual; after 1855, and perhaps as early as 1848, he was completely aware of his own nature" ("Walt Whitman: The Secret," *New Republic* 114 [April 8, 1946]:482). Cowley's essays remain refreshing and are among the best things ever written on Whitman.

44. The theory of "phases" or "stages" of development is presented most fully by Erik Erikson in *Childhood and Society* (New York, 1950). It has influenced the thinking of recent critics such as E. H. Miller (on Whitman and Melville) and Richard Lebeaux (on Thoreau). Since the final stage is "heterosexual mutuality," homosexuality can represent only arrestment if it occurs at another than its proper "phase." The idea has won large credence through vulgarization, of course. It is implicit in earlier psychoanalytic writing as well, and can be observed in Whitman criticism as early as Jean Catel, writing of "Once I Pass'd through a Populous City": "Whitman ne semble pas avoir atteint à cette différenciation des sexes où l'homme a généralement atteint à l'âge qu'avait notre poète lorsqu'il publiait la première édition des *Brins d'herbe*" (*Walt Whitman: La Naissance du poète*, pp. 422–423).

45. The manuscript versions of the 1860 edition are published in Bowers. The changes in the text of that edition for the 1867 edition have been printed and analyzed by Arthur Golden, *Walt Whitman's Blue Book: The 1860–1861 Leaves of Grass Containing His Manuscript Additions and Revisions*, 2 vols. I am indebted to both of these editions for information on Whitman's revisions. All citations from manuscript may be found in the appropriate volume.

46. Golden, 2:lvii.

47. The notebook was first published by Emory Holloway, in *The Uncollected Poetry and Prose of Walt Whitman* (Garden City, 1921), 2:94–97. Holloway printed the pronouns as "her" without comment and made no attempt to determine the meaning of "P" or "PD." Hungerford, op. cit., suggested that "16" and "164" referred to phrenological illustrations of Hope and Adhesiveness. Ingenious, but wrong. Roger Asselineau examined the manuscript again and reported that "tous les pronoms personnels masculins du texte ont été effacés et remplacés par leurs équivalents féminins, mais sous la surcharge on les discerne très nettement encore. Le doute n'est pas permis: Whitman a délibérément maquillé ces notes intimes" (*L'Evolution de Walt Whitman après la première edition des Feuilles d'Herbe*, p. 193). In a footnote Asselineau remarks on the failure of

Holloway to note this in his text. Even less excusable is the re-printing of that text without comment, as if Asselineau had never pointed out Whitman's self-censorship, in Gay Wilson Allen, *The Solitary Singer: A Critical Biography of Walt Whitman*, rev. ed., pp. 422–442.

48. In 1870, about the same time as the notebook entry, Whitman wrote to Charles Warren Stoddard, who had addressed him "in the name of CALAMUS": "As to you, I do not of course object to your emotional and adhesive nature, & the outlet thereof, but warmly approve them" (*Correspondence*, 2:97). This seems to in-dicate Whitman's approval of both a homosexual nature and homo-sexual practices.

49. Edwin Haviland Miller charges that the use of "adhesiveness" was "an evasive act, since only initiates could understand the implica-tions" (*Psychological Journey*, p. 145). There is no evidence that I know of, however, to suggest that "adhesiveness" was used in this sense by any other homosexuals.

50. Although it has been argued that homosexuality is a creation of medical science as part of a process of social control, the experience of Whitman would seem to indicate that homosexuals themselves sought an identity and a name, that they conceived of themselves as differing in specific ways from heterosexuals. Whitman's search for a word to identify his sexuality would seem to argue against the assumptions of critics like Michel Foucault and Guy Hocquen-ghem, although they are right to say that homosexuality *as illness* is a creation of nineteenth-century science. But homosexuality as identity is also a product of nineteenth-century homosexuals.

51. *The Symposium*, trans. Walter Hamilton (Harmondsworth, 1951), pp. 46–47. Whitman's text ("The Banquet," in *The Works of Plato: A New and Literal Version*, trans. George Burges 3:493) read, "as-sociate through the whole of life together, and to live in common." It is interesting to note, in this edition, the repetition of the ad-jective "manly" in describing men who love other men: they are "the most manly in their disposition" and have "a manly temper and manly look" (512). Whitman may well have been influenced by this phrasing in his own language; he would certainly also have been reassured by it.

52. For the Uranians in England, see Timothy d'Arch Smith, *Love in Earnest: Some Notes on the Lives and Writings of English "Uranian" Poets from 1889 to 1930*.

53. Carpenter, *The Intermediate Sex* (New York, 1909). Carpenter also uses the term "homogenic" love, seeming to imply that homosexu-als are a separate species. The OED does not record this usage. Akin to Carpenter's phrase, but perhaps developed independently,

is Edward I. Prime-Stevenson's "the intersexes," in his book of that
name (Florence, 1910).

54. The precise history of these terms is hard to trace, since most
philologists were, at least until recently, more prudish than responsible. The OED Supplement records uses of "homosexual" and "invert" in the 1890s and cites Symonds, Beardsley, Havelock Ellis,
and the English translation of Krafft-Ebing. They could probably
be traced back a number of years before these uses, but almost
certainly not as far back as the 1850s. "Invert" was probably used
as a modification of "pervert"; it was thought to be a more neutral
term. "Homosexual" was apparently coined in German in 1869.
    Prior to the late nineteenth century the only terms that appear
to have been in use were "sodomy" and "buggery." Both appear
in Webster's 1836 edition. But both also are terms about which
there has been a great deal of confusion, as well as being terms
which one could hardly expect the participants themselves to use.
"Sodomy" sometimes means intercourse with animals, sometimes
anal intercourse; "buggery" means anal intercourse. Neither includes the larger part of sexual activity among homosexuals nor any
of the affectional life. Symonds seems to have adopted "sods" as
an almost affectionate shortened form of "sodomite" or "sodomist."
    Even legal language is euphemistic. Most texts refer to crimes
against nature or "the crime not to be mentioned among Christians"; moreover, these references are usually in Latin. Greek had
a full vocabulary for both love and sex among men, but it was hardly to be found in nineteenth-century lexicons and even less likely
to be known by Whitman's "muscular" young men. The word
"Greek" itself, as well as synonyms such as "Hellenistic" or "Dorian," often served as a code signifier for homosexuality (see my
"Forster's Greek: From Optative to Present Indicative," *Kansas
Quarterly* 9 [Spring 1977]:69–73).

55. Gertrude Stein, "Miss Furr and Miss Skeene," in *Geography and
Plays* (Boston, 1922). See also Robert McAlmon's poem, "Revolving Mirror" (1926).

"Calamus"

56. Mark Van Doren, "Walt Whitman, Stranger," p. 82.
57. James E. Miller, *Critical Guide*, p. 78.
58. An evasion which did him very little good. As the result of a raid,
probably prompted by his socialism as much as by his homosexuality, "pornography" was discovered and Arvin was arrested, forced
out of teaching at Smith College, and driven to a breakdown.
59. Arvin, *Whitman*, pp. 272–278.
60. Taylor later turned on Whitman and became one of his greatest

antagonists (see below). But in 1866 he praised Whitman for his portrayal of the "tender and noble love of man for man." (See Traubel, *With Walt Whitman in Camden*, 2:148–149, 153.) In 1870 Stoddard exclaimed, "In the name of CALAMUS listen to me!" and sent along *South Sea Idyls*. Whitman replied in an important letter, "I do not of course object to your emotional & adhesive nature, & the outlet thereof, but warmly approve them." (See *The Correspondence of Walt Whitman*, ed. Edwin Haviland Miller, 2: 97.)

61. Noel, November 1871, quoted in Traubel, 1:425–426.

62. Dowden, "The Poetry of Democracy: Walt Whitman," *Westminster Review*, n.s. 40 (July 1871); reprinted in Edwin Haviland Miller, *A Century of Whitman Criticism*, p. 47.

63. Saintsbury, "Leaves of Grass," *The Academy* (October 10, 1874); reprinted in Miller, *Century*, p. 51.

64. Herbert M. Schueller and Robert L. Peters, ed., *The Letters of John Addington Symonds*, 2:166–167.

65. Ibid., pp. 201–203.

66. Cowley, "Walt Whitman: The Miracle," *New Republic* 114 (March 18, 1946):388.

67. Cowley, "Walt Whitman: The Secret," p. 482.

68. Fredson Bowers, *Whitman's Manuscripts: Leaves of Grass (1860)*. All manuscript citations, unless otherwise noted, are from this text. All citations from the 1860 edition are from the modern reprint, ed. Roy Harvey Pearce (Ithaca, 1961).

69. Letter to Ralph Waldo Emerson, in *Leaves of Grass*, Norton Critical Edition, p. 739.

70. Miller, *Psychological Journey*, p. 144.

71. There is considerable homosexual material in Thoreau's journals, but it can hardly be considered to have been in print in the 1850s. Miller also forgets that almost all critics, even now, deny this element in Thoreau.

72. Leslie Fiedler, *Love and Death in the American Novel* (Cleveland, 1962).

73. It is extraordinary that Melville and Whitman should not have known each other, but that appears to be the case. Whitman would certainly have enjoyed "A Squeeze of the Hand."

74. There was, of course, a classical tradition, to which we shall return. Better-educated writers such as Symonds or Pater usually called upon classical or Renaissance models, but it must be remembered that Whitman's knowledge was limited. He certainly read Plato, although we cannot date that reading accurately. Cf. note 87 below.

75. See Richard Slotkin, *Regeneration through Violence: Mythology of the American Frontier 1600–1860* (Middletown, Connecticut, 1973).

76. Floyd Stovall reports that a volume of Virgil was among Whitman's books in 1885, but he does not identify it or say when it was acquired (Stovall, *The Foreground of* Leaves of Grass, p. 48).

77. Miller, *Psychological Journey*, p. 170.

78. J. Albert Robbins, "America and the Poet: Whitman, Hart Crane and Frost," in Irvin Ehrenpreis, ed., *American Poetry*, Stratford-upon-Avon Studies 7 (London, 1965), p. 53. Robbins also claims that the "Calamus" poems "reveal the dark underside of his psyche."

79. Miller, *Psychological Journey*, p. 150.

80. On the relationship of Virgil to nineteenth-century American pastoral thought, one may wish to consult Leo Marx, *The Machine in the Garden: Technology and the Pastoral Ideal in America*, esp. pp. 19–24, 30–32.

81. Miller, *Psychological Journey*, p. 170.

82. Or as in Eliot's *The Waste Land*, another poem confronting the same problem.

83. On pretense in homosexual life, see Thom Gunn's comment, "Even in bed I lie," from his splendid poem, "Carnal Knowledge," discussed below.

84. Whitman did make some deletions (such as "sham"), but in general the sexual frankness remained.

85. Miller, *Psychological Journey*, p. 145. Although Miller says in his Preface, "It is easy to fault *Leaves of Grass*, but I am too grateful for, and humble before, Whitman's genius to find any gratification in censuring his weaknesses. Greatness too rarely walks among us; carping critics are a commonplace," there is scant evidence in his text of gratitude, humility, or even respect. Miller, like so many critics, simply doesn't *like* Whitman.

86. 1876 Preface, in *Complete Prose Works*, p. 274n. This concept enjoys a fascinating history in homosexual literature, including Mann's Tadzio and Cocteau's angels of death, as well as Forster's use of the Hermes figure.

87. Edwin Miller cites an unpublished MS on Whitman's reading of Plato and dates it "probably in the 1860's" without giving any evidence (*Psychological Journey*, p. 146). Floyd Stovall, in *The Foreground of* Leaves of Grass, says that the notes are "all apparently from Vol. I of the Bohn Library edition." I would argue, from the evidence of the text, that Whitman had read Plato by at least 1859.

88. See "The Banquet," i.e., "The Symposium," in *The Works of Plato*, 3:512–514. Burges' translation seems relatively accurate, although he translates "pederast" as "lover of youths," which seems to veil the matter slightly. The general assumption that nineteenth-century translations concealed Plato's homosexuality does not seem justified.

89. The suppression of nonprocreative sex is discussed by Freud in *Civilization and Its Discontents* and by Marcuse in *Eros and Civilization*.
90. There is a very good commentary on this poem, and several others from the "Calamus" cycle, in Joseph Cady, "Not Happy in the Capitol: Homosexuality and the *Calamus* Poems," *American Studies* 19 (Fall 1978): 5–22. Cady stresses the way the poems "identify a radical imagination implicit in homosexual experience under oppression." He argues that in this poem "the common reader is observer" as a consequence of the poet's "private" vision. Clearly public and private worlds are contrasted in the poem, but I would argue against the complete opposition to the prevailing culture that Cady finds in these poems. I find Whitman using a Romantic concept of self-sufficiency, and at the same time sustaining his role as bard by proclaiming the new adhesive order.
91. In the manuscript the phrase reads, "the moon's clear beams." The magical and love-inducing powers of the moon were already clear, as was the penetration of light into the darkness.
92. Cf. *The Symposium*, where there is a discussion of the principle of love as analogous to the principle of harmony in music. This passage is cited as the epigraph to "Atlantis."
93. Cf. Whitman's note: "That only when sex is properly treated, talked, avowed, accepted, will the woman be equal with the man, and pass where the man passes, and meet his words with her words, and his rights with her rights" (*Notes and Fragments*, ed. Richard Maurice Bucke, p. 33, n. 96). Whitman thus believed that his own greater frankness about sex might contribute to the equality of women. One should also note his sympathetic attitude to Frances Wright and the theft of her fortune by an unscrupulous husband (aided by laws that gave a woman's own inheritance to her husband!).
94. Crane often attacked "womanly men," and part of his resentment at Harriet Monroe was due to her "feminine" qualities. See, for example, the letter to Allen Tate, Brom Weber, ed., *Letters of Hart Crane*, pp. 290–291, with its attack on Ridgely Torrence as "Miss T." (Weber censors the name, but it is obvious from context.)
95. See Baudelaire's "Correspondances" in *Les Fleurs du Mal* (1857). The idea has its origin with Swedenborg, and so was common to most of the Transcendentalists, including Emerson (see his poem "Nature").
96. F. O. Matthiessen, *American Renaissance*.
97. Roy Harvey Pearce, *The Continuity of American Poetry*, rev. ed., p. 23.
98. See Virginia Woolf, *A Room of One's Own* (New York, 1929) and *Moments of Being* (London, 1976).

99. For a different view of "Song of Myself" as epic, one may compare the readings of Pearce or James Miller.
100. *Democratic Vistas*, in *Complete Prose Works*, p. 240n.
101. *The Symposium*, p. 95. In the Burges text Whitman used, this passage reads, "beauty itself, clear as the light pure and unmixed, but not polluted with human flesh and colour . . . the godlike beautiful in its singleness of form" (554).

The Academic Tradition

1. Richard Hofstadter, *The Age of Reform*, chap. iv (New York, 1955).
2. *Southern Literary Messenger* (April 1836).
3. James Grant Wilson, *The Life and Letters of Fitz-Greene Halleck*, p. 163. It is interesting to note that the "modern" biography by Nelson Frederick Adkins, *Fitz-Greene Halleck: An Early Knickerbocker Wit and Poet*, omits all this—thus testifying to a change in attitudes. Such material would now be "embarrassing."
4. "On the Death of J. Rodman Drake," in Rufus W. Griswold, ed., *Gems from the American Poets* (Philadelphia, 1851), pp. 56–57.
5. Wilson, pp. 241, 244.
6. Ibid.
7. Ibid., pp. 65–67.
8. Ibid., p. 215.
9. Ibid., pp. 81–82.

Bayard Taylor and His Circle

10. Taylor, *Critical Essays and Literary Notes*, p. 234. The speech was delivered in 1869.
11. Taylor, *Poetical Works*, Household Edition, pp. 62–63.
12. Ibid., pp. 72–75.
13. Paul C. Wermuth, *Bayard Taylor*, p. 115.
14. On the history of the Hylas myth, see Rictor Norton, *The Homosexual Literary Tradition: An Interpretation* (New York, 1974). His interpretation is quite different from my own.
15. *Poetical Works*, p. 8.
16. Ibid., p. 12.
17. Ibid., p. 25.
18. *Joseph and His Friend*, Household Edition, p. 95. The novel was first published in 1870 and reprinted in 1879.
19. *Joseph*, p. 214.
20. Ibid., p. 217.
21. The letters from Taylor to Whitman are both in Horace Traubel, *With Walt Whitman in Camden*, 12 November 1866, 2:148–149; 2 December 1866, 2:153.

22. Robert Scholnick, "The Selling of the 'Author's Edition': Whitman, O'Connor, and the *West Jersey Press* Affair," *Walt Whitman Review* 23 (March 1977): 10.
23. *Boys of Other Countries*, p. 14.
24. *Poems of the Orient*, p. 161.
25. "The Poet in the East," *Poems of the Orient*, p. 21.
26. *Joseph*, p. 355.
27. *Poems* (Boston, 1852), p. 121.
28. Ibid., pp. 70–73.
29. *Poems of the Orient*, p. 10.
30. *The Book of the East, and Other Poems* (Boston, 1871), p. 224.
31. Ibid., p. 178.
32. Boston, 1869.

George Santayana
33. George Santayana, *Persons and Places: The Background of My Life*, p. 182.
34. Ibid., pp. 183–184.
35. "To W. P." Santayana, *Sonnets and Other Verses*, pp. 28–31.
36. Lois Hughson, *Thresholds of Reality: George Santayana and Modernistic Poetics*, p. 28.
37. It will be noted that, in both Mann and Santayana, the half-Nordic, half-Latin figure may be seen as an emblem of the androgynous self.
38. *Sonnets*, p. 39.
39. Michael Angelo Buonarroti, *Sonnets*, trans. J. A. Symonds (New York, n.d. [1878]), p. 120.
40. *Sonnets*, p. 43.
41. Ibid., p. 37.

Hart Crane

Early Poems and White Buildings
1. Brom Weber, ed., *The Letters of Hart Crane 1916–1932*, p. 49. Weber deletes Underwood's name.
2. "The Visible, the Untrue," in Hart Crane, *The Complete Poems and Selected Letters and Prose*, ed. Brom Weber. All future citations from Crane are from this edition unless otherwise noted. The title of this poem is in itself a remarkable indication of Crane's Platonism.
3. Edgar Allan Poe, "The Poetic Principle," in *Selected Writings*, ed. David Galloway (Harmondsworth, 1967), p. 511. Poe goes on to distinguish between Passion and Love in terms that Crane never fully accepted. While Passion's "tendency is to degrade, rather than to elevate the Soul," "Love—the true, the divine Eros—the Uranian as distinguished from the Dionaean Venus—is unquestionably the purest and truest of all poetical themes."

4. Poe, "Alone."
5. A. E. Housman, *Collected Poems* (New York, 1940), p. 233.
6. Oscar Wilde, *De Profundis* (London, 1949).
7. Wilde, *The Happy Prince and Other Tales* (London, 1888), p. 32. The poem is criticized by R. W. Butterfield (*The Broken Arc* [Edinburgh, 1969]) for its "vapid, approximate atmospherics" (p. 15), but he misses the references to Wilde's tale. The poem is more careful, and more conscious, than he allows.
8. I am aware that the biographers do not think that Crane had had a sexual experience with another man at the time he wrote this poem. The biographers date Crane's homosexuality from the first account of an "affair" in his letters. Simple adolescent sexuality without the emotion implications of an "affair" may well have confirmed Crane's sense of his own homosexuality. In any case, it is by no means necessary for the actual experience to precede the recognition of one's own sexuality: in many cases, in fact, the recognition comes long before it is acted out.
9. See Louis Crompton, "Gay Genocide: From Leviticus to Hitler," in *The Gay Academic*, ed. Louie Crew, pp. 67–91.
10. John Unterecker's interviews for *Voyager*, included in the NET film, demonstrate to a shocking degree the hostility of Crane's friends to what they term his "sexual aberration." Crane appears to have found an understanding of his homosexuality only in his friendship with Wilbur Underwood, himself a homosexual poet. But Underwood, who lived a double life (State Department by day, park cruising and drag parties by night), can hardly have offered a model for the integration of Crane's homosexuality into his intellectual life.
11. The treatment of Emil Opffer in Crane criticism has been very misleading. The blame for this rests largely with Brom Weber, who omitted Opffer's name from his biography of Crane and censored all references to him in his edition of Crane's *Letters*. The facts are that Crane met Opffer through mutual friends, that everyone in Crane's circle knew him, that Crane wrote to his mother about him, and that Opffer was not a "sailor" or a casual sexual encounter. (M. D. Uroff calls him a "young sailor" [he was twenty-seven when he met Crane] and refuses to give his name: *Hart Crane: The Patterns of His Poetry*.) He was the publisher of *Nordlyset*, a Danish newspaper published in New York, and his brother Ivan was a talented artist whose work appeared in *The Dial*. By deleting Opffer's name entirely or calling him "E---" Weber created an atmosphere of guilt and secrecy where there was openness and joy. I think that it is likely that the affair with Opffer was so successful because Opffer combined the erotic aspects of Crane's private mythology (as "ship's writer" [Crane's phrase] he was at least symbolically a sailor) with the real intellectual and emotional needs Crane

felt. It appears to have been the only time in Crane's life that the physical and the spiritual coincided.

12. Underwood published *A Book of Masks* in 1907 and *Damien of Molokai* in 1909. He did not publish another book until 1927, when it seems certain that Crane's constant encouragement had helped him to resume publishing. One of Crane's first letters to Underwood urges, "Do, I pray you, take up a broken thread again —you really have much to give." Although Crane received a copy of the new book in 1927, his own development was such that he was no longer subject to Underwood's influence, although he did tell Underwood that his poems "remind me of the best of Blake."

13. Unpublished letter, Hart Crane to Wilbur Underwood, May 9, 1923. Unterecker's account of this letter (*Voyager: A Life of Hart Crane*, pp. 294–295) is quite misleading. The passage in question reads: "You must have guessed by now that I am in love. I told you about 'B' in my last letter. This is a quite unsensual and peculiar case, for 'B's' physical propensities are quite in opposite direction [*sic*]. This real affection is, however, sufficient in other ways. I feel a real reciprocation, and the man's beauty of manner, face, body, and attitude has made me a most willing slave. How it will end doesn't matter. At least not in my present mood. We are going to take an apartment together when I get a job." ("B" was the name given Brown in *The Enormous Room*.)

14. No one seems to have remarked on the reason for the "stumble" of the last stanza. R. W. B. Lewis (*The Poetry of Hart Crane: A Critical Study*, p. 30) terms it merely "a protective and fashionable self-irony," but he also misreads the poem by assuming that the letters are *by* the grandmother rather than *to* her.

15. Letter to Underwood, cited by Lewis, p. 37.

16. Unpublished letter to Underwood, January 2, 1921.

17. See Unterecker, pp. 230–231.

18. Lewis has suggested the influence of Blake at this point.

19. Unpublished letter to Underwood, January 2, 1921.

20. Unpublished letter to Underwood, September 2, 1922.

21. Lewis, p. 138.

22. For the verbal echoes of Melville, see Joseph Warren Beach, "Hart Crane and *Moby-Dick*," *Western Review* 20 (Spring 1956):183–196; Herbert A. Leibowitz, *Hart Crane: An Introduction to the Poetry*, pp. 93–95; and Lewis, pp. 153–155.

23. Unpublished letter to Underwood, June 15, 1922.

24. Many readers seem to have missed the point. Lewis interprets "black swollen gates" as "dark and swelling waves," which is not much help; and Sherman Paul (*Hart's Bridge*, p. 150) interprets them as "death-by-drowning," which is completely misleading. M. D. Uroff's reading of the poem is even more curious. She ar-

gues that "the poet's beloved is absent, unnecessary because the poem is not written to him or about him" (*Hart Crane*, p. 70).

Crane and Whitman

25. Unterecker, *Voyager*, p. 431.
26. Yvor Winters, "The Progress of Hart Crane" [review of *The Bridge*], *Poetry* 36 (June 1930): 163.
27. Ibid., p. 165.
28. Unterecker, p. 621.
29. Allen Tate, "A Distinguished Poet," *Hound and Horn* 3 (July–September 1930): 584.
30. Letter to Tate, reproduced in Unterecker, p. 623.
31. Review, reprinted in Brom Weber, ed., *Complete Poems and Selected Letters and Prose*, p. 205. First published in *The Pagan* 4 (September 1919): pp. 60–61.
32. For this period in Crane's development, see Dickran Tashjian, *Skyscraper Primitives* (Middletown, 1975).
33. Tony Tanner, *The Reign of Wonder: Naivety and Reality in American Literature* (Cambridge, 1965), p. 213.
34. Emory Holloway, "Walt Whitman's Love Affairs," *The Dial* (November 1920): 473–483; idem, ed., *Uncollected Poetry and Prose of Walt Whitman* (Garden City, 1921), 2:102. The complete manuscript may be found, with full annotations, in Fredson Bowers, ed., *Whitman's Manuscripts: Leaves of Grass (1860)*, pp. 64–65.
35. Holloway, *Uncollected Poetry and Prose*, 2:102n.
36. Brom Weber, *Hart Crane*, Appendix, p. 391.
37. *Moby-Dick*, chaps. lviii and cxiv. The verbal echoes of *Moby-Dick* in "Repose of Rivers" have been convincingly studied by R. W. B. Lewis in *The Poetry of Hart Crane*, pp. 213–214.
38. Unterecker, p. 431.
39. Walt Whitman, *Democratic Vistas*, in *Complete Prose Works*, p. 240.
40. Waldo Frank, *Our America*, p. 205. Cf. Crane's statement in a letter to Gorham Munson that "since my reading of you and Frank . . . I begin to feel myself directly connected with Whitman" (*The Letters of Hart Crane*, ed. Brom Weber, p. 128).
41. Frank, *Our America*, p. 232.
42. See my essay, "Hart Crane's 'For the Marriage of Faustus and Helen': Myth and Alchemy," *Concerning Poetry* 9 (Spring 1976): 59–62.
43. Crane's phrase, in a letter to Otto Kahn, in *Complete Poems*, ed. Weber, p. 252.
44. 1855 Preface to *Leaves of Grass*, in *Complete Prose*, p. 256.
45. *Letters*, p. 262.
46. Ibid., p. 267.
47. 1876 Preface to *Leaves of Grass*, in *Complete Prose*, p. 274n.

48. *Democratic Vistas*, in *Complete Prose*, p. 246.
49. See the important article by Leland Krauth, "Whitman and His Readers: The Comradeship Theme," *Walt Whitman Review* 20 (December 1974): 147–151.
50. "Modern Poetry" [1930], in *Complete Poems*, ed. Weber, p. 263. In a characteristic attack on Crane's "ignorance," Hyatt Waggoner maintained that Crane misunderstood the word "psychosis" (*The Heel of Elohim: Science and Values in Modern American Poetry*, p. 158). As Susan Jenkins Brown has shown, Crane's use of "psychosis" in the sense of "consciousness" was the prevailing one at the time (Brown, *Robber Rocks* [Middletown, n.d.], p. 136). Because Crane was not a university graduate he has come in for a great deal of ill-advised criticism from snobbish professors.
51. Harold Bloom, *The Anxiety of Influence*. Crane was certainly a strong poet, in Bloom's sense, and Whitman's heritage presented a difficult parentage. But Bloom's paradigm, rooted as it is in a Freudian view of competition between father and son, is heterosexual in its assumptions and inadequate for dealing with the more complex relationship between older and younger poet in a homosexual context, where there may be a significant element of erotic attraction involved in "influence." The master-protégé relationship might be a more useful model for such relationships. Crane was the "élève" Whitman called for, but like the younger lover of classical poetry —or Shakespeare's sonnets—he was bound to come of age and become in turn a master with his own protégés.
52. Not all critics have failed to deal with the Crane-Whitman relationship. Hyatt Waggoner has stated that "without Whitman there would have been no 'Bridge'" (*American Poets: From the Puritans to the Present*, p. 180). And R. W. B. Lewis, who offers the best study of the relationship to date, has written, "Rarely has a modern poem been so nourished by the actual writings of another poet. . . . Crane is not only paying tribute to Whitman and making use of him. He is embracing Whitman. . . ." (*The Poetry of Hart Crane*, p. 328). Bernice Slote also accepts Whitman's significance for Crane, but she is concerned primarily with Whitman's influence on what she calls the "shape" of *The Bridge* (James E. Miller, Jr., Karl Shapiro, and Bernice Slote, *Start with the Sun: Studies in the Whitman Tradition* [Lincoln, 1960]).

Some Contemporary Poets

1. "Homosexuality," in Winston Leyland, ed., *Angels of the Lyre: A Gay Poetry Anthology* (San Francisco, 1975), p. 167.

Allen Ginsberg

2. Allen Ginsberg, "Howl," *Howl and Other Poems*, p. 12.

3. Although all of Genet's major works had appeared in French, with the so-called *Oeuvres Complètes* appearing 1951–1953, the only English edition before 1956 was a limited edition of *Our Lady of the Flowers*, translated by Bernard Frechtman, five hundred copies of which were published in Paris in 1949. (See Philip Thody, *Jean Genet: A Study of His Novels and Plays* [London, 1968], p. 228.) Ginsberg apparently read Genet in French; he was introduced to his works by Carl Solomon, to whom "Howl" is dedicated, in 1949. (See John Tytell, *Naked Angels: The Lives and Literature of the Beat Generation* [New York, 1976], p. 95.)

4. *Howl*, pp. 23–24.

5. San Francisco, 1968.

6. "Who will take over the Universe?" *Planet News*, p. 7.

7. *Planet News*, pp. 33–35.

8. Ibid., pp. 89–91.

9. San Francisco, 1972.

10. "Done, finished, with the biggest cock," *Fall of America*, p. 54.

11. *Fall of America*, pp. 137–138.

12. Ibid., pp. 84–86.

13. Ginsberg, in commenting on the poem in an interview published in *Gay Sunshine* (no. 16, January 1973), reprinted in book form as *Gay Sunshine Interview with Allen Young*, relates it to mysticism— to a presumed transferal of spiritual energy: "There's a great mysticism in being screwed and accepting the new lord divine coming into your bowels."

Robert Duncan

14. *The Years as Catches: First Poems (1939–1946)*, pp. i–ii.

15. *Conceptions of Reality in Modern American Poetry* (Berkeley and Los Angeles, 1966), p. 214.

16. *Years as Catches*, p. 20.

17. *The Opening of the Field*, p. 71.

18. "Random Lines: A Discourse on Love," *Years as Catches*, p. 50.

19. *Bending the Bow* (New York, 1968), pp. 63–65. This last line cited is from Marlowe's *Edward II*. Such a reference is part of the attempt to establish a homosexual tradition; this play, more than any other, is of especial interest to homosexuals, as Marlowe's affirmation of his own sexuality through the love of Gaveston and the King. The Whitman echoes are to "Song of Myself," section 33, "I am the man, I suffer'd, I was there," and to section 52's concluding promise, "Failing to fetch me at first keep encouraged, / Missing me one place search another, / I stop somewhere waiting for you." There

is also the specific echo of Crane's "My hand / in yours, / Walt
Whitman" from "Cape Hatteras."

20. *Years as Catches*, p. 21.
21. Freud's own ideas are remarkably more advanced than those of most
    of his followers. The two most important studies of Freud in this
    regard are by Norman O. Brown and Herbert Marcuse.
22. *Opening of the Field*, pp. 22–23.
23. *Derivations: Selected Poems 1950–1956*, p. 35.
24. "An Apollonian Elegy," *Years as Catches*, pp. 71–73. Cf. also his
    "Cyparissus," from *Windings*, in *Roots and Branches*, pp. 164–
    167.
25. *Opening of the Field*, p. 70.
26. *Roots and Branches*, p. 8. The second line quoted, "lifts lifewards,"
    seems to be a verbal echo of Crane's "National Winter Garden,"
    which concluded with the lines
    > Then you, the burlesque of our lust—and faith,
    > Lug us back lifeward—bone by infant bone.
    Crane is also using sexual arousal as a metaphor for rebirth, includ-
    ing rebirth into the visionary state.
27. *Politics* (August 1944), 1:210.

Thom Gunn

28. In *Manroot*, no. 9 (Fall 1973): 32–38. Although Gunn was educat-
    ed in England, most of his writing has been done in the United
    States, and he lives permanently in San Francisco. By theme and,
    increasingly, by form, he seems very much an American poet even
    if that national identity was originally a matter of choice rather
    than of birth. The poet's identification with California and some of
    its "mythic" figures (the motorcyclist, the surfer) may be seen as
    part of the larger pattern of his rejection of "culture" and the ac-
    quisition of hardness. Gunn's American quest is an interesting re-
    versal of the European journeys recorded by James a hundred years
    ago.
29. See "The Fair in the Woods" or "At the Centre," *Moly* pp. 39–
    40, 50–51. The first is in iambic pentameter, rhyming *a b a b a*;
    the second is a modified series of three sonnets.
30. *The Sense of Movement*, pp. 11–12.
31. Ibid., pp. 28–29.
32. Ibid., p. 30.
33. Ibid., p. 32.
34. *My Sad Captains and Other Poems*, pp. 29–30.
35. Ibid., p. 23.
36. *Sense of Movement*, pp. 36–37.
37. Ibid., p. 31.
38. *My Sad Captains*, p. 40.

39. London, 1967, pp. 26–27.
40. Ibid., p. 58.
41. *My Sad Captains*, p. 24.
42. Ibid., p. 42.
43. *Sense of Movement*, p. 35.
44. *Fighting Terms*, 2d ed., pp. 20–21. The poem is widely anthologized and equally widely misunderstood. A recently published study (Alan Bold, *Thom Gunn and Ted Hughes*) calls Gunn's attitude "arrogantly masculine" (p. 21) and totally fails to see the reason for Gunn's "lying" in bed. Bold's book in general is hostile and ill-informed.
45. *Moly*, pp. 28–32.
46. Ibid., pp. 26–27.
47. *Jack Straw's Castle and Other Poems*.
48. Ibid., p. 39.
49. Ibid., pp. 21–27.

Edward Field
50. New York, 1963.
51. In *Alone with America: Essays on the Art of Poetry in the United States since 1950* (New York, 1971), pp. 116–130.
52. New York, 1967.
53. *Stand Up, Friend*, pp. 14–15.
54. Ibid., pp. 16–17.
55. Neither of his published collections include any of Field's explicitly homosexual poems. Three of them have, however, been published in Ian Young, ed., *The Male Muse: A Gay Anthology* (Trumansburg, New York, 1973). This extremely uneven anthology is most valuable for the service it has rendered in bringing together a number of poems very difficult to find and by clearly identifying the fact that they are homosexual poems by homosexual authors; it is unfortunately not always highly discriminating.
56. *Stand Up, Friend*, p. 21.
57. Ibid., p. 22.
58. Ibid., p. 24.
59. Ibid., p. 34.
60. Ibid., p. 54.
61. Ibid., p. 40.
62. Pp. 64–65.
63. *Stand Up, Friend*, p. 49.
64. *Variety Photoplays*, pp. 80–81.
65. *Stand Up, Friend*, pp. 65–69.

Richard Howard
66. *Untitled Subjects* (New York, 1969), pp. 57–62.

67. See Jeffrey Weeks, *Coming Out: Homosexual Politics in Great Britain from the Nineteenth Century to the Present*, pp. 57–59.
68. New York, 1974.
69. "Wildflowers," pp. 12–28.
70. See Lloyd Morris and Henry Justin Smith, *Oscar Wilde Discovers America* (New York, 1936), pp. 63–77.
71. *Two-Part Inventions*, pp. 40–60.
72. Ibid., pp. 61–71.
73. New York, 1974.
74. New York, 1976.
75. *Fellow Feelings*, pp. 1–5.

James Merrill
76. Susan Sontag, "Notes on 'Camp,'" *Against Interpretation and Other Essays* (New York, n.d.), pp. 275–292.
77. *Braving the Elements*, pp. 11–21.
78. New York, 1969, pp. 4–9.
79. "Mornings in a New House," *Fire Screen*, pp. 40–41.
80. Ibid., pp. 19–21.
81. *Braving the Elements*, pp. 30–35.
82. I am indebted to Andrew Dvosin's discussion of the relationship between Merrill's poem and Crane's "Voyages" in his unpublished essay, "The Homosexual Love Poem: Manners and Morals."

Alfred Corn
83. New York, 1976.
84. New York, 1978.
85. *All Roads at Once*, p. 30.
86. Ibid., pp. 55–56.
87. There is obviously an O'Hara-Schuyler-Ashbery "line of descent" in Corn's work (he has written very perceptively of Ashbery in "A Magma of Interiors," *Parnassus* 4 [Fall/Winter 1975]:223–233), but there is also an important Auden-Merrill line. Above all, Corn speaks in his own voice.
88. In his *Divine Comedies*, "The Book of Ephraim."
89. Harold Bloom, *The Ringers in the Tower: Studies in Romantic Tradition*, p. 138.
90. "Pages from a Voyage," *All Roads at Once*, p. 71.
91. Quoted on the back cover of the Penguin edition of *A Call*. I do not know the full context of Hecht's remark, but it seems to me largely inappropriate.
92. *All Roads*, pp. 68–82.
93. *A Call*, pp. 27–107.
94. 1860 text; Walt Whitman, *Leaves of Grass*, ed. Roy Harvey Pearce, pp. 372–373.

Selected Bibliography

Primary Sources

Bowers, Fredson. *Whitman's Manuscripts: Leaves of Grass (1860)*. Chicago, 1955.
Corn, Alfred. *A Call in the Midst of the Crowd*. New York, 1978.
———. *All Roads at Once*. New York, 1976.
Crane, Hart. *The Letters of Hart Crane, 1916–1932*. Edited by Brom Weber. Berkeley, 1952.
———. *The Complete Poems and Selected Letters and Prose*. Edited by Brom Weber. Garden City, 1966.
Duncan, Robert. *Bending the Bow*. New York, 1968.
———. *Derivations: Selected Poems 1950–1956*. London, 1968.
———. "The Homosexual in Society," *Politics* 1, no. 7 (August 1944): 209–211.
———. *The Opening of the Field*. New York, 1960.
———. "Poems from the Margins of Thom Gunn's *Moly*." *Manroot*, no. 9 (Fall 1973): 32–38.
———. *Roots and Branches*. New York, 1964.
———. *The Years as Catches: First Poems (1939–1946)*. Berkeley, 1966.
Field, Edward. *Stand Up, Friend, With Me*. New York, 1963.
———. *Variety Photoplays*. New York, 1967.
Frank, Waldo. *City Block*. New York, 1932 [first published 1922].
———. *In the American Jungle*. New York, 1937.
———. *Our America*. New York, 1919.
Ginsberg, Allen. *The Fall of America: Poems of These States 1965–1971*. San Francisco, 1972.
———. *Gay Sunshine Interview with Allen Young*. Bolinas, 1974.
———. *Howl and Other Poems*. San Francisco, 1956.
———. *Kaddish and Other Poems*. San Francisco, 1961.
———. *Planet News 1961–1967*. San Francisco, 1968.
Gunn, Thom. *Fighting Terms*. 2d ed. London, 1962.
———. *Jack Straw's Castle and Other Poems*. New York, 1978.
———. *Moly*. London, 1971.
———. *My Sad Captains and Other Poems*. London, 1961.

————. *The Sense of Movement*. London, 1957.

————. *Touch*. London, 1967.

Holloway, Emory, ed. *Uncollected Poetry and Prose of Walt Whitman*. 2 vols. Garden City, 1921.

Merrill, James. *Braving the Elements*. New York, 1972.

————. *Divine Comedies*. New York, 1976.

————. *The Fire Screen*. New York, 1969.

————. *Mirabell: Books of Number*. New York, 1978.

————. *Nights and Days*. New York, 1966.

Plato, "The Banquet." In *The Works of Plato: A New and Literal Version*, translated by George Burges, vol. 3. London, 1850.

Santayana, George. *A Hermit of Carmel, and Other Poems*. New York, 1901.

————. *Persons and Places: The Background of My Life*. New York, 1944.

————. *Poems*. Rev. ed. New York, 1923.

————. *Sonnets and Other Verses*. Chicago and Cambridge, 1894.

The Soil: A Magazine of Art, nos. 1–5, December 1916 to July 1917.

Stedman, Edmund Clarence. *The Blameless Prince and Other Poems*. Boston, 1869.

Stoddard, Richard Henry. *The Book of the East, and Other Poems*. Boston, 1871.

————. *Poems*. Boston, 1852.

Symonds, John Addington. *Letters*. Edited by Herbert M. Schueller and Robert L. Peters. Detroit, 1968.

Taylor, Bayard. *Boys of Other Countries*. New York, 1876.

————. *Critical Essays and Literary Notes*. New York, 1880.

————. *Joseph and His Friend*. Household Edition. New York, 1875.

————. *Poems of the Orient*. Boston, 1855.

————. *Poetical Works*. Household Edition. Boston, 1883.

Underwood, Wilbur. *A Book of Masks*. London, 1907.

————. *Damien of Molokai: Poems*. London, 1909.

Whitman, Walt. *An American Primer*. Edited by Horace Traubel. Boston, 1904.

————. *Calamus: A Series of Letters Written During the Years 1868–1880*. Edited by Richard Maurice Bucke. Boston, 1897.

————. *The Complete Poems*. Edited by Francis Murphy. Harmondsworth, 1975.

————. *Complete Prose Works*. Boston, 1898.

————. *Leaves of Grass*. Edited by Sculley Bradley and Harold W. Blodgett. New York, 1973.

————. *Leaves of Grass*. (1855) Edited by Malcolm Cowley. New York, 1959.

————. *Leaves of Grass*. (1860) Edited by Roy Harvey Pearce. Ithaca, 1961.

———. *Notes and Fragments*. Edited by Richard Maurice Bucke. London, Ontario, 1899.
Young, Ian, ed. *The Male Muse: A Gay Anthology*. Trumansburg, New York, 1973.

Secondary Sources

Adkins, Nelson Frederick. *Fitz-Greene Halleck: An Early Knickerbocker Wit and Poet*. New Haven, 1930.
Allen, Gay Wilson. *The New Walt Whitman Handbook*. New York, 1975.
———. *A Reader's Guide to Walt Whitman*. New York, 1970.
———. *The Solitary Singer: A Critical Biography of Walt Whitman*. Rev. ed. New York, 1967.
———. *Walt Whitman*. New York, 1961.
———. *Walt Whitman as Man, Poet, and Legend*. Carbondale, Illinois, 1961.
———. *Walt Whitman Handbook*. Chicago, 1946.
Arpad, Joseph J. "Hart Crane's Platonic Myth: The Brooklyn Bridge." *American Literature* 39 (March 1967): 75–86.
Arvin, Newton. *Whitman*. New York, 1938.
Asselineau, Roger. *L'Evolution de Walt Whitman après la première edition des Feuilles d'Herbe*. Paris, 1954.
Austen, Roger. *Playing the Game: The Homosexual Novel in America*. Indianapolis, 1977.
Baker, John. "Commercial Sources for Hart Crane's *The River*." *Wisconsin Studies in Contemporary Literature* 6 (Winter–Spring 1965): 45–55.
Bewley, Marius. "Hart Crane's Last Poem." *Accent* 19 (Spring 1959): 75–85.
Beach, Joseph Warren. "Hart Crane and *Moby-Dick*." *Western Review* 20 (Spring 1956): 183–196.
Bertz, Eduard. "Walt Whitman: Ein Charakterbild." *Jahrbuch für sexuelle Zwischenstufen* 7 (1905): 155–287.
———. *Whitman-Mysterien: Eine Abrechnung mit Johannes Schlaf*. Berlin, 1907.
———. *Der Yankee-Heiland: Ein Beitrag zur modernen Religionsgeschichte*. Dresden, 1906.
Binns, Henry Bryan. *A Life of Walt Whitman*. New York, 1905.
Blodgett, Harold. *Walt Whitman in England*. Ithaca, 1934.
Bloom, Harold. *The Anxiety of Influence: A Theory of Poetry*. New York, 1973.

————. *The Ringers in the Tower: Studies in Romantic Tradition*. Chicago, 1971.

Bold, Alan. *Thom Gunn and Ted Hughes*. Edinburgh, 1976.

Bowers, Fredson. "The Earliest Manuscript of Whitman's 'Passage to India' and Its Notebook." *Bulletin of the New York Public Library* 61 (July 1957): 319–352.

Briggs, Arthur E. *Walt Whitman: Thinker and Artist*. New York, 1952.

Brown, Susan Jenkins. "Hart Crane: The End of the Harvest." *Southern Review*, n.s. 4 (Autumn 1968): 945–1014.

Bucke, Richard Maurice. *Walt Whitman*. Philadelphia, 1883.

Canby, Henry Seidel. *Walt Whitman, An American: A Study in Biography*. Boston, 1943.

Carpenter, Edward. *Days with Walt Whitman*. London, 1906.

————. *Some Friends of Walt Whitman: A Study in Sex-Psychology*. London, 1924.

Catel, Jean. *Walt Whitman: La Naissance du poète*. Paris, 1929.

Chase, Richard. *Walt Whitman Reconsidered*. New York, 1955.

Coffman, Stanley K., Jr. "Symbolism in *The Bridge*." *PMLA* 66 (March 1951): 65–77.

Conwell, R. H. *The Life, Travels, and Literary Career of Bayard Taylor*. Boston, 1879.

Corbett, Elizabeth. *Walt*. New York, 1928.

Cowley, Malcolm. "Walt Whitman: The Miracle." *New Republic* 114 (March 18, 1946): 385–388.

————. "Walt Whitman: The Secret." *New Republic* 114 (April 8, 1946): 481–484.

Crew, Louie, ed. *The Gay Academic*. Palm Springs, 1978.

Dembo, L. S. *Conceptions of Reality in Modern American Poetry*. Berkeley and Los Angeles, 1966.

————. *Hart Crane's Sanskrit Charge*. Ithaca, 1960.

————. "Hart Crane's Verticalist Poem." *American Literature* 40 (March 1968): 77–81.

Deutsch, Babette. *Walt Whitman: Builder for America*. New York, 1941.

Djikstra, Bram. *The Hieroglyphics of a New Speech*. Princeton, 1969.

Donaldson, Thomas. *Walt Whitman: The Man*. New York, 1896.

Fowlie, Wallace. "The Juggler's Dance: A Note on Crane and Rimbaud." *The Chimera* 2 (Autumn 1943): 3–14.

Frank, Joseph. *The Widening Gyre*. New Brunswick, New Jersey, 1963.

Friedman, Sanford. "An Interview with Richard Howard." *Shenandoah* 24 (Fall 1972): 5–31.

Furness, Clifton Joseph. Review of Frances Winwar, *American Giant: Walt Whitman and His Times*. *American Literature* 13 (January 1942): 422–432.

————, ed. *Walt Whitman's Workshop*. Cambridge, Massachusetts, 1928.

Galpin, Alfred. "A Boat in the Tower: Rimbaud in Cleveland, 1922." *Renascence* 25 (1972): 3–13.

Gelpi, Albert. *The Tenth Muse: The Psyche of the American Poet.* Cambridge, Massachusetts, 1975.

Golden, Arthur, ed. *Walt Whitman's Blue Book: The 1860–1861 Leaves of Grass Containing His Manuscript Additions and Revisions.* 2 vols. New York, 1968.

Griffith, C. "Sex and Death: The Significance of Whitman's Calamus Themes." *Philological Quarterly* 39 (January 1960): 18–38.

Hartley, Marsden. *Adventures in the Arts.* New York, 1921.

Hazo, Samuel. *Smithereened Apart: A Critique of Hart Crane.* Athens, Ohio, n.d. (originally *Hart Crane: An Introduction and Interpretation.* New York, 1963).

Holloway, Emory. "Walt Whitman's Love Affairs." *The Dial* (November 1920): 473–483.

———. *Walt Whitman: An Interpretation in Narrative.* New York, 1926.

Horton, Philip. *Hart Crane: The Life of an American Poet.* New York, 1937.

Howard, Richard. *Alone with America: Essays on the Art of Poetry in the United States since 1950.* New York, 1971.

Hughson, Lois. *Thresholds of Reality: George Santayana and Modernist Poetics.* Port Washington, New York, 1977.

Isaacs, Neil D. "The Autoerotic Metaphor in Joyce, Sterne, Lawrence, Stevens, and Whitman." *Literature and Psychology* 15 (Spring 1965).

Jason, Philip K. "Wilbur Underwood: Hart Crane's Confidant." *Markham Review* 4: 66–68.

Kalstone, David. *Five Temperaments.* New York, 1977.

Katz, Jonathan. *Gay American History: Lesbians and Gay Men in the U.S.A.* New York, 1976.

Keller, Elizabeth Leavitt. *Walt Whitman in Mickle Street.* New York, 1921.

Knox, George. "Crane and Stella: Conjunction of Painterly and Poetic Worlds." *Texas Studies in Literature and Language* 12 (Winter 1971).

Krapf, Norbert. "Whitman's 'Calamus': Adam from the Garden to the City." *Walt Whitman Review* 19 (December 1973): 162–164.

Krauth, Leland. "Whitman and His Readers: The Comradeship Theme." *Walt Whitman Review* 20 (December 1974): 147–151.

Leibowitz, Herbert A. *Hart Crane: An Introduction to the Poetry.* New York, 1968.

Lewis, R. W. B. *The Poetry of Hart Crane: A Critical Study.* Princeton, 1967.

Lohf, Kenneth A. "The Library of Hart Crane." *Proof: The Yearbook of American Bibliographical and Textual Studies* 3 (1973).

———. *The Literary Manuscripts of Hart Crane.* Columbus, 1967.

Long, Haniel. *Walt Whitman and the Springs of Courage*. Santa Fe, 1938.

Lowenfels, Walter. "Whitman's Many Loves." *Olympia*, no. 4 (1963): 26–32.

Lynch, Michael. "Richard Howard's Finishes." *American Poetry Review* 4 (November–December 1975): 5–11.

Marcuse, Herbert. *Eros and Civilization: A Philosophical Inquiry into Freud*. New York, 1955.

Marx, Leo. *The Machine in the Garden: Technology and the Pastoral Ideal in America*. New York, 1964.

Matthiessen, F. O. *American Renaissance: Art and Expression in the Age of Emerson and Whitman*. New York, 1941.

McCausland, Elizabeth. *Marsden Hartley*. Minneapolis, 1952.

McMichael, James. "Hart Crane." *Southern Review*, n.s. 8 (Spring 1972): 290–309.

Metzger, Deena Posy. "Hart Crane's *Bridge*: The Myth Active." *Arizona Quarterly* 20 (Spring 1964): 36–46.

Meyers, Jeffrey. *Homosexuality and Literature, 1890–1930*. Montreal, 1977.

Miller, Edwin Haviland. *Walt Whitman's Poetry: A Psychological Journey*. Boston, 1968.

———, ed. *The Artistic Legacy of Walt Whitman*. New York, 1970.

———, ed. *A Century of Whitman Criticism*. Bloomington, 1969.

Miller, James E., Jr. *A Critical Guide to 'Leaves of Grass'*. Chicago, 1957.

Morris, H. C. "Crane's 'Voyages' as a Single Poem." *Accent* 14 (Autumn 1954): 291–299.

Mulqueen, James E. "'Song of Myself': Whitman's Hymn to Eros." *Walt Whitman Review* 20 (June 1974): 60–67.

Munson, Gorham B. *Waldo Frank: A Study*. New York, 1923.

Nassar, Eugene Paul. *The Rape of Cinderella: Essays in Literary Continuity*. Bloomington, 1970.

Noel, Roden. *Essays on Poetry and Poets*. London, 1886.

Paul, Sherman. *Hart's Bridge*. Urbana, 1972.

Pearce, Roy Harvey. *The Continuity of American Poetry*. Rev. ed. Princeton, 1977 (first published 1961).

Perry, Robert L. *The Shared Vision of Waldo Frank and Hart Crane*. Lincoln, 1966.

Quinn, Sister M. Bernetta. *The Metamorphic Tradition in Modern Poetry*. New Brunswick, 1955.

Raiziss, Sonia. *The Metaphysical Passion*. Philadelphia, 1952.

Reade, Brian, ed. *Sexual Heretics: Male Homosexuality in English Literature from 1850 to 1900*. London, 1970.

Riddel, Joseph N. "Hart Crane's Poetics of Failure." *ELH* 33 (December 1966): 473–479.

————. *The Inverted Bell: Modernism and the Counterpoetics of William Carlos Williams*. Baton Rouge, 1974.

Rivers, W. C. *Walt Whitman's Anomaly*. London, 1913.

Robbins, J. Albert. "America and the Poet: Whitman, Hart Crane, and Frost." In Irvin Ehrenpreis, ed., *American Poetry*. Stratford-upon-Avon Studies, vol. 7, pp. 45–67. London, 1965.

Runden, John P. "Whitman's 'The Sleepers' and the 'Indiana' Section of Crane's *The Bridge*." *Walt Whitman Review* 15 (December 1969): 245–248.

Saez, Richard. "James Merrill's Oedipal Fire." *Parnassus* 3 (Fall/Winter 1974): 159–184.

Sarotte, G. M. *Comme un Frère, Comme un Amant: L'Homosexualité masculine dans le roman et le théâtre américains*. Paris, 1976.

Scholnick, Robert. "The Selling of the 'Author's Edition': Whitman, O'Connor, and the *West Jersey Press* Affair." *Walt Whitman Review* (23 March 1977): 10.

Schlaf, Johannes. *Walt Whitman homosexueller?* Minden, 1906.

Schyberg, Frederik. *Walt Whitman*. Translated by E. A. Allen. New York, 1951.

Slote, Bernice. "The Structure of Hart Crane's *The Bridge*." *University of Kansas City Review* 24 (March 1958): 225–238.

Smith, A. E. "The Curious Controversy over Whitman's Sexuality." *One Institute Quarterly: Homophile Studies*, no. 4 (Winter 1959): 6–25.

Smith, A. Helen. "Water Imagery in *Leaves of Grass*." *Walt Whitman Review* 17 (September 1971): 82–92.

Smith, Tomothy d'Arch. *Love in Earnest: Some Notes on the Lives and Writings of English "Uranian" Poets from 1889 to 1930*. London, 1970.

Spears, Monroe K. *Hart Crane*. Minneapolis, 1965.

Spitzer, Leo. "*Explication de Texte* Applied to Walt Whitman's Poem 'Out of the Cradle Endlessly Rocking.'" *ELH* 16 (September 1949): 229–249.

Stovall, Floyd. *The Foreground of Leaves of Grass*. Charlottesville, Virginia, 1974.

Sugg, Richard P. *Hart Crane's "The Bridge": A Description of Its Life*. University, Alabama, 1976.

Symonds, John Addington. *Walt Whitman: A Study*. London, 1893.

Tate, Allen. "American Poetry since 1920." *The Bookman* 68 (January 1929): 503–508.

Taupin, René. *L'Influence du symbolisme français sur la poésie américaine*. Paris, 1929.

Traubel, Horace. *With Walt Whitman in Camden*. New York and Philadelphia, 1908.

Unterecker, John. "The Architecture of *The Bridge*." *Wisconsin Studies*

in Contemporary Literature 3 (Spring/Summer 1962):5–20.
————. *Voyager: A Life of Hart Crane*. New York, 1969.
Uroff, M. D. *Hart Crane: The Patterns of His Poetry*. Urbana, 1974.
Van Doren, Mark. "Walt Whitman: Stranger." In *The Private Reader*, pp. 69–86. New York, 1942.
Van Nostrand, A. "*The Bridge* and Hart Crane's Span of Consciousness." In *Aspects of American Poetry*, edited by Richard M. Ludwig. Columbus, 1962.
Vince, R. W. "A Reading of 'The Sleepers.'" *Walt Whitman Review* 18 (March 1972):17–28.
Waggoner, Hyatt H. *American Poets: From the Puritans to the Present*. Boston, 1968.
————. "Hart Crane and the Broken Parabola." *University of Kansas City Review* 11 (Spring 1945):173–177.
————. "Hart Crane's Bridge to Cathay." *American Literature* 16 (May 1944):115–130.
————. *The Heel of Elohim: Science and Values in Modern American Poetry*. Norman, 1950.
Walcutt, Charles C. "Voyages." *Explicator* 4 (June 1946), no. 53.
Weber, Brom C. *Hart Crane: A Biographical and Critical Study*. New York, 1948.
Weeks, Jeffrey. *Coming Out: Homosexual Politics in Britain from the Nineteenth Century to the Present*. London, 1977.
Weirick, Bruce. *From Whitman to Sandburg in American Poetry*. New York, 1930.
Wermuth, Paul C. *Bayard Taylor*. New York, 1973.
Whicher, Stephen E. "Whitman's Awakening to Death: Toward a Biographical Reading of 'Out of the Cradle Endlessly Rocking.'" In *The Presence of Walt Whitman: Selected Papers from the English Institute*, edited by R. W. B. Lewis, pp. 1–27. New York, 1962.
Willingham, John R. "'Three Songs' of Hart Crane's *The Bridge*: A Reconsideration." *American Literature* 27 (March 1955):62–68.
Wilson, James Grant. *The Life and Letters of Fitz-Greene Halleck*. New York, 1869.
Winters, Yvor. "The Progress of Hart Crane" (review of *The Bridge*). *Poetry* 36 (June 1930):153–165.

Unpublished Sources

Burlingame, Robert N. "Marsden Hartley: A Study of His Life and Creative Achievement." Unpublished Ph.D. dissertation, Brown University, 1954.
Crane, Hart. Letters to Wilbur Underwood. Yale University Library.

————. Manuscripts and Correspondence. Columbia University Libraries.

Dvosin, Andrew. "The Homosexual Love Poem: Manners and Morals." Unpublished essay.

Foster, Margaret. "Arthur Rimbaud and Hart Crane: An Essay in Influence and Parallels." Ph.D. dissertation, Ohio State University, 1940.

Hartley, Marsden. Manuscripts. Yale University Library.

————. "The Spangle of Existence: Casual Dissertations" [1942]. Typescript in library of the Museum of Modern Art, New York.

Schwartz, Alan Howard. "Hart Crane's Poetry: A Critical Edition." Ph.D. dissertation, New York University, 1967.

Sixbey, George L. "Walt Whitman's Middle Years: 1860–1867." Ph.D. dissertation, Yale University, 1940.

Tashjian, Dickran L. "The Influence of European Dada on American Visual Arts and Letters: 1913–1925." Ph.D. dissertation, Brown University, 1969.

Index